TO END POVERTY

By the same author:

Pamphlets

'Who's Starving Them.'
'The Natural Society?'
'The Theory of Alternative Green.'

TO END POVERTY

THE STARVATION OF THE PERIPHERY BY THE CORE

RICHARD HUNT

ALTERNATIVE GREEN

First published in 1997 by
Alternative Green
20 Upper Barr, Cowley Centre, Oxford. OX4 3UX.

A CIP catalogue record for this book is available from the British
Library.

ISBN 0-9528871-0-7

Typeset in Garamond by Laserset, Abingdon.
Printed by Information Press, Eynsham, Oxford.
Bound by Green Street Bindery, Oxford.
Design, graphics and jacket by Richard Hunt.

Contents

1.   Before Poverty   **1**

Primitive societies are not hungry. They have been called the "original affluent society". They do not cultivate because they do not need to and because it is harder work. They obey the Law of Least Effort. Today people work harder partly to climb the peck order.

2.   The Birth of Tyranny   **14**

Tyranny starts with a leader and his companions. Gods are invented to create inherited kingship to preserve the companions' position. Religion legitimises taxation which takes from the many to give to the few, creating wealth at the core, the city, and poverty on the periphery.

3.   Does Trade Create Wealth or Poverty?   **34**

Primitive societies prefer to share rather than exchange. So they do not trade. Governments force people to trade in order to increase their income and power from indirect taxes on trade. Rulers, traders and periphery rulers collude to force periphery peoples to grow cash crops to increase trade and feed the cities.

4.   Does Industry Reduce Poverty?   **52**

The Theory of Division of Labour was welcomed in order to justify clearing the land to grow cash crops to increase trade which would create wealth which would 'trickle down' to the poorest on the periphery. It didn't The Theory of Comparative Advantage was worked out to justify international trade which forced periphery countries to accept core industrial goods. Periphery industries were destroyed. Industry is caused by high labour costs caused by high cost of living caused by high taxation.

5.   Regression   **78**

If a government loses resources to feed its army, it can no longer extract the crops and loses control. Taxation goes down and with it technology. Regression took place as after the Roman Empire.

6.   Technological Progress   **86**

Medieval monasteries led the 'first industrial revolution' by their need to cut labour costs to pay for their extravagant building programme. Overpopulated Flanders, Northern France and Italy industrialised to obtain food from eastern Europe which therefore starved. The impoverished periphery was expanding.

7.   The Pattern in Britain 107

How was this new model of development reflected in Britain? There was a regression of technology and dereliction of cities after Rome withdrew its soldiers. Less taxed, the peasants were better off. But the Anglo-Saxon kings quickly learned about indirect taxation on trade until William I who didn't understand, so there was a short regression. Then towns were planted to raise indirect taxes, and wool was exported. Britain was an agricultural periphery to the Flanders core.

8.   Stagnation 123

Before the Black Death grain overproduction in eastern Europe caused grain prices to fall. Monasteries with less income from their grain couldn't repay their loans to their bankers who went bankrupt. Depression followed. This fall in grain prices from overproduction caused the same pattern as the Great Depression of the late 19th Century and the Depression of the 1930s.

9.   Economic Growth and its Poverty 129

The industrial revolution happened in Britain because a century of high indirect taxation to pay for the wars with France had given Britain the highest cost of living in Europe. Therefore it had the highest wages and labour costs. So its goods were being priced out of the market. It was forced to industrialise to reduce labour costs. The consequent cheaper goods destroyed local industries throughout the world.

10.   The Modern World 149

Europe and America were forced by British competition to industrialise also. America led because it had the highest labour costs and it bribed periphery rulers to give it their trade with the most guns. Three trading blocks might develop, Europe with its resources periphery in Eastern Europe and Africa, America with its resource periphery in South America and Japan with its resource periphery in Asia.

11.   The Third World 168

The Third World is now the impoverished periphery of the developed world. It is starving because we are using its land to grow crops for us instead of food for itself. We are using up its timber because we have already used up our own. Aid is used to encourage cash crops for us.

12.   The Crisis of Industrialism 183

Environmental problems such as global warming, the destruction of the ozone layer, nuclear waste, deforestation, erosion, biocides, industrial wastes and pollution are making industrialism untenable.

13. Solutions Which Won't Work   **193**

Solutions offered by governance, capitalism, socialism, religions and the Greens cannot work.

14. To End Poverty   **199**

Revolution on the Periphery; political break-up; cutting taxes to cut the power of government.

Postscript   **204**

Authors quoted   **205**

Index   **210**

Chapter 1
BEFORE POVERTY

TODAY TENS OF MILLIONS OF PEOPLE die of starvation or related diseases every year. That didn't happen before. For two or three million years people lived fairly happily, warm enough, with enough to eat, like the few remaining hunter-gatherer societies today: "Despite the poverty of their existence the Yahgan make no attempt to store food from one day to the next, since all that they need is readily available at all times of the year. They spend only a fraction of the day in hunting or gathering food and the rest of the time is free for conversation or recreation." (Pearson. 1.)

"Surrounded by a wide variety of plant and animal life, the Pygmies have no difficulty in finding food, and while the men hunt game with bows and arrows, the Pygmy women and young girls gather mushrooms, fruits, nuts and edible roots. In fact the forest is so generous a provider of food that the Pygmies do not have to trouble to hunt every day, and they happily laze around their camp whenever the previous day's work has brought them all they need." (Pearson. 2.) For the Andaman Islanders: "Food is abundant, both the land and sea offer an inexhaustible supply." (Cipriani. 1.)

Even for Kung bushmen in the Kalahari Desert: "During this period (a year of drought) meat makes up 37% of the diet, mongongo nuts 33% and other vegetables 30%. Sufficient supplies were obtained daily to provide each member of the group with 1.4lbs of food or some 2140 calories, about 165 calories more than the basic daily requirement. Furthermore, obtaining food is by no means a full time job. Individuals engaged in hunting and gathering devoted only from one to three days a week to the job and had the rest of the week free for resting and playing games and visiting friends at nearby camps." (Pfeiffer. 1.)

Of the Hazda in Kenya: "Although visitors from the affluent lands described their land as 'an inhospitable wilderness' and their life as a bitter struggle against starvation, they had a generous food supply and no enemies and a surfeit of leisure. The people considered themselves to be hunters and game was abundant. But more than 80% of their diet consisted of wild honey and various plant foods collected by the women: about half the men did practically no hunting at all. From early morn-

1

ing until dark, they spent a major part of their time gambling, betting arrows on whether wooden disks tossed against a tree would land barkside up or barkside down," (Haviland. 1.)

Social Control

There are no policemen to keep order in these groups, no prisons to punish wrongdoers. Yet they manage. "Disputes between individuals are invariably harmful to the success of the band as a whole, and the pygmy who jeopardises the welfare of the group may find himself subject to public insult and ridicule. To be laughed at and humiliated may serve as a far more effective reprimand than a fine or a thrashing... The threat of social ostracism, however brief that ostracism may be, functions as a powerful instrument of social control among the Mbuti. Resort to permanent exile is virtually unknown among the Pygmies." (Haviland. 2.)

Murder is very rare indeed. In one recorded instance an eskimo killed another member of the band. Then he killed another. Obviously social life becomes impossible under such circumstances. So four members of the group ambushed him and shot him, to the relief of the whole group.

It seems that fighting is very uncommon amongst hunter-gatherer societies. An anthropologist was being told by a pygmy how they fought with pygmy intruders. "Kenge saw that I was taking all this very seriously, and he took me to one side. 'Old Masisi's head is unsteady,' he said, 'it has worms in it. He will only fight with words. Every year those pygmies come into our land and we go into theirs. There is plenty of food. So long as we do not meet there is no fighting. If we do meet, then those who are not in their own land run away and leave behind whatever they have stolen. That is the only way we fight. We are not like villagers.'" (Turnball.) Of the Aborigines: "adults are generally peaceful. Although personal clashes between individuals occur fairly often, there are neither social hierarchies or warfare." (Haviland. 3.)

And health ? Of the Bushmen "10% were determined to be over sixty years of age, a proportion which compares favourably to the percentage of elderly in industrial populations." (Lee.) "Australia presents us with a spectacle of a continent from the pathology of which entire classes of disease prevalent in other divisions of the globe were, until comparatively recent times, completely absent. Thus the whole class of eruptive fevers, smallpox, scarlet fever, and measles, so fatal elsewhere, were unknown. Epidemic choleras, relapsing fever, yellow fever, whooping cough and diphtheria were equally absent, as also was syphilis." (S. Davidson.) Primitive man was healthy.

It is now accepted in the anthropological world that the lives of 'primitive' peoples were not "solitary, poor, nasty, brutish and short", but that they are well-fed, long-living, healthy and peaceful. Marshal Sahlins has

2

called them "the original affluent society." So we cannot look to 'primitivism' and ignorance for the causes of poverty.

Nomadic hunter-gatherer groups number about 25 people. When they coalesce into settlements, the group seems to number about 500, about the maximum number that one person can know. "There is an architects' rule of thumb to the effect that the capacity of an elementary school should not exceed 500 pupils if the principal expects to know all of them by name – and it has been stated that when a group exceeds 500 persons, it requires some form of policing." (Pfeiffer. 2.)

How then, without policing or institutions of justice, do the villages maintain peace and acceptable behaviour? The key is that everyone knows everyone else and nearly everyone is related to everyone else. "Conflict was first of all a matter between individuals, then a concern of the families and finally of the band. The delinquent person was cautioned, ridiculed, gossiped about and shamed into conformity." (Haviland. 4.) "In the 'vito', an old Spanish custom paralleled among various Mediterranean peoples, an individual who has offended community standards may be visited by a noisy delegation of his neighbours in the middle of the night. This unwelcome group of visitors may proceed to make such abusive noises or subject the offender to such inconveniences that he cannot possibly mistake or ignore its disapproval of his behaviour." (Haviland. 5.)

Individual unacceptable behaviour reflects on the whole family. So there is strong family pressure on him to behave. Also, if he has caused harm, it is usually the case that his whole family has to make compensation. "Among the Masai, pastoral nomads of East Africa, a murderer is usually concealed by his relatives while the victim's family searches for him to avenge their kinsman's death. The culprit is protected until the mood has cooled and negotiations can begin. The traditional fine for murder is forty-nine cattle. When people collect their blood property, they go armed as for war. Thus the deeply rooted need for revenge is satisfied by a symbolic show of anger, punishment of the aggressor and compensation to the victim's relations." (de Waal.)

Such disputes are often given to the arbitration of an influential member of the group. But the Leopard-skin chief "gave his final decision as an opinion couched in persuasive language and not a judgement delivered with authority . . . The verdict is only accepted because both parties agree to it." (MacDermot.) Of course, the community, like every other animal society, will have a peck order: but it will be of respect and influence, not authority. "The chieftain is usually spokesman of his group and master of its ceremonies with otherwise little influence, few functions and no privileges. One word from him and everyone does as he pleases." (Sahlins. 1) "There is no centre of authority in the village

3

and moreover it is customary to avoid public responsibility . . . for fear of exciting jealousy." (Douglas.) "A 'chief' is a sacred person, without political authority. Indeed the Nuer have no government and their state might be described as an ordered anarchy." (Evans-Pritchard.) "the influence of chiefs was uncertain, and no one would acknowledge any authority to his own will . . . A chief received deference indeed, but not obedience . . . No chief could carry his will against a single dissentient." (Diamond.)

Sharing the Wealth

Because of the close family ties there is no disparity of wealth. "most of these people hold very strongly to the view that wealth should not be too unevenly distributed." (Mair). "Over the past 50 years in Thak, there has been a gradual equalisation of land holdings towards the five plot level. MacFarlane suggests that the numerous cross-cutting bonds, linking everyone with everyone else, (*jat*, age group, real and fictional kinship) has reduced conflict and maintained a kind of non-competitiveness." (Gellner and Humphrey.)

In fact in a small community wealth is a bit of an embarrassment. "The possession or acquisition of wealth created difficulties for a rich villager. His fellow citizens who considered themselves his equals, and were as often as not related to him, overwhelmed him with requests for gifts of grain and money." (Gourou.) "So it was firmly built into the ancient democracy of the Dinka that no family, and certainly no individual, could be allowed to possess more goods than other families possessed." (B. Davidson.)

Agriculture

For reasons which will be discussed later the hunter-gatherers had to start cultivating. And this means harder work! "A thinly spread population begins to do a little agricultural work as a supplement to food collection and hunting. When their territory becomes more crowded, they must work more and provide nearly all their food by agricultural work, but this can still be done by a few hours work now and then and requires no regular daily work. When the further growth of population compels them to change over from forest fallow to bush fallow and to shorten the bush fallow or prolong the periods of cultivation, a point is eventually reached where they must accept to do really hard work in one or two relatively short peak seasons. Still, they continue to have long periods with no or very little agricultural work." (Boserup. 1.)

People were reluctant to cultivate because, in spite of conventional wisdom, agriculture is harder work. Agriculture started, not because we were suddenly imbued with the Protestant Work Ethic, or conversely, because it was less work, but because we were hungry. There was just not enough game or wild fruit and veg. One of the first places to start cultivation, Mesopotamia, had suffered a disastrous change of climate when the rain belt moved north at the end of the Ice Age. The 'Fertile Crescent' was in fact a desert by 5,000 BC. during the Thermal Maximum.

Agriculture means more work. More food is produced, but the labour input is higher per unit of food. The hunter-gatherers don't cultivate because, intelligently, they know it is more work. "Careful comparative study of swidden gardeners and hunter-gatherers would probably bring into question the traditional view that the neolithic 'revolution' gave men relief from the food quest and 'the leisure to build culture'." (Sahlins. 2.) "On the debit side, farming, particularly primitive farming, makes heavier demands than food gathering on time and labour, leading to a decrease in leisure rather than the increase that was once thought." (Trump.)

The first form of cultivation in forested areas is known as 'cut and burn' or 'swidden gardening', where a small area of forest is cut down and burnt, or just burnt, cultivated for a few years, then left to grow wild again to recoup its fertility, and a new area is cleared. But as the population increases, all the forest has to be cut down and subsistence agriculture has to replace 'cut and burn'. And it means more work. "But even after 'cut and burn' has been abandoned, when the work admittedly becomes more laborious, most cultivators in Africa are still only occupied for a fraction of what we would regard as a normal working year; two to four hours a day on average." (Clark. 1.) In West Africa, "The number of hours worked in farming and associated activities was low, perhaps averaging half a day throughout the year, and sometimes rather less." (Hopkins.)

As agriculture becomes more intensive they are forced to make better tools. A digging stick is no longer adequate to grow enough food. "After the burning of real forest the soil is loose and free of weeds and hoeing of the land is unnecessary. By contrast, when the period of fallow is shortened and therefore the natural vegetation, before clearing, is thin or grassy, the land must be prepared with a hoe or similar instrument before the seeds or roots can be placed. Thus, the hoe is not introduced just as a technical perfection of the digging stick. It is introduced, typically, when an additional operation becomes necessary, i.e. when forest fallow is replaced by bush fallow." As the fallow is reduced, only grasses have any time to grow. When they are burnt: "the roots are left intact and with many types of grasses these roots are exceedingly difficult to remove by means of hoeing. Thus the use of a plough becomes indispensable." (Boserup. 2.)

To increase output, irrigation often becomes necessary. And again this is harder work. "Total labour input per crop hectare of a given crop may be twice as high as for dry cultivation." (Boserup. 3.) "These succeeding stages each call for more labour per unit of food produced. When draught animals have to be kept, it is rarely if ever possible to find natural grazing in sufficient abundance to keep them all the year round." (Clark. 2.)

Whereas hunter-gatherers move round their territory as certain trees come into fruit or certain animals move their annual way, the cultivators, in order to protect both their growing and stored food, are forced to stay put. This has certain advantages. They can build more comfortable dwellings; they can use pottery utensils which would have been too heavy to carry around. But these advantages are only the side effects of a deteriorating situation forced on them by their growing numbers.

Thus the first important development of 'progress', instead of being the invention of a creative species which brought leisure and freedom from poverty, is found to be caused by a scarcity of resources brought on by a growing population and it means less leisure and harder work.

Leisure Preference

But even though the cultivators are having to work harder, they don't overdo it, and certainly don't produce a surplus. In America: "The pure Indian . . . seems never to work unless compelled. As for storing up anything for the future, the thought seems scarcely to enter his head. If he has enough to eat, he simply sits still and enjoys his life until hunger again arouses him to activity. His wants are few and easily supplied . . . He is hardly to be blamed for his apparent laziness. He is certainly lazy according to our standards; but he has little to stimulate him and it is easy to get a living without much work." (Huntington.) In South America: "The majority of Andean Indians are still outside the monetary economy. They have been accustomed for generations to an extremely low standard of living and cannot easily be persuaded to grow more food than is necessary for themselves. They have no ambition to better their material existence." (Pendle. 1.) On the northern edge of the Roman Empire: "the Goths, with good soil at their disposal, could not, or would not organise an agriculture . . . The abundance of land excludes all thought of economising its use." (Koener.) "For they take no pains to make the best of the fertility and extent of the land. They plant no fruit trees; they mark off no meadows; they irrigate no gardens; the land simply has to yield the corn crops." (Tacitus.)

But even when they have been compelled to start cultivating, they still do as little as possible. The peasants of sixteenth century England: "preferred leisure to a higher income secured at the cost of further toil.

These attitudes, in particular the preference for leisure, were also shared by other groups who received a larger proportion of their total income in money, notably the petty craftsmen and the labourers of both town and country." (Clay. 1.) In 1718 Governor Rogers of the Bahamas bemoaned the fact that the people would not work to earn money to pay their taxes. "For work they mortally hate it, for when they have cleared a patch that will supply them with potatoes and yams and very little else, fish being so plentiful. . . . They thus live poorly and indolently, with a seeming content, and pray for wrecks and pirates; and few have an opinion of a regular orderly life under any sort of government, and would rather spend all they have at a Punch house than pay me one tenth to save their families and all that's dear to them."

Congressman Porter in New York State in 1810 couldn't get them to work either. "Such is the fertility of the land that one half their time spent in labour is sufficient to produce every article which their farms are capable of yielding, in sufficient quantities for their own consumption, and there is nothing to incite them to produce more. They are therefore naturally led to spend the other part of their time in idleness and dissipation." (See Wilkinson. 2.)

Regression

But if they only work as little as they need to, one should suppose that, given the opportunity, if it meant less work still, they would revert to a lower technological level. They do. When early American colonists first arrived in the almost uninhabited lands of the eastern seabord, they brought with them the relatively sophisticated techniques of European agriculture. But with all the virgin land available there was no need for their old intensive methods. They quickly reverted to 'cut and burn' because it was easier. "The large size of the original land grants had encouraged the development of less intensive methods of land use than those practised in Europe: in conventional terms there had been a regression in agricultural techniques." (Wilkinson. 1.)

When a tribe in Java was driven off its cultivated land into the jungle by the Dutch, it forgot its agriculture and reverted to hunter-gathering. It did not find the comforts of agriculture worth the extra work – Law of Least Effort. "there are certain segments of the Latin American farm population which, according to field investigators, have been descending in the technological scale rather than ascending. They are going the wrong way. Observers such as Warbel and Lynn Smith who have studied the relatively recent European colonisation in South Brazil, for example, tell us that these colonists, who came (or whose ancestors came) from countries like Germany and Italy with relatively advanced techniques, have lost many of these techniques. This is true of such fairly simple practices as the use of the plough and crop rotation and the inclusion of livestock and forage crops in the farm economy for the maintenance of soil fertility." (Boserup. 3.)

In Russia in the sixteenth century there was: "extensive depopulation... which was the joint result of war and famine and of the flight of peasants to the free frontier lands of the south – depopulation of a magnitude to cause anything from a half to nine tenths of the cultivated land to be abandoned, and a reversion of the three field system to more primitive and extensive methods of cultivation." (Dobb. 1) "Certainly there have been historic examples of economic retrogression, in parts of early modern Italy or Spain, for example." (Gould. 1.)

Other technologies vanish too. In pre-classical Greece: "the sole function of writing in the Mycenaean world known to us was to meet the administrative needs of the palace. When the latter disappeared, the need and the art both went with it." (Finley. 1.) When the Roman Empire collapsed and the French were no longer forced to produce the extra food for Rome, France regressed. "The fall of Rome was thus made manifest in the restoration of a culture designed not for cultivation but for the exploitation of the natural wilderness." (Duby. 1.) "Even the potter's wheel fell into disuse in Western Europe, pots again being made by hand." (Thomas. 1.)

Another indication that advanced technologies are not necessarily welcome is the number that have existed long before they were exploited. "Thus while the Iron Age begins around 1400 BC., iron beads from before 3000 BC. have been found." (Mumford. 1.) "Even modelling in clay produced paleolithic animal sculptures long before it formed Mesopotamian houses and pots." (Mumford. 2.) "The ancient inhabitants of America had wheels on their toys, yet they never used wheeled transport. The lack of draught animals was the main reason, the unsuitability of the terrain to roads another." (The Economist.)

Least Effort

Each regression and non-use of technology indicates an unexpected motive of human behaviour. Like every other organism in nature, people obey the Law of Least Effort. "In simple terms the Principle of Least Effort means, for example, that a person, in solving his immediate problems, will view these against the background of his probable future problems, as estimated by himself. Moreover he will strive to solve his problems in such a way as to minimize his total work and his probable future problems. That in turn means that the person will strive to minimize the probable average rate of his work expenditure (over time). And in doing so, he will be minimizing his effort, by our definition of effort. Least Effort is therefore a variant of Least Work. . . . The sheer idea that there may be only one dynamic minimum in the entire behaviour of all living individuals need not by itself dismay us. The physicists are certainly not dismayed at the thought that all physical processes throughout the entire time-space continuum is governed by the one single superlative, Least Effort." (Zipf.)

The dynamic minimum is perhaps better put as 'the avoidance of discomfort by Least Effort'. That this is true of humans is supported by observations of anthropologists, frustrated planners and economists whose grandiose schemes have fallen apart because people, given a choice, won't work. It is such a common phenomenon that it has been given a jargon name – 'the leisure preference'. As a Kung bushman put it: "Why should we cultivate when there are so many mongongo nuts in the world?"

The Peck Order

Nevertheless, if it is true that people obey the Law of Least Effort, there's an awful lot of explaining to do. Climbing Everest or a two car garage don't look like Least Effort.

Millions of years ago animals found that fighting to get the best mouthful of meat from a carcase was a fairly silly way of going about things. They evolved a system we call the 'peck order' (or pecking order or rank order or dominance hierarchy). They all agreed just to fight once to establish their position relative to each other. After that a look, or a peck, was enough to remind the other of the result of that fight, so they didn't need to go on fighting.

The peck order not only stops fighting; it protects the weaker. "In jackdaws, and in many other social birds, ranking order leads directly to protection of the weaker ones. All social animals are 'status seekers', hence there is always particularly high tension between individuals who hold immediately adjoining positions in the ranking order; conversely, this tension diminishes the farther apart the two animals are in rank. Since high-ranking jackdaws, particularly males, interfere in every quarrel between two inferiors, this gradation of social tension has the desirable effect that the higher ranking birds always intervene in favour of the losing party." (Lorentz.)

Amongst baboons: "In troops where the rank order is clearly defined fighting is rare. We observed frequent bickering or severe fighting in only about 15% of the troops. The usual effect of the hierarchy, once relations amongst the males are settled, is to decrease disruptions in the troop. The dominant animals, the males in particular, will not let the others fight. When bickering breaks out, they usually run to the scene and stop it. Dominant males thus protect the weaker animals against harm from inside as well as from outside." (Washburne and DeVore.)

Keeping Up With The Jones

The peck order is observed in all species which live together in groups, humans as well, as a means of living peacefully together with Least Effort. Many species have evolved different ways of establishing a peck order without fighting – it's less effort, fewer people get hurt. For humans speed and dexterity, for example, are qualities which lift people in the peck order. In order to measure these qualities, humans have found that instead of chasing each other and dextrously beating each other over the head, it's much more fun and less dangerous to compete to get a ball between two posts. It is agreed what the goal is and it is agreed what are the limitations to achieving that goal – in football you can only use your feet. So a common way of agreeing on the peck order without fighting is 'conventional means to conventional goals'. In primitive societies it might be who has the biggest bone through his nose. In our urban society one agreed measure is who has the bigger car. If you've got two cars, even better. So the two car garage does not contradict Least Effort after all. It's a way of asserting a superiority in the peck order over your neighbour without having to hit him over the head every morning. Conventional means to conventional goals. Keeping up with the Jones is a very necessary pattern of behaviour for keeping the peace in the community with Least Effort.

The Consumer Society, materialism, conspicuous consumption are all examples of this necessary behaviour. If we've got enough money to waste on electric toothbrushes, we must be well-off, high in the peck order.

The need to be high in the peck order is millions of years old, deeply engrained, automatic. Don't knock it. We all compete in our different ways, how we dress, what we eat, how we travel, whom we know. Some groups reject the 'conventional means'. Thieves accept the conventional goal of success as money, but break the conventional rules for acquiring it. But that doesn't work. You have to acquire the money in ways that are agreed. Criminals don't get status.

Some groups reject both what is conventionally agreed to be the goal and the conventional means to get there. But such groups still have their own peck order and simply evolve different goals and different means. They might reject conspicuous consumption but carefully present all their books on their open shelves, eat ecologically-sound beans and, within their own groups, compete to be holier than the others. Amongst political groups the agreed means might be how many papers you sell or how many of the right books you've read; better still, how many you've understood.

Climbing Everest is the same behaviour pattern. The one who climbs highest is the best. Children and kittens compete in the same way. "I'm the king of the castle." Frazer-Darling watched fawns doing the same thing. Competing in the peck order starts early, but it gets complicated later on because modesty is another 'conventional means'. So the mountain climber can't, like Tarzan, shout, "I'm the king of the castle." He has to pretend that he only climbed the mountain "because it's there". But he knows, and we all know, that he has climbed the peck order.

Another way to compete is what we put on our walls. The multi-millionaire shows that he is right at the top of the peck order by competing at an auction (conventional means) to buy what is generally agreed to be the most desirable oil painting, Van Gogh's 'Irises' (conventional goal). And everyone agrees what is more and less desirable to have on our walls. An oil painting is better than a water colour. Both are better than prints. Exceptions are understood. An eighteenth century penny print is better than the popular 'Green Lady'. We state our position in the peck order by what we put on our walls and what we know about it. It's less effort than fighting. So climbing Everest and the two car garage do not contradict Least Effort.

We all obey Least Effort. How hard would you work if you were warm and well-fed and all your family and friends were outside in the sun. How bored with leisure would you have to get to go and work on a factory production line? Many people say they enjoy their work. What they mean is that they enjoy the company of their colleagues, they enjoy the competition of business or the exercise of authority. It's not the work itself they enjoy.

Summary

At this point we are trying to determine what causes poverty. We have seen that it is not 'primitivism' or ignorance since hunter-gatherer societies are not poor and hungry. We have seen that agriculture was developed to avoid the hunger and poverty caused by population pressure, and that it was not seen as progress at all since it meant harder work. We have seen that though people work hard to climb the peck order, they still obey the Law of Least Effort and would revert to a lower level of technology if the opportunity occurred.

Chapter 1. Before Poverty
References

E. Boserup. "The Conditions of Agricultural Growth." George Allen and Unwin. '65. 1: p.53., 2: p.24., 3: p.63.

L. Cipriani. "The Andaman Islanders." Weidenfeld and Nicholson. '66. 1: p.62.

C. Clark. "Population Growth and Land Use." MacMillan. '67. 1: p.139., 2: p.42.

C.G.A. Clay. "Economic Expansion and Social Change." Cambridge University Press. '84. 1: p.4.

B. Davidson. "The Story of Africa." Michael Beasley/Channel 4. '84, p.55.

S. Davidson. "Human Nutrition and Dietetics". Edinburgh. '69. Quoted by R. Wilkinson.

A.S. Diamond. "The Evolution of Law and Order." Watts. '51. p.32.

M. Dobb. "Studies in the Development of Capitalism." Routledge Kegan Paul. '46. 1: p.68.

M. Douglas. "The Lele of Kasai" in "African Worlds" Ed. C. Darryl Forde. O.U.P. '54. p.14.

G. Duby. "The Early Growth of the European Economy." Weidenfeld and Nicholson. '74. 1: p.21.

The Economist. 16.2.91.

E.E. Evans-Pritchard. "The Nuer". Clarendon Press. '40. p.5.

M.I. Finley. "Early Greece: The Bronze and Archaic Ages." Chatto and Windus. '81. 1: p.61.

Frazer-Darling, F. "A Herd of Red Deer." O.U.P. '37.

D. Gellner and C. Humphrey. "Gurkha Swords into Ploughshares." 'New Society'. 17.8.78.

J.D. Gould. "Economic Growth in History." Methuen. '72. 1: p.425.

R. Gourou. "Man and Land in the Far East." Longman. '75. p.215.

W.A. Haviland. "Anthropology". Holt Rhinehart and Winston. '82. 1: p.337., 2: p.482., 3: p.317., 4: p.467., 5: p.477.

A.G. Hopkins. "An Economic History of West Africa." Longman. '73. p.17.

E. Huntington. "The Climatic Factor as illustrated in Arid America." Carnegie Institute of Washington 1914. Publication no. 192. p.180.

R. Koener. "Settlement and colonisation of Europe." in "The Cambridge Economic History of Europe." Ed. Postan. Vol 1. C.U.P. '71. p.15.

R.B. Lee. "What hunters do for a living." in "Man, the Hunter." Ed. Lee and Devore. Chicago '68. p.36.

K. Lorentz. "On Aggression." Methuen. '66. p.36.

B.H. MacDermot. "Cult of the Sacred Spear." Hale. '73. p.179.

L. Mair. "An Introduction to Social Anthropology." O.U.P. '65. p.192.

L. Mumford. "The Myth of the Machine." Vol. 1. "Technics and Human Development". Secker and Warburg. '66. 1: p.111., 2: p.136.

R. Pearson. "Introduction to Anthropology." Holt Rhinehart and Winston. '74. 1: p.327., 2: p.346.

G. Pendle. "A History of Latin America." Penguin. '63. 1: p.123.

J. Pfeiffer. "The Emergence of Man." Harper Row. '72. 1: p.344, 2: p.334.

M.D. Sahlins. "Tribalism." Prentice Hall. '68. 1: p.12., 2: p.30.

H. Thomas. "An Unfinished History of the World." Hamish Hamilton. '79. 1: p.29.

D.H. Trump. "The Prehistory of the Mediterranean." Allen Lane. '80. p.26.

C. Turnball. "The Forest People." Jonathan Cape. '61. p.247.

F. de Waal. "Peacemaking among Primates." Penguin '91. p.262.

Washburne and Devore. "The Social Life of Baboons." Scientific American. Vol. 204. No. 6. pp. 62–71.

R. Wilkinson. 'Poverty and Progress.' Methuen. '73. 1: p.152., 2: quoted by R. Wilkinson. p.168.

J. Zipf. "Human Behaviour and the Principle of Least Effort." Hafner. '65. pp. 1 and 3.

Chapter 2
THE BIRTH OF TYRANNY

ON AN ISLAND there was a large group of monkeys, one of which was particularly strong and charismatic. He and his mates began to bully the others and gradually he developed into a simian Hitler. For fifteen years he and his companions terrorised the island. But finally he died and life returned to normal. There's nothing new or particular to the human species about the pleasure of bullying.

This pattern shows itself in street gangs today. It depends on a strong, charismatic and probably paranoid-schizophrenic individual with the necessary callous ruthlessness, driven by his internal fear, who can persuade a few others that they would benefit by grouping together to bully the rest. Such groups grow and die all the time. Throughout history these little tyrants, the so-called Age of Heroes, have risen, thrived and died. We can never stop that. But, as we'll see, we can stop it becoming hereditary.

In the 1870s in Tanganyika, now Tanzania, was such a tyrant, Nyungu. Even then it wasn't a totally natural situation. Arab traders were already seeking ivory and slaves. Control of this trade bought guns from the Arabs which increased the tyrant's power. But it does show how such men started.

The Kimbu tribe were mainly hunter-gatherers living in a fairly sparsely populated forest area, 2$^1/_2$ people to the square mile. They did a little cultivating, but preferred to hunt and gather.

Nyungu got himself a gang of thugs, a 'ruga ruga', and started to terrorise the neighbourhood. "They were noisy and excitable, their hair plaited in long hanks. They were almost naked, but wore ivory bracelets and their heads were adorned with 'ghastly finery' designed to inspire terror. Their arms bore the medicine marks of the elephant hunter. We are not told what the 'ghastly finery' on their heads was, but oral sources confirm that it was the custom to wear parts of their victims bodies, scalps, beards and so on, as caps. Tradition states that they also wore belts made of human entrails and necklaces of human teeth. The White Fathers, who were attacked by Nyungu's ruga-ruga in 1878, described them as dressed in feathers with bands of beads on their foreheads and pieces of brilliantly coloured cloth on their heads. For weapons they carried bows and arrows, two or three spears and an ancient musket." (Shorter. 1.)

Nyungu and his companions terrorised, bullied and killed the local population. And he disarmed them, so that he had total control. He took the crops and anything desirable and handed them out to his companions. He was gradually able to control the ivory trade. With the profits from this he bought guns which he distributed to his companions, and thus was able to control an increasingly large territory. His expansion was finally ended by the British colonists doing exactly the same thing on a vast scale.

The reason a gang develops round a leader is the loot that they can get. In Scotland c. 730 AD. "Royal power was thus precarious, dependent above all on success in battle which brought riches to the king and his followers. Failure meant no more plunder and rewards in land and consequently desertion by the followers." (Duncan)

The loot belongs to the leader and he gives it out to his companions. In Germany c. 100 AD.: "The companion looked to the generosity of his chieftain for the war horse he covets, for the bloody and victorious spear, and for the meat, drink and entertainment which, abundant if rough, serve instead of pay. Only with opportunities for war and booty can chieftains so reward their followers." (Tacitus.)

The system depends on the leader rewarding his companions. But a leader, as his power increases and controls a larger population, can extract the plunder without fighting by demanding 'gifts' from subordinate chiefs. In East Africa: "A conqueror . . . demanded that conquered chiefs should greet him regularly in this manner. This meant they had to bring him gifts of ivory, slaves and cloth." (Shorter. 2.) This is the precursor of taxation. These 'gifts' are then distributed by the leader to the companions, (which is what taxation is all about, taking from the many to give to the few.)

To maintain power, the first thing a conqueror does is to disarm the defeated. The leader and his companions stay in power because they are the only ones with the arms. In all these 'Heroic' societies it is only the few 'freemen' who are allowed to bear arms. It's about 5-10% of the population. In Ireland: "Below them (the kings, nobles and druids) were the non-noble freemen, like gentlemen farmers . . . the rest of the population consisted of unfree members of society, people without franchise, men who were not allowed to bear arms." (Ross). In 4th cent. BC. Crete: "The typical Cretan polity was a military aristocracy with a Dorian citizen body dominating the rural 'dwellers around' . . . forbidden to bear arms." (Burn. 3.) In Japan: "Beneath the *daimyo* was the main body of samurai, or warriors, among whom there were wide variations in power and wealth. Together with their families they are estimated to have numbered around 2,000,000 persons or about one sixteenth of the total population." (Moore. 1) "The peasants were strictly forbidden to own firearms or carry swords." (Moore. 2)

Once an elite, the schizophrenic leader and his companions, have disarmed the people, there is a massive campaign of terror to cow them into total submission with bloodshed sometimes on a horrifying scale. It's all part of the pattern.

There is another intriguing aspect to schizophrenia. It has a close connection with psychic ability. I am told that many schizophrenics are psychic. Officially the paranormal doesn't exist, so there's no mention of it in the textbooks. The doctors and nurses won't admit it. But the patients all recognise the connection. So if the paranoid-schizophrenic leader is psychic too, is a healer perhaps, that's a formidably persuasive combination.

Population Growth

It's beginning to look as though it was at this point, the creation of hierarchies of obedience in a hunter-gatherer society, that the population began to increase. It seems that populations grow when a group or a family becomes no longer self-sufficient; when it is not limited by the amount of food on its own land. When it could get food from elsewhere, it could have more children. In parts of Africa, Asia and Latin America before colonialism: "It appears as if several of these societies strove to maximise labour productivity. This involved limiting the population to the number that could be supported with a fairly modest effort. The methods of achieving this limitation varied. Sexual taboos – e.g. the prohibition of intercourse during a nursing period of 3-5 years – was common, as were various abortion methods. Different ways of legitimising abortions also appear to have existed. The condition for the functioning of the system was that the land was collectively owned and that the food was distributed according to need." (Anell and Nygren.)

This is an important quote because it indicates the significance of self-sufficiency, common ownership of land and the sharing of food as the mechanism to stabilise population.

So when a local bully and his companions or a shaman and his acolytes can force the people to hand over some of their food, they are no longer constrained to have only the number of children that can be supported by their own land. Perhaps it was the rich that got the children. The usual view is that population started to increase after they had discovered agriculture. They had more food so they could feed more children. As we've seen, agriculture is harder work and unpopu-

16

lar, so the agriculture came because of the children, not the children because of the agriculture.

There's another intriguing thing. We always thought that people started settling in villages because of agriculture, but, "At Mureybit in South West Asia, storage pits and year-round occupation indicated that its occupants had definitely settled down between 8200 BC. and 7500 BC. yet the remains and artifacts indicate that the occupants were hunter-gatherers and not domesticators." (Haviland. 6)

In Ancient Egypt: "Its wide distribution (of pottery) may bear witness to the growing sedentariness made possible by a highly successful collecting economy which flourished along the southern fringes of the Sahara during a period of increased rainfall, in the fourth millennium (BC.) or earlier." (Trigger. 1.)

In Japan about 10,000 BC. they started settling down, but still as hunter-gatherers. "Stone Age men in Japan also caught fish and hunted and ate wild animals including birds, deer, wild boar and bears. In addition, they ate nuts and wild berries, but they did not, at least in the early periods, grow any crops.

"Stone Age men in Japan lived in small communities in pit houses of square shape and simple construction . . . they made wicker baskets . . . pots were used both for storage and preparation of food." (Cortazzi. 1.)

So agriculture is probably not the cause of settlement and population growth but their effect. Something else caused them. We have seen how tyrants do it. Another culprit is religion. As we shall see later, a shaman was able to instil religious obedience into the tribe and force them to hand over some of the results of their hunting and gathering. This fed a small elite who could settle down in a fortified place. It would be in their interests to have more people hunting and gathering for them, so they might find religious excuses, as religions have done ever since, to forbid curbs on births. Certainly the Japanese had a significant organised religion. "In the late Jomon period stone circles were built apparently for burial and fertility rites. The most notable of these circles is at Oyu in Akita prefecture where numerous stones were formed into two concentric circles in a sundial pattern around a standing pillar. It seems probable that a form of shamanism developed and that the Jomon people felt a fear of the dead and the spirits . . . in the final period rice cultivation seems to have been introduced from the continent of Asia." (Cortazzi. 1.) Stone circles in Britain are closely associated with a growing hierarchy.

So it seems that religion, obedience to hierarchy and settlement pre-dated agriculture, and that the increase in population was not caused by the agriculture but by the ability of groups or individuals to take food from others to feed their extra children. Having got the children,

17

it then became necessary to increase food production with agriculture.

Inherited Kingship

The little tyrants like Nyungu die and nearly always their tyrannies die with them. But when the tyrant dies his companions lose their power and wealth. The companions depended for their arms, their wealth and privileges on the generosity of the leader. If the leader dies then the whole thing collapses. Sometimes the leader is supplanted and the new leader has his own companions who look to the new leader's generosity for their wealth and privileges. The companions of the previous leader lose everything. To avoid such a distressing situation the companions, foreseeing the death of their leader, try to arrange an orderly maintenance of the status quo. They put it out that the leader was not only leader because of his personal qualities but was descended from the gods, and that therefore the leader's son, also descended from the gods, should inherit the kingship, and the companions stay the companions and keep their wealth.

This means pulling an enormous great con trick on the people – that there really are gods from whom the king could be descended. It must have taken many years of brainwashing, propaganda and terror until the people were cowed into accepting such nonsense. Religion is a political construct.

The Invention of Religion

The seeds of this nonsense lie in the animist beliefs amongst primitive societies, though they were far less significant or demanding than we had thought.

In the Andaman Islands, "The Onges do not love Eiuga or any other of the spirits. They merely fear them and seek to evade their anger by various expedients. It is curious that they never hesitate to try and deceive the spirits and think themselves very clever when they manage to steal roots or tubers from the ground. Nor do they revere the spirits of their ancestors: these are to be feared and propitiated by preservation of their bones . . . they have no 'practices' of any kind, no concept at all of holy places, prayers or images." (Cipriani. 2.) "their corporate sense is such that they have no need of leaders to give orders: such as there are, their leaders are chosen on the basis of outstanding powers, such as supposed clairvoyance." (Cipriani. 3.)

There's the key to the problem. Someone's starting to tell them what to do based, not on logic or self-interest, but supposed revelation. "Long established customs may be altered overnight as a result of a 'revelation' by some seer, only to have the new customs overthrown themselves in the course of time by the next 'revelation'." (Cipriani. 4.)

When the population grows, the numbers in the village rise above 500, too many for everyone to know; the sanctions for good behaviour are weakened. The village has a choice. It can either split into two separate communities, or, to maintain its strength against neighbouring communities, it can look for a new sanction for good behaviour, a bogey man, religion.

The behaviour of the Eskimos suggests that the development of religion is indeed not a progress in thought, but an accommodation to more densely populated living in a more anonymous grouping: "the people have two ways of grouping themselves, and to those two ways correspond two judicial systems, two moral systems, two sorts of domestic economy and of religious life. To a real community of ideas and interests in the dense agglomeration of the winter, are opposed an isolation, a social atomisation and an extreme moral and religious poverty in the dispersal of the summer." (Mauss.)

But the desire for a religious fiat brought far more dangers than advantages. The people are now beginning to accept obedience to the shaman. With the advent of religion people are no longer doing what they perceive to be logical or in their best interests, but what they are ordered to do by a few whose motives are not above suspicion, pretending to have the ear of the spirits. General human behaviour becomes irrational.

So when the companions of a dying leader are looking round for a reason to put his son in his place to preserve their privileges, they've got a god-given excuse – that the family of the leader is descended from the gods. And the leader's son must inherit the leader's position. And the companions keep the goodies. So it looks as though the development of religion from animism to heroic god was a political construct to preserve the wealth of the rich. But it wasn't a simple operation persuading the people of this dodgy nonsense. It involved savage blood-letting, terror, torture and mass deaths to impose the belief in the gods and obedience to the laws of the ruler. The people had first invented spirits as explanations for the natural world including psychic phenomena. They had used these spirits as a sanction for good behaviour. But they had to be forced to accept the final personification of the spirits into the gods which could be used as ancestors of tyrants.

The companions invented religion to preserve their wealth. Previously the heroes had not been too interested in such wimpish ideas. Heroes fight, fornicate and drink. But as the uses of this concept became apparent they got religion in a big way. The leaders became priest-kings.

Moses is a useful early example because it is so well documented in the Bible. Moses was schizophrenic. He was having what they called visions and what we call hallucinations. Whether he was paranoid or not it's difficult to tell, but he was fairly ruthless in protecting his own position. "Execute all the tribal leaders of Israel." (Numbers 25.4.) And he certainly had the reputation of being psychic, making bushes burn etc. His first job was to impose obedience.

"Moses told the people, 'You must obey all the commandments of the Lord your God, following his directions in every detail, going the whole way he has laid out for you: only then will you live long and prosperous lives in the land you are to enter and possess'." (Deuteronomy. 5. 32.) Just in case the carrot wasn't enough to enforce obedience, the stick was applied. "He (the Lord) issued the following command to Moses. 'Execute all the tribal leaders of Israel. Hang them up before the Lord in the broad daylight so that his fierce anger will turn away from the people.' So Moses ordered the Judges to execute all who had worshipped Baal." (Numbers. 25.4.)

The Effects of Obedience

Having established the principle of obedience to the law, the Lord proceeded to take His people to the cleaners. "A tenth of the produce of the land, whether grain or fruit, is the Lord's and is holy. If anyone wants to buy back this fruit or grain, he must add a fifth to its value. And the Lord owns every tenth animal of your herds and flocks," etc. (Leviticus. 27. 30) That is to say income tax and wealth tax at 10% or 12% in cash.

And where did all this wealth go? To the Chief Priest, of course, who just happened to be Moses brother, Aaron. Surprise. Surprise. And who collected the wealth, the taxes? Moses' tribe, the Levites. When the Israelites thought that this was pushing it, Moses said, "That'll be all right. We'll say that the Levites can't possess any land." Who needs land when you can extort the produce from everyone else's?

The people, having gone along with the fiction of a god as convenient sanction for good behaviour in a crowded society, now find themselves being fleeced by the priests of that fictitious god. The bible is a hilarious testament to the hanky-panky of this priestly establishment. A tenth of everything produced was handed over to the priests. "The priests shall wave these offerings before the Lord along with the loaves representing the first sampling of your later crops. They are holy to the Lord and will be given to the priests as food." (Leviticus 23. 20.) And a tenth of that tenth was handed over by the priests to the Chief Priest, Moses' brother. And if not "you will die". (Numbers 18.32.)

For the priests to get their hands on the crops one thing that had to be stopped was people sacrificing to the god anywhere else. The priests needed it to be done in the sanctuary. So make a rule. "You must not make sacrifices to your god just anywhere, as the heathens sacrifice to their gods. Rather, you must build a sanctuary for him at a place he himself will select as his home." (with a priest) "There you shall bring to the Lord your burnt offerings and other sacrifices – your tithes, your offerings presented by the gesture of waving before the altar." (Deuteronomy. 12. 4.) The sanctuary was doubling as a tax office and the priests were the tax collectors. Now one begins to see why the religions were so keen about corporate worship.

Notice that it is the people who are taxed, not the land. So that the more people there are, the bigger the tax take. It is in Moses' interest, Aaron and his sons' interest, the Levites' interest, to increase the population. It is in no one else's interest. Is that why the religions talk so much about the sanctity of human life? Quite certainly they and the Establishment have always strongly opposed any sort of birth control.

One way the people tried to avoid paying their taxes was to say that they were too busy in their fields to come to the sanctuary. This involved a big rewrite job for the priests. A new creation myth was worked out (in addition to the Adam and Eve story), which involved God creating the world in six days and taking the seventh day off. It was then decreed that everyone must follow God's example and not work on the seventh day, but come to the sanctuary, and pay their taxes.

Another way of increasing the income of Moses and his companions was an all-embracing sin list which needed 'atonement'. "The same instructions apply to both the sin offering and the guilt offering – the carcase shall be given to the priest who is in charge of the atonement ceremony for his food. (When the offering is a burnt sacrifice, the priest who is in charge shall also be given the animal's hide). The priests who present the people's grain offerings to the Lord shall be given whatever remains of the sacrifice after the ceremony is completed. This rule applies whether the sacrifice is baked, fried or grilled. All other grain offerings, whether mixed with olive oil or dry, are the common property of all the sons of Aaron." (Leviticus 7. 7.)

But as well as the grain, mixed or not, the Levite priests had to hand over a tenth of all the tithes they received to the Chief Priest, Aaron. "Tell the Levites to give to the Lord a tenth of the tithes they receive – a tithe of the tithe, to be presented to the Lord by the gesture of waving before the altar. The Lord will consider this as your first-of-the-harvest offering to him of grain and wine, as though it were from your own property. This tithe of the tithe shall be selected from the choicest part of the tithes you receive as the Lord's portion, and shall be given to Aaron the priest." (Numbers 18. 25.)

The fine detail of these laws was necessary to ensure the priests' income. Two of Aaron's sons, in a ceremony, got into a muddle with their incense burners and didn't do it quite according to instruction. "So fire blazed forth from the presence of the Lord and destroyed them." (Leviticus 10. 3.) Now the Lord's reaction might at first seem a trifle over the top. But he was quite right. If they couldn't get a little detail right like swinging a censer, what other little details might they get wrong – like that 10 per cent of all that is holy!

Of course all this only applies to Jews who worship at the sanctuary. Strangers in the land who weren't Jews couldn't be taxed. Highly undesirable. So the rules were rewritten. A verse which starts: "Any Israelite who sacrifices an ox, lamb or goat anywhere except at the Tabernacle is guilty of murder . . ." (Leviticus 17. 3.) is followed by an inserted verse "I repeat: Anyone, whether Israelite or foreigner living among you who offers a burnt offering or sacrifice . . ." (Leviticus 17. 9.)

The Temple of Solomon at Jerusalem was truly wealthy. It had storehouses bursting with grain, hides, oil etc. It had craftsmen with great skill producing sophisticated works of art. It had writers, philosophers and a growing body of knowledge.

But all this was at the specific expense of the peasants who had to feed the artisans, the writers, the experts. Jerusalem created no wealth at all. It generated no jobs. It was the food which generated the jobs. With this taxation the rulers could feed their artists, their philosophers, their architects, builders and workmen, their servants, their master-craftsmen. From the peasants' food were made the great buildings, the epic poems, the statuary, the philosophies, the roads, the bridges, the ports which are called civilisation, the culture of cities. Without that taxation of an agricultural hinterland a city and its culture could not exist.

By now the people must have realized the pickle they'd got themselves into. But there were three convincing reasons why they put up with their religious masters. The most immediate was that if they didn't, they got themselves killed by the priests' soldiers. That's always a very persuasive argument. The second was that the most intelligent amongst them, those whose opinion they valued, said that, yes, there was indeed a god. The elite was always very careful to buy the intelligentsia, to give them well-paid jobs and status – as long as they supported the elite and the ideas that kept the elite in power. So the intelligentsia duly persuaded the people to live with their chains. And still does!

The third reason is the unexplained powers of the shaman. There's an awful lot of anecdotal evidence that faith-healing works. There are persuasive examples of clairvoyance very often linked with religion. When a seer who is a successful healer and proven clairvoyant says with total conviction that there is a god, that's persuasive.

The problem is that when priests/shamans go into trances, whether by breathing techniques, meditation, energetic dancing etc., their brains go on the blink; they start to hallucinate, hear things, see things. And what they hear and see, the products of their own brains, is what they expect to hear and see. If they go to Lourdes they hallucinate the Virgin Mary – not the Buddha. William Sargent in 'The Mind Possessed' shows that in certain deep states of altered consciousness part of the result is an unbreakable conviction about the validity of the hallucination. That conviction, a chemical change in the brain, lasts for about seven years before it needs a recharge. That conviction is very convincing.

So the people, persuaded by the threat of death, the opinions of the intellectuals and the conviction of their seers, continue to accept the gods which give them the sanctions for good behaviour, but which impoverish them.

The Bible is the best account we have of the growth of religious power and the change from priest-king to king but it must have happened in every early city state. The secularisation of power, though still founded on obedience to the law of a god, continued until today when the communist powers even reject the god from which their power is derived, a very unstable position.

Thus is wealth and poverty created by religion. Moses' successors now had a continuing supply of food to feed their soldiers and police, their judges, their bureaucrats, their builders, cooks, artists, philosophers. They could buy better weapons, and more of them, to make war on neighbours. They were able, after a little chat with the Lord, to rewrite the rules when changed circumstances might threaten their income.

It's not clear from the Bible how the later secular kings raised their funds. Presumably they got a cut from all those sacrifices 'waved in front of the altar'. But there were many other techniques available. "a central institution . . . may demand tribute, levy assessments, mobilize labour, decree consumption standards etc. And, in a similar vein one of the most common of all means of surplus accumulation has been the power of arms to plunder and secure booty. Corvée, book days, tithes, censuses, tax farming, auctions, markets by decree, these are some of the paraphernalia of surplus mobilization." (H.W. Pearson).

We are trying to identify the causes of poverty. This excursion into Bible study has been to show the early techniques of taxation, and how that taxation produced great wealth, great culture, but it didn't make the people in general wealthier. We don't know whether the Jewish peasants were hungry after they had been taxed; but we do know that it was they and only they who created others' wealth. We judge a civilisation as great by its buildings, its literature, its artifacts. But none of these things mean that the people are well fed. It usually means they are hungry. The major cause of poverty is government taxation.

Mesopotamia and Egypt

The intricate tax laws of a small kingdom in the Middle East 3000 years ago have survived because they have been politically useful to kings ever since. They are still read out in churches all over the world because they form the legal basis of taxation (Obey every law of God's representative on Earth, the king). But Israel was not a great ancient civilisation like those across the desert to the east on the Tigris and Euphrates. The Mesopotamian empires in what is now called Iraq started much earlier, lasted much longer, were much bigger and were much, much richer.

Why were they rich? In Sumer, c.2500BC., "Almost all the land and cattle belonged to the gods, that is to the temples. Each temple possessed its own fields and pastures (the main temple having, of course, the greater share). The cultivated land was divided into three parts: one part was 'the land of the Lord' and as such, was worked by the whole community for the sole benefit of the temple; another, 'the food land', was allotted to the dependants of the temple for their support, and the third part, 'the plough land', was let out to tenants against one seventh or one eighth of the harvest." (Roux. 1) Sumer was rich because it forced or conned the peasants into obeying the priests' laws. The land now grew crops for the rich, not the poor. With these crops the rich could now feed soldiers, arm them and attack other cities less tyrannical, who levied less taxation and were therefore less well armed.

In Assyria: "The men, horses, cattle and sheep brought into Assyria by the thousand, the enormous yearly income in silver, gold, copper, iron, grain and other commodities so accurately registered by palace scribes, all this was generally not purchased but taken by force. Wealth was constantly being transferred from the periphery to the centre, from the dependencies and 'protectorates' to the Mesopotamian homeland. The Assyrians took much and gave very little, with the result that if the state was rich, its distant subjects were destitute." (Roux. 2.)

The state stole from their own people too. In Egypt: "Ramasses III gave over 900 square miles carrying 86,486 people to endow his new foundations at Thebes and very considerable though less amounts to Heliopolis and Memphis representing altogether something like 10% of the cultivable land of the kingdom." (Hawkes. 1.)

In Nubia, a colony of Egypt; "All of the Egyptian temples received produce from their nearby estates and some were authorised to levy duty on goods produced in their vicinity or passing them on the river. These profits were used to support not only priests, administrators and their servants but also specialists such as traders, miners, shipbuilders, and a wide range of other craftsmen." (Trigger. 2.)

The peasants were now forced to produce a surplus, for a surplus is never produced voluntarily, the Law of Least Effort – grain carefully stored against the seven lean years is not a surplus. This was stored in the palaces, temples, garrisons and castles. Therefore the poorest with the least land were forced to go to where the surplus was kept to earn back by labour the food which had been taken from them. "As for land on lease-hold the normal return expected from the tenant was one third of the crop. It is therefore small wonder that the poorer people were engulfed in debt to the point of selling their children as slaves, and that a large proportion of the population preferred to work for the local temples or for the king against regular wages paid in grain, food and clothing." (Roux. 3.)

Notice at this point that the interests of those poor now change. Previously, as peasants, the more that was taken from them by the king, the poorer they were. Now as servants or artisans of the king or the temple, the more the rulers can squeeze from the peasants left behind in the villages, the better chance those in the towns have of eating. Urban artisans do not make products for the peasants in exchange for their food but eat by making baubles for the elite who own the food. Urban workers depend for their subsistence on a strong ruling class. There are indeed two classes, not the workers and the bosses but the workers with the bosses against the peasants; the town against the countryside.

It was the extortion of a food surplus from the land by the elite which brought the *need* to invent writing. "Year by year the quantities of grain, sesame seed, vegetables, dates, cattle, large and small, preserved fish, wool, skins and the rest brought to the temple stores increased as did the number of citizens bringing them . . . The most advanced attempts made during these birth throes of literacy were wage lists – signs representing individuals followed by an indication of daily pay in terms of bread and beer. Writing was invented in Sumeria solely for the administration of the temple economy." (Hawkes. 2.) Likewise in order to get the crops in from the furthest outposts, roads and bridges *had* to be built, the wheel *had* to be 'invented' to get the crops into the temples and castles of the elite.

Trade

Today's conventional wisdom is that trade creates wealth. It was not so in Mesopotamia. There is no evidence of any local trade at all. "Babylonia, as a matter of fact, possessed neither market places nor a functioning market system of any description." (Polanyi. 1.) So whatever wealth there was in Mesopotamia was not created by local trading. (Local markets were imposed, with coinage, later, as an extremely efficient hidden taxation, to be described in the next chapter.)

But there was considerable royal trade with other countries. Partly it was for status. But it could also be a source of income by taxation. "Copper was imported in enormous quantities on which the palace made a tidy profit in income dues." (Oates.) And timber was imported, for example the cedars of Lebanon used to build the royal palaces and temples. This may have been barter, which doesn't create wealth, but it doesn't sound as though the two parties were equally enthusiastic. "Sargon lists among his military achievements the fact that he was the first king to have compelled Egypt . . . to establish trade relations with Assyria." (Oppenheim. 1.) That sounds more like theft than wealth creation.

And up in the hills of Turkey the same thing was going on. "The prominence of armed men, and the squat heaviness characteristic of Hittite sculpture, certainly suggest the heavy tread of conquerors, who found themselves in a position to require rents and services from their victims on a scale sufficient to maintain small cities in which artisans and other specialists could cater to the conquerors' tastes." (McNeill. 1.)

Nowadays peasants are usually made to produce a surplus by taxation, which will be described later; but sometimes brute force is used even now. In Russia Stalin decided to "use force to make the villages contribute the food and raw materials needed for expansion of the urban and industrial sector of the economy . . . This was done by compulsory collectivization of agriculture. Peasants were compelled to pool their land and draft animals to equip collective farms; and each collective farm was required to deliver part of its harvest to the state as a kind of tax before distributing anything to the peasant members as payment for their work." (McNeill. 2.) Stalin took so much that there was mass starvation in the Ukraine, where the grain was grown.

Cities

The cities of Mesopotamia grew up round the castles, palaces and temples. They have no independent economic validity. They produce no wealth. They generate no jobs. It is the food from the peasants which generates the jobs. The cities are simply places where the extracted surplus is spent. If a king goes away and the surplus is no longer brought to the city, that city dies. In 1570 Akbar the Great built a city at Fatehpur Sikri in India. Fourteen years later he left, taking the surplus with him. So the people had to leave too. All that remained was an elegant skeleton of a beautiful sandstone city. "the private dwellings and shops decayed and disappeared; the walls, mosque, mint, treasury, caravansary, palaces and other public places remained; no industry has since come near." (Galbraith.)

"The capital of Bengal was Rajinahal in 1592, Dacca in 1608, Murshihad in 1704. In each case and in the same way, as soon as its prince abandoned it the town was jeopardised, deteriorated and occasionally died." (Braudel. 10.)

London is said to be a capital and a great port because of its geographical advantages. For a thousand years since William the Conqueror London has prospered. But for a thousand years before that, the geographical advantages to the Romans, the Anglo-Saxons and the Danes were irrelevant. The Romans put their capital at Colchester in spite of the large 'trade' through London to Rome. The Anglo-Saxons were even less impressed. The wealth went to Winchester or Wallingford or Canterbury or York, wherever the kings took their surplus, and they never took it to London. London became a village.

A town can be created by a natural resource surplus. But if the surplus runs out the town dies. In America they discovered oil at a place they then called Pithole where a town suddenly grew up. "At its peak Pithole in 1865 had 10,000 inhabitants, eight hotels, two telegraph offices, a theatre, a daily newspaper." Then the oil ran out and the town vanished. "It lived for 500 days." No industry was created. When the oil went, the people went. Today there is "no sign of the main street, the theatre or the churches." (Sampson).

The phenomenal growth of cities in the Third World today is for exactly the same reason; that's where the surplus is spent. The agricultural land grows the crops, cotton, oil crops like palm and ground nuts, coffee, tea etc. in great plantations. The profits from these crops do not go back to the countryside. They are spent in the cities. So the peasants with inadequate land are forced into the shanty towns of those cities to work for those with the surplus to spend.

But even those with land are heavily taxed, taxes which are spent in the cities. "Direct taxation in Nigeria, nearly all from rural producers, yielded 38% of all revenue." (Davidson. 1.) And they paid nearly all the indirect taxation too. "Of a gross one million pounds a year earned by Kenya Africans in registered employment direct and indirect taxes for the sample period 1920-23 annually subtracted £750,000; only a quarter of their earnings remained to the earners." (Davidson. 2.)

There are other reasons for towns and cities, military and administrative, no more natural than cities built from the surplus expropriated from the periphery. Right from the beginning towns had been planted to control the local population. Today it's called 'hamletisation'. In East Timor, Guatemala etc., recalcitrant natives are forced into villages where any rebellious activity can be more easily suppressed. In Mesopotamia: "Many cities of ancient Iraq had some town planning for military purposes on a grid-iron pattern." (Thomas. 6.) "The Assyrian kings constantly founded new cities and peopled them with prisoners of war. These were ruled by royal officials and paid taxes to the king. All this and a road system

27

built for policing, as well as for the collecting of taxes and tributes, served to support the king's household and his army . . . a conscious and ruthless execution of the political concept of forced urbanization can be said to have created the Assyrian Empire." (Oppenheim. 2.)

In twelfth century east Germany "Everywhere considerable coherent villages were set up – some in compact form, about a central 'place', a street or a village green and pond: some in the looser form of the strung out 'Waldhufen' village. All were planned. This orderly procedure. . . was associated with the urgent need to strengthen political supremacy." (Koener. 2.)

In Algeria: "Nomads in particular had been subjected to considerable pressure to settle in villages as part of the quest for security . . . New villages were established and the dispersed rural population were re-housed in an attempt to isolate them from guerilla forces. The first villages were established in 1955 and by 1961 half the rural Moslem population of the country (35 million people) had been resettled or moved . . . Similar programmes were undertaken by the Portuguese in Mozambique and Portuguese Guinea, and by the Rhodesian government in the 1970s." (Christopher.)

The grid-iron pattern is an indication of towns planted by a government, whether for administrative, military, or, as we shall see later, for tax-raising purposes. "All the towns in China, Korea, Japan, peninsular India and colonial America (not forgetting those in Rome and certain Greek cities) were planned according to the chess board pattern." (Braudel. 2.)

'Justice'

The power to demand crops, to force the peasants to produce extra for an elite, a surplus, depends on the fiction that the ruler has the ear of God; that he is in some way superior, better. The elite, to stay in power, must reinforce this fiction. The whole Old Testament of the Bible is a justification for the elite to impoverish the people. Children had to be conditioned to obey every word of the Bible. They were taught to recite it by heart. If any part of that Bible is questioned, then the power of the elite to remove the crops is questioned. Questioners were burnt or otherwise dissuaded. And the whole edifice of 'Justice' was built up to perform this service for the elite. While it was pretended that judges were wise and fair, their main function was to extirpate any hearsay which might threaten the legitimacy of their employers.

The object of 'Justice' is injustice. 'Justice' was imposed by the sword and by religion to enforce the unjust laws which took from the many to give to the few, the taxation, tithes, forced labour, share-cropping, slavery, whichever technique that could be found to expropriate the crops and labour from the people. In every village a Lord meted out 'Justice'. In medieval France: "Of all the seigneurial rights over people, justice was the one which would most readily permit lords to relieve workers of the money that they had managed to earn." (Duby. 2.)

At first 'Justice' took the crops, then it took the land on which those crops were grown. The Lords in Britain, in their Parliament, passed the Acts of Enclosure, acknowledged as legalised theft, which took the people's land, making it into the private property of the rich. Those laws are still operating, enforced every day in nearly every case involving property. Final Appeal against these laws is to those very Lords in that same Parliament who made those laws.

The Superiority of the Elite

To maintain its authority an elite must appear to be better people than those it rules, more noble, the nobility: aristocrat derives from the Greek 'aristos', the best. It must employ architects to make their houses into palaces. It must use artists and writers to portray their superiority. The function of the artist has always been to reinforce the authority of the elite. That's what they're paid for. That's why the naive ones, who thought that art was for art's sake, starved in their garrets; and hence the yawning gap between 'modern art', associated with the present elite, and popular culture. When a ruling elite changes, the artistic styles of the old elite are discarded. With the arrival of 'democracy' the pretty realism of the kings was replaced by the modernism of the new governing elite. Jazz, the vernacular art of the American Negroes, was unacceptable in artistic musical circles unless it had been reworked by Gershwin or Stravinski. Today electro-funk, or whatever, has replaced jazz as the vernacular style, so jazz, safely sanitised, no longer a threat, can be heard on Radio 3.

The rulers enforce their own values; their particular dialect becomes 'correct' pronunciation; their way of spelling, however silly, is enforced by education; their cultural values are lauded in their schools. The object of education and culture is to reinforce the superiority of the lawmakers.

One of the earliest ways that the rulers justified their power was to claim descent from the gods. Each of them ordered their intellectuals and writers to produce the sagas linking them with the gods, such sagas as Gilgamesh of Mesopotamia, the Odyssey, the Iliad, the Aeneid, Boewulf. When the monotheistic religions, Christianity, Islam, Judaism developed, a blood relationship to a single god with no wife was a bit tricky. The Jewish kings tried to relate themselves to Adam and Eve, but it didn't have quite the same ring. Instead the justification to rule was that the king was God's representative on Earth. So the king didn't need a saga. The sagas stopped being written.

Moving the Loot

The elite now own the crops which finance the jobs in the towns; but to secure them they need to get them into their stockades, fortresses and castles, and they have to get the soldiers out to the villages to get the crops in and to keep the peasants in order, ie. paying their taxes. They have to build roads and they have to invent wheels. That's why Rome built roads all across her empire and that's why they all led back to Rome. In the 1st cent BC. "The laying out of roads may have been the chief activity for highly mobile legionary troops stationed in the hinterland of Gaul in the 20s . . . Three hundred years later an Aeduan orator could complain that the roads served military rather than civilian purposes." (Wightman).

In Roman Africa, "that (logical network of roads) was in the first place military, in the second administrative – for the collection of corn and taxes – and only a very poor third, however useful, for the benefit of the inhabitants." (Raven. 1.) "Many waterways in China, though serving a secondary purpose for irrigation, were primarily designed to ensure efficient movement of the grain tax from the provinces to the capital and the frontiers." (Bray.) In medieval France: "It should also be emphasized that the entire road system at this time was organised to facilitate communications between Paris, the fairs of Champagne, the producer-towns of the north and the foreign markets." (Bautier. 2.)

In the Third World today: "If you examine the transportation network, for instance, in nearly any poor country, you will see that the roads and railways have not been geared to facilitating commerce between neighbouring countries or even between regions of the same country; but to getting food and other raw materials moved from the hinterlands to the capital and the ports and from thence northwards" to the developed countries. (George.) In Mali in one year nine tenths of the development aid was spent on roads. All but one of the roads went from the agricultural areas down towards the ports. The other went from nowhere to nowhere but was militarily important (for subduing its own people).

In Argentina, Rosas "did not finally subdue the provinces; the central authority still needed railways for the completion of that task." (Pendle. 2.)

The object of roads, of railways and ports is not to get the people to the seaside, but to get the troops to the people. The object of roads is not to create wealth but to remove it.

The Monopoly of Arms

Having established obedience to the law with a mixture of force and religious persuasion, the elite, to maintain its power, had to disarm the people. It's a tricky operation because the elite still needs an armed force to discourage importunate neighbours. It seems usually that free-men, the upper middle classes, kept their arms and an obligation to fight for the elite, while the poor, the slaves, serfs etc., the vast majority of the population, were forbidden to have arms. The freemen benefited enough from the status quo for the elite to risk arming them. But the implication is that there weren't that many freemen. If a state was rich enough, it could afford a professional army, well-paid and heavily disci-plined to avoid mutiny, and very often foreign.

While the monopoly of arms guaranteed their continuing power within their area of control, it made the kings very vulnerable to attack from armed 'barbarians' outside. The Huns, Goths and Visigoths were able to devastate the Roman Empire because the Roman population was dis-armed, protected only by insufficient paid soldiers. The Vikings were able to attack the coasts in the British Isles with impunity because the inhabitants were disarmed, defenceless. When William the Conqueror invaded England, he didn't have to defeat the whole English people, only the few arms-bearing freemen Harold could muster.

The elite had three answers: invade the barbarians' territory, which of-ten over-extended the elite's power, or build a wall to keep the barbar-ians out, the Great Wall of China, Hadrian's Wall, the Antonine Wall, Offa's Dyke. It didn't usually work. So it was in the interests of a ruler that the neighbouring lands should also be controlled by rulers who would dis-arm those free, arms-bearing peoples, and he gave them help to do it.

So that's the main thesis of this book, that poverty is caused by govern-ment, by its taxation and, as we shall see later, governments' theft, legal or otherwise, of the land.

The next section is about what is not the cause of poverty, the lack of trade and industry, capitalism.

Chapter 2. The Birth of Tyranny
References

L. Anell and B. Nygren. "The Developing Countries and the World Economic Order." Francis Pinter Ltd. '80. p.24.

R-H Bautier. "The Economic Development of Medieval Europe". Thames and Hudson '71. 2: p.114.

F. Braudel. "Capitalism and Material Life". Weidenfeld and Nicholson. '73. 2: p.385., 10: p.412.

F. Bray. "The Rice Economies". Blackwell. '86. p.64.

A.R. Burn. "The Lyric Age of Greece". Arnold. '60. 3: p.67.

A.J. Christopher. "Colonial Africa". Croom Helm. '84. p.44.

L. Cipriani. "The Andaman Islanders." Weidenfeld and Nicholson. '66. 2: p.43., 3: p.144., 4:p.76.

H. Cortazzi. "The Japanese Achievement". Sidgewick and Jackson. '90. 1:p.3.

B. Davidson. "Africa in Modern History". Longman '83. 1: p.134., 2: p.118.

A.S. Diamond. "The Evolution of Law and Order". Watts. '51. p.32.

M. Douglas. "The Lele of Kasai". in "African Worlds". Ed. Darryl Forde. O.U.P. '54. p.14.

G. Duby. "The Early Growth of the European Economy". Weidenfeld and Nicholson. '74. 2: p.227.

A.A.M. Duncan. "The Kingdom of the Scots" in "The Dark Ages". Ed. L.M. Smith. MacMillan. '84. 1: p.135.

E. Evans-Pritchard. "The Nuer". O.U.P. '74. p.5.

J. Galbraith. "The Age of Uncertainty". B.B.C.–Deutcsh. '77. p.304.

S. George. "How the Other Half Dies". Penguin. '76. p.36.

W.A. Haviland. "Anthropology" Holt, Rhinehart and Winston. '82. 6: p.224.

J. Hawkes. "The First Great Civilizations". Hutchinson. '73. 1: p.391. 2: p.43.

R. Koener. in The Cambridge Economic History of Europe. ed. Postan. C.U.P. '71. Vol.1. 2: p.83.

B.H. MacDermot. "The Cult of the Sacred Spear". Hale '73. p.179.

M. Mauss. "The Gift". '54. I read this quote in another book which seemed to attribute it to "The Gift", which I later read but couldn't find the quote. Perhaps I missed it, or perhaps it's a different book.

W.H. McNeill. "A World History". O.U.P. '79. 1: p.40., 2: p.50.

B. Moore Jnr. "The Social Origins of Dictatorship and Democracy". Penguin. '66. 1: p.232., 2: p.262.

J. Oates. "Babylon". Thames and Hudson. '86. p.59.

A.L. Oppenheim. in "Trade and Market in Early Empires". Ed. K. Polanyi. Free Press. '57. 1: p.35., 2: p.36.

H.W. Pearson. in "Trade and Market in Early Empires". Ed. K. Polanyi. Free Press. '57. p.336.

G. Pendle. "A History of Latin America." Penguin. '63. 2. p.136.

J. Pfeiffer. "The Emergence of Man". Harper Row. '72. 2: p.43.

K. Polanyi. "Trade and Market in Early Empires". Free Press. '57. 1. p.16.

S. Raven. "Rome in Africa." Longman. '84. 1. p.70.

A. Ross. "The Pagan Celts". Batsford. '86. p.28.

G. Roux. "Ancient Iraq". George Allen and Unwin. '64. 1: p.113., 2: p.238., 3: p.145.

A. Sampson. "The Seven Sisters". Hodder and Stoughton. '75. p.19.

A. Shorter. "Chieftainship in Western Tanzania". Clarendon. '72. 1: p.276., 2: p.130.

H. Thomas. "An Unfinished History of the World". Hamish Hamilton. '79. 6: p.29.

B.G. Trigger. "Ancient Egypt. A Social History". C.U.P. '83. 1: p.16. 2: "Nubia under the Pharaohs". Thames and Hudson '76. p.118.

E.M. Wightman. "Gallica Belgica". Batsford. '85. p.49.

Chapter 3
DOES TRADE CREATE WEALTH OR POVERTY?

CONVENTIONAL WISDOM SAYS that the formation of cities was a natural step in the progress of mankind. So far we have seen that there was nothing natural about it at all; that it was forced on people by poverty caused by religious laws. But conventional wisdom says that trade and industry, stimulated by cities, create wealth, and that therefore everyone is richer, outweighing the poverty of the peasant. So, does trade create wealth?

In fact trade in any quantity has to be forced on people. With the advent of coinage rulers were able to generate an enormous income by their taxation on trade, a hidden tax on the consumer. But before coinage there was no benefit to the rulers to enforce trade. Trade between ordinary people did not happen to any extent. In the 5th century BC. "The Persians do not frequent market places and in effect do not possess in their country a single market place." (Herodotus, writing at the time. 1.53) "Archaeological evidence speaks against the existence of 'market places' within the cities of the Ancient Near East." (Oppenheim.) In Mesopotamia: "common people seldom did any trading." (McNeill.)

The Mesopotamian kings all engaged in trade with neighbouring countries. But even this sometimes had to be enforced. What the kings wanted was high status goods, cedar and scented woods for their temples and palaces, marble and diorite for their statues, precious stones for their jewellery. All this trade was kept closely in the hands of the kings. It benefited the townspeople giving them raw materials on which they could work to earn their living. But it brought no benefit to the peasants.

The Phoenicians have a wide reputation of being some of the earliest traders. And they didn't do it from choice. They had been driven off their land by the Assyrians and left to starve on the coast of the Mediterranean. The Assyrians didn't seem to like the coastal regions. The Phoenicians, by trading; "maintained themselves, after they had lost the interior, in their seaports and island strongholds." (A.R. Arnold. 2.)

In the Adriatic c.1000 AD.: "The rise of Amalfi, though not easily comprehensible at first sight, is explained by the port's early privileged contacts with Islam, as well as by the very poverty of its infertile hinterland, which drove the little town to commit itself single-mindedly to maritime ventures." (Braudel. 9.)

Core, Hinterland and Periphery

(The meaning of 'core' is fairly clear. The 'hinterland' is usually considered to be the crop-producing land which supplies the city. This might be understood to include the periphery, the outer areas. Similarly the periphery might be understood to include the hinterland. But now it is necessary to find two different words to describe various functions of the hinterland/periphery, the area closer to the core and the area further away. So we'll call the area closer to the core the 'hinterland' and the area further away the 'periphery'.)

The city depends for its existence on removing the crops from its hinterland and periphery. Because of the cost of transport, the difficulty of control and the perishability of some of the crops, there is a pattern of concentric circles round the core supplying various crops. The areas furthest away, the periphery, supply the forest products, tar, furs, wax, hides. The nearer parts of the periphery supply the timber, because of transport costs.

Early on this periphery is quite close to the city, but gradually all the trees are cut down. The rain runs off the cleared land and causes erosion.

In Assyria: "In early times hills quite near to the capitals would have carried substantial trees (the occasional one still remains where some favourable circumstances has protected it). As these became exhausted, Assyrian control was reaching out, so that the extensive forests of the Zagros and Tauros became available, the conquered population being used to fell them and transport them." (Saggs. 1.)

After all the trees are cut down a city has to import them from further away, sometimes overseas from a different country. Thus the periphery sometimes becomes politically separated from the core. But the periphery and the core are two essential parts of an economic whole. The city cannot exist without the periphery. The periphery is not peripheral. Today the Third World is that essential periphery to the core of the developed world.

Within this outer concentric ring of the periphery is the hinterland. On its furthest parts are raised the horses and cattle which can be walked to the core, and sheep for wool and the grain areas and the crops like flax and cotton. Closest to the core are the market gardens for fruit and vegetables which perish and must quickly be brought to market. Within the core is usually the industry and at the heart of the core the financial area.

Because of the higher density of population nearer the core, land prices are higher than at the periphery. Therefore it is necessary to grow crops closer towards the core which can command a higher price. In Renaissance Italy: "it was more profitable to grow vines than wheat (that is if someone else grew the wheat for you), more profitable to be in the secondary sector (industrial) than in the primary (agricultural) and in the tertiary sector (service and financial) than in the secondary." (Braudel. 2.)

As the core exhausts the timber of its periphery, it has to extend that periphery. So what was forest becomes cattle country, what was cattle country grows grain etc. And the transport system expands and innovates to cope with the greater distances.

Sometimes in sparsely populated countries like Colonial America or Russia there is an almost empty periphery into which to expand, usually killing off or enslaving the indigenous population. "For a long time the central zones siphoned off the populations of their outer margins: these were the favourite places for recruiting slaves. And where do the unskilled workers come from today, to work in the industrial area of Europe, the United States and the Soviet Union?" (Braudel. 7.)

Food prices and therefore wages and labour-costs are always highest at the core and lowest at the periphery where food is mostly free and where the 'social relationship economy' (see below) encourages people to minimise their profit. On the periphery: "money prices, if they exist at all, are laughable. A low cost of living is indeed in itself a sign of under-development. The Hungarian preacher Martino Szepsi Combor, returning to his native country in 1618, "noted the high price of food-stuffs in Holland and England; the situation began to change in France, then in Germany, Poland and Bohemia, and the price of bread went on falling all the way until he reached Hungary." (Braudel. 8.)

Since food is so cheap in money terms, the periphery always has to exchange far more food for the same manufactured goods than those closer in. For the periphery, manufactured goods are much more expensive.

Does Trade Harm the Periphery?

'Primitive' peoples engage in very little trade. Pygmies do not trade amongst themselves. But they do sometimes trade with negro villagers living nearby. They do this by leaving fruit etc. which they collect in the forest, at a certain spot. Then they go away. The negroes come and leave what they consider a suitable barter next to the piles of fruit, such as steel knives or axes. They go. The pygmies come back and take

36

either the offered barter or take back their fruit. But this barter only happens outside the group with people they don't really get on with.

Within the group "most of these peoples hold very strongly to the view that wealth should not be too unevenly distributed." (Mair) So if one individual has more than he needs, he is expected to share it. He is not expected to swap it. The more he has to share out, the bigger man he is. If he were to take his surplus food out from the group and trade it, the group would not benefit. To exchange food and not to share it would be seen as extremely anti-social. So they would be very ambivalent about trade, wanting the steel knife, but under pressure to share everything with the rest of the group, and not wanting to see food and timber leaving the community. "Primitive societies have the concept of 'property in use' but the idea of something not intimately associated with the owner, because of 'value in exchange', does not exist. There is no trade or barter within the group, and all material assets which contribute towards the survival of the band, such as land, are shared as need be." (R. Pearson. 3.) "Karl Blucher noted that, far from being of a trucking disposition, primitive man was strongly averse to acts of barter." (Polanyi. 1.)

'Primitive' societies don't trade amongst themselves. They trade very little with other tribes. And they don't seem to want to trade with us for our industrial luxuries. In the northern interior of East Africa: "The tribesmen were rarely attracted by the traders' products like cloth. It was only the prospect of acquiring cattle that moved them." (Low.) The Bolivian Indian "feels no inducement to produce agricultural surpluses to sustain the life of the towns and obtain for himself the conveniences and amenities of factory-produced consumer goods." (Osborne.)

Of course they exchange gifts, as we do at Christmas. But they, like we, do not expect the gifts to be of equal value. Today a mother exchanging gifts with a young daughter does not expect a gift of equal value. (It is the very opposite of the market economy.) Social status is a strong factor in the gift exchange. In the Trobriand Islands: "Within the sociologically defined relationships – of which there are many – the exchange is usually unequal, as benefits the relationship." (Polanyi. 2.) The higher up the peck order the higher the value of the giver's gift. A chief was expected to be very generous indeed. But such gift exchange is not trade. Gift exchange is impossible where there are no defined social relationships – with another tribe for instance. In the Trobriand Islands: "Exchange was carried on by gift-giving and ceremonial distribution of goods; barter existed only with persons outside the tribe: buying and selling were non-existent." (Fusfield)

The concept of gift-exchange has been worked out to try to analyse tribal behaviour in economic terms and it simply doesn't work because 'economic' behaviour can only take place in an anonymous society unaffected by social relationships.

In societies where cash is beginning to appear, the price is still related to social position. "In Lesu, New Guinea, a rich man might pay 5 tsera for a pig for which another man would pay 4. The more he pays the more prestige the buyer has. Everyone then knows he is a rich man." (Dumont and Cohen.)

Thus there is a third type of economy beyond the market (capitalist) economy where the free market determines the price, and the command (socialist) economy where the state or the town determines the price. In this third economy the price is determined by social relationship.

What the traders want from the periphery are the raw materials, the pelts, the timber, the labour. The more of these are traded away, the poorer are the peoples of that periphery. They cannot use the baubles of civilization to eat and keep warm. Their forests are cut down so that the land can support fewer animals to be hunted for food. When the forests go, the rain erodes the bare soil. The land produces less while more is traded away. It is not surprising that periphery peoples nearly always have to be tricked or forced into trade. Today in Sarawak the forest hunter-gatherers find that they have traded away their forests for two crates of beer. A common tactic by traders is to offer arms to chiefs of enemy tribes to force the tribes to deliver up the raw materials. Where previously those chiefs had great influence but no authority, with guns they now had power. And all power corrupts. The traders had brought wealth and power to the few and social division and poverty to everyone else. These peoples are quite right to fear strangers.

Ancient civilizations didn't bother much with trade. They just took the resources by force. But as the periphery receded it became difficult to muster sufficient military strength, so they had to resort to trade, or blackmail, or corruption. And few are immune to corruption. Antonio Cavazzi wrote in about 1660 that: "for a coral necklace or a little wine, the Congolese would sell their own parents, their own children, or their brothers and sisters, swearing to the purchasers that these were household slaves." (Braudel. 21.)

But most often and most successfully they used credit. Fur trappers would be allowed credit to buy alcohol. Before they could have any more, they had to go and trap the furs which paid off their debt, so they could have more alcohol. From the vast loans to Third World governments today it is obvious that credit still works.

Trade breaks down the co-operative instinct of the group – the need for mutual aid, the inter-dependence. Successful individuals in the group no longer depend for their wellbeing on the others inside the group, but on the traders. It is the first symptom of the dog-eat-dog society. For the Pygmies all the goodies of western civilization are available via the negro villages. But the pygmies do not want them. Part of the reason is perhaps that they are aware of how divisive these goodies are. They have seen how chiefs of a tribe can be bought with the traders' guns and alcohol, and how those chiefs, corrupted by the power of those guns, dependent no longer on the goodwill of their people but on the traders for their power, betray their own people, forcing them to produce the required surplus of crops and selling off their forests.

The Kula Ring

It has always been presumed that 'primitive' societies didn't trade because they didn't have money or they didn't have transport or competitive bargaining. But in the Trobriand Islands they had all these facilities, but they still didn't trade. They used them for our equivalent of international football matches.

The Kula Ring was an association of islands, a ring. Highly desirable, named shells moved one way round the ring, another set of shells travelled in the opposite direction. The object of the 'game' was to achieve status by obtaining the incoming shell by exchange of other shells, promises of friendship, redeeming old agreements etc. It was a highly ritualised process. It involved all the processes of trade – long distance travel, competitive exchange, agreements, 'credit'. But it definitely wasn't trade. It has been quoted as a sort of proto-trade. It wasn't. They knew how to trade but chose not to. Sometimes they traded outside the ring but only with their enemies.

The Triangle of Corruption

Trade makes the periphery poorer. Therefore the traders had to force the periphery into trade. "The Dutch in Indonesia could find no economic incentive to stimulate the production of spices for the European market. They had to resort to warfare, to peddling supplies of arms, to the exactions of 'contingencies' and forced deliveries from the native rulers whom they maintained in authority." (E.E. Rich.) The only source of arms to keep the puppet rulers in power were the traders' governments, since, as we have seen, governments always keep a monopoly of arms.

We now have the complete pattern of economic imperialism, which has operated ever since, the Triangle of Corruption. The core rulers supply arms, via the traders, to periphery rulers to suppress their own people and extract the crops to sell to the traders for use at the core. The periphery rulers depend on the traders for their income and power, and they depend on the core rulers for their guns. The traders depend on the periphery rulers to supply the crops and the licences to mine, and they depend on their own core rulers to provide those guns and also the transport infrastructure and military cover. The core ruler depends on the periphery ruler for the crops which provide his income and power and which feed the core cities. He depends on the trader to obtain and transport the crops and collect the taxes. It's an interdependent triangle of corruption.

For example, in the 1670s one of the early multinationals, the Hudson Bay Trading Company, obtained exclusive British trading privileges in Canada from Charles II, the core ruler, in return for cash and a share of the profits. For beaver skins (used for expensive London hats) it traded cheap glass beads with the Canadian Indian trappers. The trappers, having enough glass beads and not wanting to strip the country of its resources, stopped bringing in the beaver skins. So the Hudson Bay Trading Company (the trader) went to Charles II (the core ruler): "Supply us with guns and military cover and we'll keep your profits coming." The guns, and alcohol, were passed over to enemy Indian chiefs (the periphery rulers) on condition that they forced the trappers to produce the skins. The Triangle of Corruption delivered. The trader got the skins and the profits: the core ruler got his cut: the puppet government got its guns and power, the workers in London got their employment refining the raw materials; we got our hats. The Indians got exploited.

Today, the British government (the core ruler) supplied President Marcos of the Philippines (the periphery ruler) with military equipment (for example, personal carriers from GKN Sankey). In return Marcos drove 2000 peasants and tribespeople off 4000 acres for our Commonwealth Development Corporation with Guthrie Inc. (the trader) to grow palm oil for our margarine etc. Our government kept Marcos in power with our guns. In return he handed over his people's land to the traders to make its profit on crops grown for us. More than 80% of Philippines farmland now grows crops for export. Marcos has gone but nothing else has changed. We supported President Aquino instead. She's a wealthy landowner and her friends made sure that she, and they, kept their land and kept the crops being exported.

In Portugal the king, threatened by Spain, in 1703 asked Britain for help. Again the price was high and paid by his people. Britain demanded that all tariffs on their products in Portugal be eliminated. To keep his crown the king allowed Portuguese industry to be destroyed. Fifty years later the Marquis of Pombal complained that "two thirds of our necessities are now supplied by England. The English produce, sell and resell everything which is needed in our country. The ancient manufacturers of Portugal have been destroyed". "The Treaty of Methuen brought on the destruction of Portugal's textiles industries, the take-over by Great Britain of its foreign and even domestic trade, and the conversion of Portugal into a mere entrepôt between Great Britain and Brazil and other Portugese colonies." (Frank. 1.)

The Marquis could complain but they were crocodile tears. To start with he was still a marquis only because his king was still on the throne. He depended as much as the king on British support, and his wealth probably came from the export of wine from grapes grown on his estates to Britain, so that the land was not growing crops for his own people. The whole Portuguese upper class benefited from the betrayal of the country by the puppet.

In Bengal the British installed a puppet on the throne on condition he gave the British merchants trading privileges. "As a result the group was able to offer higher prices for local products than the Bengal merchants, who had to pay the local taxes, yet sell them more cheaply; and by this means the merchants were quickly forced out of business. The group then used the virtual monopoly it had acquired of the entire marketing system to compel producers to accept lower prices and to compel consumers to pay more, the Company's sepoys being called in to persuade anybody who raised objections." (Inglis).

For a hundred years America has supported corrupt regimes in South America, getting rid of those unwilling to 'co-operate'. The United Fruit Company owned vast tracts of Guatemalan land to grow bananas, thanks to previous corrupt regimes maintained in power with US. arms. In 1954 the Guatemalan President was initiating a series of mild land reforms. The United Fruit Company moved into action. High American officials, who had shares in the company, got the CIA to start destabilising. They found a Colonel Armas who could be bribed to front a coup. "The CIA offered him three million dollars and the United Fruit Company said that they would run him guns on the company-owned railway. The understanding was that the firm would recover its old privileges under the new regime . . . To support the "Liberators'" claim to be operating on their native soil, some radio transmissions came from the US. Embassy in Guatemala City." (Guardian. 7.5.82.)

The CIA was successful. America had found and imposed a small boss, who was prepared, by exporting the crops, to betray and starve his people. The quid pro quo was a return of the land and privileges to the United Fruit Company to export bananas, for the profit of the US.

For more than a hundred years America has supported corrupt regimes in South America. That is where its wealth has come from. That is why it is now rich and powerful for the moment. In the same way Britain's wealth came from Africa and around the world. "Any countries which did not care to enter into relations were forced to do so with gunboats and marines; the last 'closed' countries of the world, China and Japan, were thus forced into unrestricted intercourse with the modern economies between 1840 and 1860." (Hobsbawm.)

In each case the core government in return for military support has forced the puppet into trade with the core government and on very unequal terms. And in each case it is not just the puppet who benefits but the whole of his upper class. It is the poor who suffer.

The Dependence of Multinationals

There's a myth that multinationals are all powerful. They are not. They are only one side of the interdependent Triangle of Corruption. Their income depends on both their home government and the puppet government. When Iran nationalised its oil industry in 1953 and withdrew its oil concessions from BP, BP, without British government gunboats, was powerless. BP had started life as the Anglo-Iranian Oil Company. It kept the first Pahlavi Shah on the throne with British guns in exchange for the exclusive oil concessions. To keep these oil concessions BP needed Britain to use military force. It refused, and BP lost most of its concessions to the American oil companies who then kept the Shah of Iran in power. BP, one of the most powerful multinationals in the world, was powerless without the military support of its own government. When the USA would no longer support the Shah, the American multinational oil companies lost their oil concessions too.

Money

The elite have now established total obedience to their laws. They have built their temples and palaces in their cities, financed by the peasants' food. They have their professional armies to suppress their populations; they have a transport infrastructure to remove the loot, and a growing technology invented to administer and hold on to it.

The next major step in the impoverishment of their subjects is the introduction of money. Herodotus says that coinage was first introduced in the 7th cent. BC. by the king of Lydia. Now why should the king of Lydia do a thing like that? No doubt he quoted Keynes about transactions, contingencies and speculation, and was very virtuous about the whole thing. But kings are not altruistic.

A government makes laws to give the monarch sole rights to all gold mines, 'Regalian Rights': it forbids anyone else to mint coinage: it forbids any other coinage to be used as legal tender, and then it forces taxes to be paid in its own coinage. So to obtain the coins to pay the taxes, the people must work for the elite, *the only source of the coins*. Or they must give their crops to the elite for the coins which they then give back in taxes.

It's a neat trick. The people are forced to produce natural resources for cash; they are forced into growing crops for cash, cash-cropping, the Formal Economy. They are forced to work for the elite, their henchmen and their hangers-on, the Establishment, who are given the coinage in return for their support or their work.

For example in Africa: "a Cape Colony Act of 1894 imposed a tax in cash of ten shillings on 'fit adult males' so that, as Prime Minister, Cecil Rhodes, blandly explained, rural producers might be removed from their life of sloth and idleness and made to give some return "for our wise and good government". The idea took on fast. To pay cash taxes Africans would have to earn cash: almost invariably in that period this meant leaving the village for European employment. If they faulted to pay they must naturally be punished and would work as prison labourers instead." (Davidson. 2.) And that was the way they forced the Africans down the mines, with cash taxes. And "one thinks of the deliberate use of money taxes to induce the production of cash crops in Tsarist Russia." (Gould. 1.)

The king of Lydia introduced coinage in the 7th century BC. Within a hundred years the king of Lydia was Croesus, the richest man in the world. There were no flies on the kings of Lydia.

Certainly money has its uses in transactions etc. And if the production of a goldmine in the form of coinage were distributed freely and equally, there would be no problem (except for inflation), no unequal distribution. But Establishments make sure that the people always have to work for the money, work for them.

If all the money in a country vanished, would that country be any poorer? All the things which had been desirable and obtainable would still be there, still available. It would mean only that those who manufactured the money could no longer remove the desirable objects with their enforced legal tender. Gold or any other kind of money is not the desirable object in itself but only the means to acquire the desirable objects.

Money is not wealth. It is simply an I.O.U. When a king gives out gold coins, it is understood that the gold will acquire a certain volume of goods. When he gives a gold coin for support given or work done, that coin is an I.O.U. for food or raw materials, or goods and services. The king prints the money, his I.O.U.s, and buys his food and baubles with them. I.O.U.s are redeemable. But coinage is never redeemed.

The peasants are forced to exchange their wheat for cash. The king who printed the money now has the wheat, the desirable object. The peasants have the cash. Until the peasants can get rid of the cash to some other sucker in exchange for other natural resources, the king is richer, the peasants are poorer. Money is a means of taking wealth from the periphery and giving it to the core, taking it from the poor and giving it to the rich.

In the same way if a country sells its crops for cash, who is richer, the buyer or seller? While one country is holding another country's cash, it is poorer. Liberia has no currency of its own. It was set up by America and uses American dollars. So America can print dollars and remove Liberian crops.

Legal Tender

It is important for a king, in order to get the crops, that only his coins be used. If the country's crops are bought with another king's coins (IOUs), then that other king is ultimately getting the crops. So if a country starts minting coins, all the neighbouring countries have to quickly mint their own to prevent an outflow of crops in exchange for the coins of the other country's king. It is in the king's interest to allow only the use of his coins. It is in other countries' interest to force him, if he is weak, to use their coins as well, making their currencies convertible, so that they can cream off the crops. After the last war: "The Americans, anxious for the restoration of the international economy" (taking the wealth from the Third World to the Developed World) "and resentful of the discrimination against the dollar that the machinery of the sterling area made possible through the close control of the sterling/dollar exchange transaction, agreed to make Britain a loan on the condition that sterling was made convertible within a year." (Harrison. 1.)

So money is not only a means of taking wealth from one man and giving it to another but it also takes from one country and gives to another.

International Trade

Using this new method, money, for removing the crops from the people and getting them to work for him was much less effort than the previous force of arms or the religious confidence trick. It was much more efficient. But it depended on a supply of coins. If a king had no gold or silver mines in his country, he had to export his own crops to obtain them, and re-mint them as his own coins. A king without gold mines needed foreign trade. So he encouraged foreign traders who had gold. In fact he gave then concessions, free trade zones, putting his own traders at a disadvantage. And to get the gold he had to increase still further the crops available for trade. He gets his support and keeps his position by the amount of gold he can dole out to his supporters. If someone else has more gold they might go to him. He'd lose his crown and probably his head. So he must increase external trade to get the gold to buy support.

For Edward III the main English export was wool exported to Flanders to be made up into cloth. England was a Third World country supplying raw materials to the industrialised towns of the Low Countries and Italy. England's sheep produced a short fine hair, suitable for expensive cloth. Edward, the periphery ruler, encouraged wool production and export. Land was taken from the peasants by the Church and by acts of enclosure. Instead of growing food the land was now growing wool for export, the profits of which went to the land owners, the Church, the king, not to the peasants. They starved and were forced into the towns and cities as in the Third World today. The international trade was in the hands of foreign not English traders because it was the foreign trader who had the gold.

Indirect Taxes

But having invented money and found it a very useful way of bleeding the population, the rulers now found that in money they had a tool to tax the population so that they hardly knew what was happening, a hidden tax – indirect taxation on trade. Bingo! The rulers taxed the traders with market dues. The traders immediately increased the price of the goods by the amount of the dues. The consumer paid the tax without knowing it. And still does. With the invention of money, most of the rulers' income came from indirect taxation on trade.

Market dues don't sound much more than the cost of a stall. Not so. In Poland it paid the defence budget. "The military force which kept the tribal unity of early Poland together was an organised royal guard numbering 3000 men and paid in cash from the market places." (Lönnroth.)

Having discovered this unexpected gold mine, the rulers set about exploiting it. As we have seen, 'primitive' societies don't actually like trading. It's seen as anti-social. Before the use of money there were no markets in the villages and towns of the ancient Near East.

So the kings, to increase their income from indirect taxation on trade, had to force the people to trade. Instead of taking their crops, he demanded taxation to be paid in cash. To get this cash the peasant had no choice but to grow extra crops to sell off for cash at the new local market and to hand over that cash to the king. But being able to tax the trader as well, the king was able to tax the taxation.

The people had not only to be forced to trade, they could only trade at certain specified times and places so that the trade could be taxed. All trade was forbidden that did not take place in official markets and at official times. In 18th century Dahomey in West Africa: "The market is presided over by an officer who expects a toll from every vendor . . . Access to the market is no less strictly controlled. Toll houses are located at the entrance to Whydah, as to every market town throughout the kingdom. The collection of tolls on all persons carrying goods serves not only as a revenue measure but as a device to ensure control of entry into the market." (A.R. Arnold. 3.) And when the traders tried to avoid the toll houses it became necessary to build walls round the market towns to force the traders to pay their dues at the toll gates. At Madrid: "A new line of walls was begun in 1782, but its purpose, like that of the Farmers General Wall around Paris, was rather to delimit the city's jurisdiction and to check smuggling than to provide an effective military defence." (Pounds. 2.) The reason for town walls is much less to do with defence and much more to do with tax collection.

Walls allowed them to charge an entrance fee too. The wall in Peking "is guarded at night as if it were war-time, but in daytime the gates are not guarded except by Eunuchs who stay there rather to collect entrance fees than for the safety of the town." (Braudel. 3.)

Towns

The function of the town now changes. From now on towns and cities are not only the places where the surplus is stored and spent and the countryside 'administered', but it is now a tax office. The traders, not the priests, are now the tax collectors. Towns are given charters by the king to hold markets. The reality of that charter is that every neighbouring village is forbidden to have a market. All trade must be done at the chartered market where that trade is taxed.

The traders of a town compete with other towns for the charter to hold the market for that area. Without that charter there is no trade. The traders are bankrupt. So they get together and offer gold to the king to hold his market at their town. In return for the gold and their collection of his taxes he gives them monopoly rights on all trade. In the General Charter to all burgesses of Scotland, signed by the King of Scotland in 1364, it says: "none shall sell but to the merchants only of such burghs within whose privilege he resides, whom we strictly charge to bring such merchandise to the Mercate and Cross of the burghs that the merchants may purchase thereof, make an effectual monopoly of the same without restriction." It was blatant. In return for the monopoly on all trade the traders passed on the market dues to the king.

The town was also given control over the surrounding countryside. "In Germany the cities regularly carried on a battle against the surrounding countryside for the control of the food and industrial raw materials. In some cases a *Bannmeile* was created and within it any food or materials produced had to go to the city. No industry was allowed which might compete with the city's handicrafts." (C.H. Wilson.) This privilege was often the only reason for a town's existence. In the German cities east of the Elbe in the fourteenth and fifteenth centuries. "The guild regime retained its hold within the town boundaries, but not over a rural hinterland; and, stripped of their special trading privileges, the prosperity of many of these towns faded." (Dobb. 1.)

In Norway: "The urban monopoly of commerce had been redefined as late as 1818 by a law distinguishing between small-scale retail trade, which was available to any duly registered burgess of a town, and the business of a merchant for which a four year training and familiarity with a foreign language and book-keeping were prescribed . . . Although it was still deemed important to avoid 'distracting the mind of the countryman from his natural pursuits to trade and barter', he could now be assigned a royal trading licence without paying for the status of burgess in the nearest town." (Derry)

"Towns became distinctive economic and social units just when and because certain places were set apart and defended by laws and privileges making them market and production centres and denying some or all such rights to the countryside around. In origin and essence the early towns depended on such segregation of economic functions and so in a definite though particular sense on the existence of monopoly. They *were* because others were not, they *had* because other places had not. They grew when and where lords restricted trade to a centre, granted special protection or privileges to those who settled or did their business at a defined place, gave a legal market to some locality and so denied economic activities to somewhere else." (A.B. Hibbert)

Towns were not only built by kings. Local lords were also able to increase their income by planting towns and taking the market dues themselves. These towns would be sited on bad agricultural land on the edge of their estates where good roads or bridges could attract passing trade. The object was to attract the wealth from other estates.

The lords made their money by charging higher rents, turning agricultural land into building plots; they could charge an entry toll on any visitor to the town; they took market dues, perhaps 10% on all sales, and they charged rent on the market stalls. "With the increase in the number of market centres, the lord of a town had an interest in the prosperity of market places that went beyond the rent of his burgage plots. In the first instance he was the recipient of all the tolls paid by those outsiders who used the market. Every town had the grant of a market (and usually a fair) that derived from the lord of a town, or from the crown's grant to a lord. Markets also gave the lord of a town further rents from the booths and stalls that were set up in the market place itself." (Beresford. 1.)

The area of the town was a tiny proportion of the estate but it contributed a useful proportion of income. Where did that income come from? Conventional economics claims that the town generated the wealth itself. In fact, in the end it all came from the peasants on and off the estate. The lords tried to site their towns on the edges of their estates so that they could attract passing trade, ie. money, ie. tokens for food which could be bought from other estates. From the lord's point of view towns were a means of increasing his income by acquiring food from other lords' estates. The town created no wealth. It simply attracted it from other estates. The higher taxes paid by the town burgesses were simply a proportion of the food which they had acquired from peasants of their own or other estates.

Peasant Versus Worker

The reason a peasant would go to a town to work harder and pay higher taxes was that either he could not produce enough food for himself or often that he could be free of the control of his lord; he was no longer a chattel. 'The free air of the town'.

But when a peasant moves to a town, his interests change. As a peasant the less food that was expropriated the better he fed. As a town worker the more food expropriated from the peasants he left behind, the better he fed. Marx got it all wrong. The class struggle is not between the bosses and the workers but between the bosses with the workers against the peasants. The workers depend on a strong ruling class for the expropriation of their food. When a peasant moves to the town, he is selling out the other peasants. He is going over. The great divide is between those who produce the food and those who consume it.

The people who suffered from the growth of the towns were the peasants who were forced to take their crops to the town markets where they received a lower price, because of the monopoly rights granted to the wholesalers by the king or the lord and because of the market dues they had to pay.

People don't go to the cities because of the bright lights but because they are hungry and that's where the food is. Cities are biologically unhealthy; the fertility rate declines as the population density increases; growth is mainly by immigration. Cities are medically unhealthy: "the mortality rate for all causes is often well above the national average." (Coates and Rawstrom). As for crime: "statistical studies have shown that the frequency of crime is several times higher in the cities than in the rural areas." (Glozer). And mental problems: "In an American study Paris and Dunham found that there were 326 cases of schizophrenia per 1000 people in the centre of Chicago. The quotient drops to 55 near the city's outer suburbs. The incidence of alcoholic psychoses is 240 per 1000 in the centre of the city, 60 in the outer suburbs. Similar differentials occur in the figures of delinquency, suicide and drug addiction. And the numbers for the periphery of the city are still greater than those for small towns." (Munck.) Even though these figures seem excessive, the pattern is clear.

So once again we find that towns and cities are not a natural step in the progress of mankind, but a means whereby the core can become richer at the expense of the periphery. Towns and trade do not create wealth, do not alleviate poverty. They do not create wealth, they simply move it around.

Trade flourishes because governments get most of their income, and therefore their power, from it. Because trade creates poverty, people have to be forced to trade by cash taxes.

What happens when countries don't tax trade?

Neither China nor Japan encouraged trade because they didn't think to tax it. In China most taxation was direct taxation on the peasants. In Japan all of it was. In both countries merchants were treated with disdain. So neither country had reason to encourage trade, or towns and cities. These were built for military and administrative purposes. Because the rulers saw no benefit in trade, industry which flows from trade never got started. By 1644 the rulers forbade any foreign trade at all. For nearly 300 years China stagnated.

In Japan the Tokogawa regime also forbade all foreign trade. It also stagnated. In 1853 Commander Perry forcibly reminded them of the West's superior armanents. Up till this time the government had got all its taxation from the land and none from trade. "Taxation was based exclusively on land, hence merchant wealth remained untapped." (Lehman.) So the government hadn't encouraged trade or industry. But, terrified of becoming another Western colony, Japan in 1868 determined to industrialise. For this they needed more money so they started to tax trade. "Until 1890 the land tax represented 70-80% of the total government revenue. Following 1890 it dropped to just under 40% and in the last decade or so of the Meiji period it corresponded to about a quarter." (Lehman. 2.) Japan then started its economic miracle.

Summary

Primitive societies hardly trade at all. They feel that trade is anti-social because they prefer to share rather than exchange. Trade, because it can make no allowance for unequal social relationships, is only possible in an anonymous society. Even though the manufactured goods are available, they do not grow the extra crops to buy them. Primitive societies consider not only that trade is not worth the effort but that it is anti-social as well. So trade is not innate to human behaviour. There's nothing natural about trade.

In fact people have to be forced to trade. Money is introduced by the ruler to make it easier to remove the crops and to make the people work for him by demanding taxes be paid in cash which was only available from him. Money then allows him to impose a hidden tax on trade. To collect this tax all trade has to be restricted to towns where the traders are given a monopoly on trade in return for collecting the tax. By demanding cash taxes people are forced to grow extra crops, which they must sell in the new markets to raise the cash to pay the tax. Towns were planted to increase the tax take on trade.

Towns did not grow because it was a natural progress but because of the rulers' laws to remove the crops from the countryside. Towns are parasitic on the countryside. They depend on the expropriation of the crops. And so do the workers of those towns.

In order to increase trade (and therefore the tax on that trade) beyond their jurisdiction, rulers bribe periphery rulers with military support to use their land to grow crops for the core and to give the core traders privileges over the periphery traders, destroying periphery trade and industry. If periphery rulers can't be bribed, they are replaced or forced to trade.

In even fewer words, trade is caused by the rulers' desire for the tax on that trade. And if the king and his friends are richer then everyone else is poorer.

We'll cover the major reasons for industrialisation in the next chapter. It is sufficient here to show that, without government interest and taxation on trade, it does not happen. With it, it does.

Chapter 3. Does Trade Create Wealth or Poverty?
References

A.R. Arnold. in "Trade and Market in Early Empires". Free Press. '57. Ed. K. Polanyi. 2: p.43., 3: p.185.

M. Beresford. "New Towns in the Middle Ages". Lutterworth. '67. 1: p.63.

F. Braudel. "Capitalism and Material Life". Weidenfeld and Nicholson. '73. 3: p.383. quoting a traveller of 1697. "The Perspective of the World". Collins. '84. 2: p.48., 7: p.64., 8: p.40., 9: p.106., 21: p.435.

B.E. Coates and M.E. Rawstrom. "Regional Variations in Britain." '71.

B. Davidson. "Africa in Modern History." Allen Lane '78. 2: p.110.

T.K. Derry. "A history of Modern Norway". Clarendon. '73. p.109.

M. Dobb. "Studies in the Development of Capitalism." Routledge Kegan Paul. '46. 1: p.158.

R. Dumont and N. Cohen. "The Growth of Hunger". Marian Boyars. '80. p.206.

A.G. Frank. "Capitalism and Underdevelopment in Latin America". Monthly Review Press. '67. 1: p.155.

D.B. Fusfield. in "Trade and Market in Early Empires". Ed. K. Polanyi. Free Press. '57. p.345.

Glozer. Penguin '36.

J.D. Gould. "Economic Growth in History". Methuen. '72. 1: p.400.

'The Guardian'. 7.5.82

A. Harrison. "The Framework of Economic Activity", MacMillan. '67. 1: p.93.

A.B. Hibbert. "The Economic Policy of Towns" in "The Cambridge Economic History of Europe". C.U.P. Ed. Postan. Vol. III. p.197.

E.J. Hobsbawm. "Industry and Empire". Weidenfeld and Nicholson. '68. p.114.

B. Inglis. "The Opium War". Hodder and Stoughton. '76. p.18.

J.P. Lehman. "The Roots of Modern Japan". MacMillan. '82. 1: p.72., 2: p.221.

E. Lönnroth. "The Baltic Countries" in "The Cambridge Economic History of Europe". C.U.P. Ed. Postan. Vol III. p.365.

D.A. Low. in "History of East Africa". Ed. Oliver and Matthew. Clarendon. '63. Vol. 1. p.325.

L. Mair. "An Introduction to Social Anthropology". O.U.P. '65. p.192.

W.H. McNeill. "A World History". O.U.P. '79. 2: p.36.

E. Munck. "Biology of the Future". Collins. '74. p.69.

A.L. Oppenheim. in "Trade and Market in Early Empires". Ed K. Polanyi. Free Press. '57. 2: p.17. Quoted by Polanyi.

H. Osborne. "Bolivia, a Land Divided". O.U.P. '64. p.95.

R. Pearson. "Introduction to Anthropology". Holt Rhinehart and Winston. '74. p.218.

K. Polanyi. 1: "The Livelihood of Man". Academic Press Inc. '77. p.63. 2: "Trade and Market in Early Empires." Free Press '57. p.74.

N.J.G. Pounds. "A Historical Geography of Europe" C.U.P. '79. 2: p.120.

E.E. Rich. Preface of Vol IV. "The Cambridge Economic History of Europe". Ed Postan. p.xxi.

H.W.F. Saggs. "The Might that was Assyria". Sidgewick and Jackson. '84. 1: p.182.

C.H. Wilson. "Trade, Society and the State" in "The Cambridge Economic History of Europe". Ed Postan. C.U.P. Vol IV. p.497.

Chapter 4
DOES INDUSTRY REDUCE POVERTY?

IN THE ANCIENT WORLD the cities were built on the poverty of their hinterlands and peripheries. Those cities created no wealth; they stole it. But to steal it, the empires needed large armies. Or they needed to trade the more expensive, luxury core crops, such as olive oil and wine, for the cheaper necessities, corn and timber. The Greeks, unable to afford a large army, took this one step further by manufacturing cloth and pottery to exchange for the necessities of life from the periphery.

Did the manufactured goods create wealth? Was everyone therefore better fed? Does industry reduce poverty?

By the time of the Mycenaean Age, 1700–1200 BC., there was a ruling elite and an obedient and disarmed population producing the surplus in sufficient quantities for the temples to need to invent writing. Then for unknown reasons the ruling elite lost power and their cities became derelict. After that: "The population was smaller and very much poorer than before; that is not to say that the ordinary farmers and craftsmen were poorer, but that the upper classes were." (Finley. 1.)

During these so-called Dark Ages, with no temple stores to record, writing was no longer needed and was forgotten. When the need arose again later, they used a different alphabet. "The sole function of writing in the Mycenaean world known to us on the available evidence was to meet the administrative needs of the palace. When the latter disappeared the need and the art both went with it." (Finley. 2.)

A major factor in a population's exploitation is a foreign ruling class. A foreign invader is not influenced by any kinship ties and can be far more ruthless. In Greece the tradition had it that the Dorians, the Sons of Heracles, invaded from the north and imposed their rule. The population was now again forced to produce a surplus which was taken to the stockades of the Dorians. The larger the area which the different Dorian groups could control, the larger the surplus they could extract and the more supporters and artisans they could feed in their stockades, growing into towns and cities. "The size, wealth, population, power and importance of every early Greek city depend on the size and fertility of its plain. Big cities have big plains, small cities have small plains. No cities have no plains." (Burn. 2.) The cities created no wealth. They were parasitic totally on their plains, their hinterlands and peripheries. If they engaged in trade, they were exchanging crops with other hinterlands. Trade simply transferred the crops from the hinterland of one city to the core of another.

By about 700 BC Athens had exhausted the timber on her own periphery in Attica, Athens' plain. Plato writes: "The soil, which kept breaking away from the highlands . . . keeps continually sliding away and disappearing into the sea. . . What now remains, compared with what existed earlier is like a skeleton of a sick man, all fat and soft earth having wasted away and only the bare framework of the land being left . . . What are now mountains were lofty soil-clad hills; the stony plains of present day were full of rich soil, the mountains were heavily wooded – a fact of which there are still visible traces. There are mountains in Attica which can now support nothing but bees, which were clothed, not so very long ago, with fine trees, suitable for roofing the largest buildings – and roofs hewn from the timber are still in existence . . . The country produced boundless pasturage for cattle.

"The annual supply of rainfall was not lost, as it is at present, through being allowed to flow over the denuded surface into the sea, but was received by the country, in all its abundance into her bosom, where she stored it in her impervious clay and so was able to discharge the drainage of the heights into the hollows in the form of springs and rivers with an abundant volume and a wide territorial distribution. The shrines that survive to the present day on the sites of extinct water supplies are evidence for the correctness of my present thesis." ('Critias')

The reason for this destruction of its periphery was population increase. For whatever reason all the Greek city states had suffered big population increases. Most of the other cities had solved this by emigration, founding colonies round the Mediterranean and Black Seas. Athens did not. Without a hinterland large enough to supply her growing population she was forced to import food and other raw materials. There are two ways of doing this, barter and theft. Athens did a bit of both. She got herself an empire, making her subjects pay taxes with which she bought their food, leaving them to starve, and she got herself industrialised.

She had a large urban population who needed somehow to earn its food. They had to make products to exchange with the rich who owned the food. The place where the Athenian workers got much of their food from was Scythia on the northern coast of the Black Sea, the Ukraine today.

The Scythians had come out of Central Asia and conquered the local population. The Scythians were nomads; the local population were agriculturalists. "The Scythians were typical nomads: they lived in tent-like carriages dragged by oxen and counted their riches by the number of horses, which also served them as food . . . The Scythians established a strong military state in Southern Russia. . . in spite of the nomadic nature of the Scythians themselves, agriculture went on flourishing in the steppe north of the Black Sea." (Riasonovski.) It went on flourishing because the Scythians were forcing the population to grow for export. "The basic exchange was Scythian grain for oil and wine produced in the city states of the Aegean coastlines. As a result of such trade, by 500 BC. the Scythian aristocracy of Southern Russia was beginning to acquire a very sophisticated taste for Greek luxuries." (McNeill. 3.)

It was these luxuries, mainly pottery and cloth, that the Athenian workers produced in exchange for the grain. The people who owned the crops that Athens needed were not the peasants on the periphery, but the Scythian aristocracy who could force the peasants to grow the surplus and remove it. So the pottery which Athens made was a luxurious status symbol product which would persuade the Scythian lords to exploit their people, take their crops and exchange them for the posh Greek pots. No wealth was created, no poverty alleviated by this manufacture. The Greek artisans and slaves exchanged their labour for the Black Sea food. The Greek traders made their profits and ate better. The Scythian lords got their pots and their status. The Scythian peasants went hungry. The pottery industry had simply moved their crops to Athens and moved the poverty of Athens to the Black Sea.

If the peasants of the Black Sea had been free and not disarmed, they might have sold any occasional surplus. But they were not free. They had to work harder feeding both themselves and Greece, and if they bought food, it was more expensive because of Greek competition.

But it was worse than that. If there was local pottery production, that would be badly affected too. There's not much variation in demand for pots. So if the local rich population is buying Greek pots, then they are not buying local pots (The poor make their own). The local potter loses business and goes hungry because the food has gone to Athens.

Worst of all, the cost of living in cities is higher because the necessities of life, food, fuel, water, all have to be bought, so wages have to be higher. So labour costs are higher. Therefore it is necessary to introduce labour-saving devices to cut down the amount of labour in a product. (The worker still has to work just as long. Labour-saving devices save labour in the product, not labour for the worker.) As long as the cost of the labour-saving devices can be covered by the profits from the extra production, then the product of the core will always be cheaper than the low labour-cost periphery. So the pottery industry of the Black Sea would be destroyed by the cheaper Athenian product.

The periphery rulers have the option of protecting their local industry by imposing a tax on imported products to bring them up to, or above, the local price. The core rulers use every trick in the book to avoid this, but their main tactic is bribery. Because of the core higher labour costs, their technology is more advanced and their weapons superior. So they can offer the periphery rulers better arms to keep them in power, as long as they allow in the core products tax-free. Nowadays they euphemistically call this 'Free Trade'. Also, periphery rulers don't like to impose tax because it makes the luxuries from the core more expensive for them.

To show the superiority of the core arms there's a quote from Polybius: "The Gaulish sword being only good for a cut and not a thrust . . . from the way their swords are made, only the first cut takes effect; after this they at once assume a shape of a strigil, being so much bent lengthways and sideways that unless the men are given leisure and rest them on the ground and set them straight with a foot, the second blow is quite ineffectual." That would turn an epic film like Ben Hur into slapstick comedy!

The Athenian workers, although they probably didn't realize it, depended for their food on the power of the Scythian aristocracy to produce the extra crops from their peasants to feed Athens. Core workers depend on a strong ruling class on the periphery able to extract the surplus. The Athenian elite would be far more conscious of the need to support and increase the Scythian rulers' control of their people in order to continue the flow of grain. To get the crops the Athenians would have offered all the necessary sweeteners, credit, silver, manufactured status symbols like pottery and fine cloth, arms and the expensive core crops like olive oil and wine.

Athens not only had to import grain. Presumably she imported her timber from the Balkans via the Black Sea. The eastern coast of the Black Sea was known as the Land of the Golden Fleece, where Jason went with his Argonauts. So it's likely that that is where she got her wool from.

Athens, having exhausted her own resources had had to expand her periphery into the Black Sea. Athens and the Black Sea were two essential components of one economic whole. But while the people of the Black Sea could do without Athens, Athens could not do without the Black Sea. Today, the Third World can do without us. We can't do without the Third World.

So we have come to the final stage of economic development – industry. Athens, to obtain her natural resources, started manufacturing and exporting pottery and cloth. Conventional economic theory says that people were therefore better fed. We have seen that this is not so. So where has conventional economic theory made its mistake?

Specialisation

The first step towards industry is specialisation and division of labour, page one of the economic textbooks.

It was previously thought that hunter-gatherers had to work all the time getting their food and that they never produced a surplus and so never had any time or surplus to spare to allow for specialisation. We now know that this is not true. Hunter-gatherers only work about two to three hours a day. So they had plenty of time to produce a surplus and plenty of time to specialise. They did neither; so specialisation is not caused by spare time from a surplus of food.

It was previously thought that when man invented agriculture, it enabled him to produce a surplus and allowed time to specialise. We now know that agriculture is harder work. Early cultivators work at least three hours a day, so they have less time to specialise, not more. But it does still leave them with a bit of time on their hands and they do, in certain circumstances, start specialising. And they don't like it!

In Nepal: "Each of the larger settlements in the valley has, attached to it, a number of low-caste families, either blacksmiths, leather workers or tailors." (Gellner and Humphrey.) In Polynesia, "in some villages there is the despised community of craftsmen and traders, highly skilled in wood-carving and basketry." (Diamond) In Baluchistan, "they still lived in their own segregated camps and were employed by the Company in their traditional menial capacity of sweepers and blacksmiths . . . In the corner of the yard sat Mansoor, the blind musician." (Matheson.)

The circumstance in which specialisation takes place is poverty. When people have insufficient land they are forced into the undesirable situation of having to specialise, to do the jobs that other people don't want to do in order to persuade them to let them have some of their food. Where there is a choice specialisation does not occur. When it does, it's looked down on. Have you tried selling things to people? It's fairly demeaning business. A Macdonalds local manager says, "It's a degrading job - having to clean tables and scrub floors in front of all the customers." That's the reality of specialisation.

The people were in no doubt of this when they started creating their gods. These gods needed their weapons, but armourers and blacksmiths, though vitally important and highly skilled, were menial specialists. So when it came to creating a blacksmith god, an excuse had to be found for a god doing a menial job. He was made lame. Hephaestus was lame. Vulcan was lame. Wayland Smith was lame. "The dwarf smiths were also unpleasant, greedy, unscrupulous folk whom anyone might cheat or rob." (Clapham.)

Division of Labour

If a despised potter became successful enough, and if he could find someone even poorer than he, he could offload his more menial and unpleasant jobs to that someone. That's called 'Division of Labour'. It benefits the potter; it does not benefit the menial who never gets more than the minimum wage however successful is the potter.

In medieval times the elite had justified the life of drudgery of the workers by saying that it was God's will. "It is seemly that men should plough and dig and work hard in order that the earth may yield the fruits from which the knight and his horse will live; and that the knight who does a lord's work should get his wealth from the things on which his men are to spend much toil and fatigue." (The Blessed Raimond Lûll in 'The Book of the Order of Chivalry'.) (No one suggested the peasants were growing a surplus of food to exchange with the products of the urban artisans.) In the Age of Reason and religious scepticism that was no longer an acceptable reason for exploitation. So they looked for a new justification.

In 1776 Adam Smith published his "Wealth of Nations" to identify what is wealth and how to increase it. Smith thought that wealth was created not by the crops but by trade and industry. The traders and the industrialists would become wealthy and this wealth would 'trickle down' to the middle classes, then to the working classes and then to the peasants. This convenient theory happily justified forcing the peasants to produce more crops because, it was said, the crops would stimulate trade and industry which would create wealth which in the end would trickle down back to the peasants and make them wealthier. It also justified driving them off their land so that it could both grow more cash crops to stimulate trade and force the peasants into the factories which would then create wealth to trickle down to the workers. It did trickle down to the workers, but never back to the peasants.

To start with, Adam Smith worked from two false premisses: first, that the lives of 'primitive' societies were "solitary, nasty, dull, poor, brutish and short." (Hobbes). Adam Smith writes: "Such nations are so miserably poor that from mere want they are frequently reduced or at least think themselves reduced to the necessity of sometimes directly destroying and sometimes abandoning their infants, their old people and those afflicted with lingering diseases to perish with hunger, or to be devoured by wild beasts."

We now know that this isn't true (or that it isn't done from poverty). Marshall Sahlins has described hunter-gatherers as the 'original affluent society' whose food and fuel is abundant and free. This misconception about who is rich and who is poor is the false premiss on which the 'Wealth of Nations' is built. So although Smith could see the poverty of peasants, particularly during the Highland Clearances, he could still think, wrongly, that even so it was an advance on 'primitivism'. Smiths's second mistake was to see the evident wealth of Britain's towns and cities, but not to realize that the wealth was only built by workers paid with food (and other necessities of life) extracted from the peasants and that the wealth of the towns was only created by the poverty of the countryside.

Smith was quite right that the wealth of the rich, their food, 'trickled down' to the middle classes in return for their services and that some of that food which the middle classes had received from the rich would in turn 'trickle down' to the working classes in return for their labour. But Smith assumed that it continued to 'trickle down' to the peasants. It didn't. The wealth of the traders and industrialists was the food and other necessities of life taken from the peasant. Some of that food the middle classes ate, and destroyed. The rest trickled down to the workers who ate it, destroyed it, all. All that was left to trickle down back to the peasants was soot, sewage, scrap and shoddy.

The theory of 'Division of Labour' tries to show that if all members of a firm concentrate on what they are best at, then the firm will produce more overall. That is true. The theory then says that all members of that firm therefore benefit because all get an increase in wages. That is not true. The management indeed benefit . But it is in the management's interest to keep the wages of the workers down in order to keep the product cheaper; and the wages of the lowest paid are not determined by the success of the firm but by the hungrier unemployed outside, who would be prepared to work for less.

The conventional economist's answer to this is that in a situation of full employment workers cannot be starved into accepting lower wages. Their position is based on the false premiss that full employment is the natural condition. But there has never been full employment and no one thinks there ever will be. They used to argue that unemployment was theoretically impossible, Say's Law, which said that production created its own demand, so that there must always be enough wealth to buy the products of the factories, so there can never theoretically be unemployment. It is universally agreed that J.M. Keynes killed off Say's Law. But no one seems to have noticed that he therefore also inadvertently killed of the Theory of Division of Labour which depended on the non-existence of unemployment.

The theory also doesn't mention that one firm benefits only if another firm loses. There is only a certain amount of food to be earned by producing goods. If one firm earns that food, it is no longer available to another. The theory would have us believe that the peasants, captivated by industry's products, grow more and more crops to buy them. We have seen that this is not true of primitive societies. We have seen that it is not true of peasant societies when they have the choice. And we have seen that it has certainly never yet been true since industrial products have always been made for the rich, not the peasant. So both observed behaviour and the Law of Least Effort disprove the idea that peasants increase production of the crops to buy the goods.

Therefore there is only a limited amount of goods to buy the crops. Therefore economics is a zero sum game. The success of one firm means the failure of another.

Smith was quite right to realize that by separating the various jobs in the manufacturing process, so that each worker concentrates on one small aspect, more is produced in shorter time, so that, given the same wages and working hours, the product is cheaper to the rich consumer. So they could buy more products. So, he presumed, they were wealthier. So division of labour creates 'wealth'. Certainly, in return for the same amount of food to feed the worker, the consumer receives more goods. (But the worker is having to work the same number of hours and for the same wages if the goods are to be cheaper. Division of Labour does not save labour for the worker, only the amount of labour in the product.)

The wealthier the consumer, it is said, the more he can buy and therefore the more wealth is created. Thus wealth creates wealth and we get the concept of the self-generating engine of economic growth. But it's based on equating two different meanings of the word 'wealth'. In order to buy more goods a consumer has to be wealthy (in terms of food to feed the worker) to produce the wealth (in terms of goods) So that wealth (food) creates wealth (goods). That's correct. But they leave out the bracketed 'food', misleading the reader into believing that wealth (goods) creates wealth (goods).

The government and the rich loved this analysis. For the government it meant more trade and industry and therefore more income from the taxation on trade. For the rich it meant a justification to drive the peasants off their land to grow more cash crops (food wealth) to buy more manufactured wealth. And it meant more landless labour to fill the factories producing the manufactured wealth.

In France Louis XIV forced his peasants to provide him with food (and the other necessities of life). At his glittering court at Versailles he distributed this food to his ministers, mistresses, soldiers, cooks, builders and artisans; even the beggars at his gates benefited from this 'trickle down'. The French peasants starved. One of the worst famines ever to hit France was accompanied by plague and perhaps one tenth of France was reduced to beggary. 'Division of labour' showed that the cooks could provide more and better cakes for the king, and the artisans could make more and better baubles for his mistresses. But Smith was wrong to think that therefore the whole of France was wealthier, and therefore better fed.

59

'Division of Labour' is only half the story. It is a half truth with intent to deceive. The other half of the truth, in France, was that the periphery starved to feed the palace – the king, the cooks, and even the beggars at the gate. The village craftsmen also starved because the small crop surplus which they had received in exchange for their artifacts had been removed to Paris in return for the cheaper Parisian products. The village crafts had been destroyed by the cheaper core industries. 'Division of Labour' had produced cheaper goods to give a living to fewer workers at the core at the expense of the many village craftsmen.

Giving up the struggle, the craftsmen themselves went into the factories, but there was no one left in France with any food to buy the extra products. So the French government in the 19th century had to invade African countries and turn them into colonies where those who had previously bought the products of local craftsmen became the market of the cheaper products of the new French industries. So the local African craftsmen starved instead. There were no more markets left for them. There were no new peripheries.

Industrialism in France had simply moved the starvation on the French periphery into the Third World, the periphery of the developed world. Division of Labour creates wealth at the core at the expense of that wealth on the periphery.

Does industry create wealth?

In the France of Louis XIV all the structures, institutions, infrastructure of trade and industry were by now in place, the roads, bridges, harbours, the factories, the shops, the wholesale markets. Yet they created no wealth. It was all 'financed' by the peasants' food. The transport infrastructure was paid for by the king with the peasants' food. The Gobelin tapestry factory was set up by the king and its products bought by the rich with food received from the king, his nobles or the church which owned vast tracts of farmland.

The wholesale market in Paris took in the crops from a wide area. Everything sold at Les Halles paid a tax to the king and no wholesale trade was allowed outside Les Halles. The produce for sale was a result of the king levying taxes in cash on the peasants, who therefore had to grow extra crops, cash crops, to sell for the cash which they handed over to the king. The crops were bought by the middle and working classes with the cash which had 'trickled down' from the king via his state employees, soldiers and contractors, the only source of the cash.

"Paris received vast quantities of foodstuff, fuel and raw materials for its crafts, but little ever left the city. It was a consumer rather than a producer. Its income derived from the tax revenues of the kings and the rents paid to nobles who gathered to his court. Paris, like classical Rome, had little basic industry before the nineteenth century, and for much of its livelihood it was parasitical on the French nation." (Pounds. 1) So we all seem to be agreed that some sort of trade is not wealth-creating. For instance the existence of the vast wholesale trade created no wealth but was purely parasitic. And so was the built infrastructure, the roads, bridges, buildings, factories. And so were the highly skilled craftsmen producing the luxuries for the French nobility, the superb furniture, the carpets, the cloths, the paintings, the literature, the palaces. All this we are agreed is 'parasitical'. It is not wealth which has been created by Paris but by the crops from the French peasants. So what remains at issue is whether the existence of a 'basic' industry in a city, or 'crafts' which 'have left the city' have created wealth.

If fine cloth bought by a nobleman in Paris with food from his estates in Lyon creates no wealth, then that fine cloth, exported to Lyon and bought by another man with food from another estate in Lyon creates no wealth either. In both cases the food from Lyon has been sent to Paris to feed the weaver to produce the cloth. Exporting cloth is simply another way of importing the necessary food into the city. It creates no more wealth than internal trade.

If two craftsmen exchange products with each other, each has more wealth (goods) but no more wealth (food). Neither is better fed unless they can exchange those goods for food later. So if two cities exchange manufactured goods, neither is better fed. And the object of making goods is to eat.

But what about 'basic industry' in a city? Does that create wealth? Does it generate jobs? Does it reduce poverty both in the city and on the periphery? We seem agreed that making a luxury Louis XV table is parasitical. But so, surely, is the brass foundry that produces the decorative ormolu mounts for that table. A basic industry is still, in the end, producing goods for the consumer. It is still the nobles with the money (the tokens for the crops) who are the consumers. The brass foundry, basic industry or not, is still parasitical.

If the noble, with a finite amount of crops, spends those crops in his local town, creating employment there, he cannot spend those crops in Paris, creating employment there. Employment in Paris must be at the expense of employment on the periphery. Towns and cities are specific cause of poverty in the countryside.

Provincial towns were just as parasitic. Bayeux on the eve of the French Revolution, was "predominantly . . .composed of shopkeepers and petty tradesmen and those involved in the administration of the town and surrounding area. Over half of those rated in the tax lists hovered dangerously on the fringe of destitution . . . the rest lived either by exploit-

61

ing someone else or were dependent on income from property. The town in fact was parasitic upon the countryside." (Hufton.)

Smith justified the division of labour whereby some do the clean, well-paid jobs and most do the menial, low-paid jobs by saying that both gained thereby. He suggested that because each does what he is best at, the business is more efficient and therefore more successful, so that both benefit. That is certainly true for the management. But the wages of the lowest paid are not determined by the success of the firm (whose interests are to keep the wages down) but are determined by hungry people at the factory gate prepared to work for even less. So, today, factories are being sited in the Third World where hunger forces wages down.

Goods for the workers

Nevertheless that analysis doesn't seem to apply in Britain where workers are clearly not starving and in fact most are enjoying the products of their manufacturing industries. So are the workers really worse off? In global terms the many are. The few are not.

Once the elite had given up the fiction that they ruled because they were the god's chosen ones and found a new justification to despoil the peasants by the theory of Division of Labour, the logic of that theory forced them to share a larger part of the loot with their servants, artisans and henchmen, the urban workers. If some of their wealth wasn't seen to 'trickle down', then their justification was blown. The rulers are under another pressure too. No government can contain an angry city mob. No government can allow too much hunger at the core. So a government will always have to buy off the mob at the core at the expense of the periphery. In Ancient Rome, to preserve their own wealth, the elite had a policy of buying off the urban poor with free 'bread and circuses'. In 19th century Britain, terrified of further urban discontent, the government repealed the Corn Laws to reduce the price of bread. The Welfare State was introduced for the same reason. So for the relatively few workers at the core in the developed world life is all right.

They have enough to eat, they are warm enough and they have a little money left over to spend. Perhaps 5% of their income is 'discretionary' after they have paid out for housing, food, water, heating, clothing, taxes and travelling to work. Their 5% discretionary income is spent with one eye on the peck order – fashionable accessories, holidays at popular places, or books and furniture etc. So some of the factories which originally produced expensive goods for the elite can now make a living supplying goods to their servants and artisans.

Nevertheless the vast proportion of industrial goods made for the worker are not peck order baubles bought by the 5% discretionary income but the necessities of life which are now almost all produced in factories – prepared food, heating appliances, clothing, and household goods. If you live on the fifth floor of a concrete block, a cooker is a necessity. Building a bonfire in the middle of the floor is not an option. And if you have children, and downstairs is a concrete wilderness, traffic and strangers, a television set is not a luxury but a necessity.

Driving them into the factories

Although for years the economists have been telling us that we are all better off if we work in their factories, the people are unconvinced. It is only hunger which drives them into the factories. What they dislike above all is the indignity of taking orders: "those who can stay on the land have seldom been willing, short of starvation, to leave it for employment as wage earners . . .wage earners who can get hold of land quit their employments – that was the experience of the colonists in America and Australia." E.H. Phelps attributes "the dislike of wage labour to a desire to preserve one's freedom and independence." "As far as wage earners were concerned it (industrial work) was . . . regarded as tantamount to serfdom, because it placed a man in a situation of total dependence upon the whims and the probity of an employer or his overseer." (Clay. 4.) "Not so much manual labour – as the farmer's ever respected position shows – but dependence upon another man's personal whim and command causes the serving man to be despised." (Polanyi. 4.) "The strongest economic pressures are necessary before people are willing to sacrifice their independence and accept terms of factory employment profitable to an employer." (Wilkinson. 1.)

In a lecture in 1840 Professor Merivale said, "A certain Mr Peel took out to Australia with him: 300 individuals of the labouring classes; but they were all fascinated by the prospect of obtaining land and in a short while he was left without a servant to make his bed or fetch water from the river." Huberman comments: "Shed a tear for Mr. Peel who had to make his own bed simply because he did not realize that as long as workers have access to their own means of production – in this case the land – they will not work for someone else. We have been inured for so long, and educated and brainwashed into taking orders that we have almost forgotten that pride, that we want to be our own bosses."

In the newly colonised Kenya that pride was still alive. Lord Delamere said: "If this policy is to be continued that every native is to be a land holder of a sufficient area on which to establish himself, then the question of obtaining a satisfactory labour supply will never be settled." Lord Delamere quite understood that the natives wouldn't take orders unless they were starved into it.

So South Africa starved them. They took away their land. "In 1913 there duly followed a Land Act which abolished all African land ownership in rather more than 90% of South Africa . . . its immediate motivation was to increase the labour supply . . . it opened the way for a more effective pressure on rural Africans, by hut or poll tax, to quit their own economy for the cash and wage economy of their new masters." (Davidson. 3)

Gibbon Wakefield put it quite clearly: "Where land is cheap, where everyone who so pleases can obtain a piece of land for himself, not only is labour very dear as respects the labourer's share of the profit, but the difficulty is to obtain combined labour at any price." So the factory system cannot work if everyone has access to enough land.

The first workers in the factories were prisoners and orphans, later women and only finally men. "Some of the earliest factories were attached to gaols and poorhouses in order to give profitable and disciplined employment to their inmates." (Pounds. 4.) "Men were at first loath to enter factories . . . It has been estimated that at least three quarters of the employees in the early cotton factories were women and children." (Viljoen. 1.) Much manufacture was done outside the factories, for example, weaving in the peasants' homes. But that still wasn't from choice.

Working Hours

It is generally thought that as we 'progress' so we work less hard, helped by labour-saving machinery. It's not so. Primitive societies work 2-3 hours a day collecting and preparing food etc. Cultivators work perhaps half a day. In West Africa: "The number of hours worked in farming and associated activities was low, perhaps averaging half a day throughout the year, and sometimes rather less." (Hopkins) But even full time farming is hardly back-breaking. In Ancient Greece: "The extent of the dormant periods meant that for almost half the year there was little to do on the farms." (French) If they hadn't had to feed the cities as well there'd have been even less to do.

In Ancient Roman North Africa the farmers, as well as working their own farms, had to work on the imperial farms. But it wasn't exhausting. An inscription, thanking Hadrian for honouring the law, says: "We ask that in accordance with the clause of the Lex Hadriana we owe not more than two days work per year of ploughing, two of cultivating, two of harvesting."

In medieval times they didn't have to work on Saints' days. And there were an awful lot of saints. In Italy a Lombard document of 1595 says: "the year consists of 365 days but 96 are holy days and thus one is left with 269. Of these a great many are lost, mostly in wintertime and even at other times because of rain and snow." In France: "even when only the Apostles' days were observed the total annual holiday would be longer than now, particularly since work commonly stopped at the midday dinner bell on the vigil of each feast as laid down for instance in the weavers' ordinances of Douai and St. Omer. The ordinances of Arras in the thirteenth century decreed that there should be no work for four days at Christmas, eight days at Easter and eight at Pentecost." (C.E.H.E.II.)

In the seventeenth century governments started to crack down. Up till then: "In what some craftsmen may have regarded as the golden era before the advent of Colbert, Parisians celebrated 103 holidays a year." (Treasure. 3.)

With the onset of the industrial revolution the population in the factories, perhaps 3%, had to work very hard indeed, but much of the population were still on the farms working only half the year. As the nineteenth century progressed and more and more were forced into the factories, so the harder the population worked as a whole, 10 hours a day, six days a week for those in the factories. But it got rougher for the farmworkers too. "Farmworkers were being compelled to consume cheaper foods than those to which previous generations had been accustomed and also they were working many more days in the year, and hours in the day." (Clark. 2.)

Today the nominal working week is shorter but the number of hours actually worked is only marginally fewer because of the amount of overtime. But much more than that (even if one discounts the vastly increased travelling time) today over half the female population works. So the population as a whole is working harder than ever. "In the U.S. the numbers of people working more than 48 hours a week rose from 13% of the work force in 1948 to 20% in 1965. While the number of people who were moonlighting, or holding more than one job, has doubled since 1950." (Ward.)

To sum up: "Certain orthodox views of evolution are better turned around: the amount of work per capita *increases* in proportion to technological advance and the amount of leisure decreases." (Sahlins. 3.)

Living Standards

And just as we think we work less, we also think living standards improve. But in fact living standards started to deteriorate noticeably in the Middle Ages. "The paradox must be emphasised since it is often thought that hardship increases the further back towards the Middle Ages one goes. In fact the opposite is true, as far as the standard of living of the common people – the majority – is concerned. Before 1520–40, peasants and craftsmen in Languedoc (still little populated)

65

ate white bread. The fact cannot be misleading. The deterioration becomes more pronounced as we move away from the 'autumn' of the middle ages; it lasted right up to the middle of the nineteenth century." (Braudel. 2.) "Abel has argued that the annual consumption of meat in Germany declined from the fifteenth century from an average of 100 kilograms or more per person (a sort of biological maximum) to not more than 14 kilograms per person in the mid nineteenth century." (Cipolla. 1.) "I am convinced that at no period of English history for which authentic records exist, was the condition of manual labour worse than it was in the forty years from 1782–1821, the period in which the manufacturers and merchants accumulated fortune rapidly and in which the rent of agricultural land was doubled." (Rogers. 2.) The deterioration in Europe stopped once the wheat started coming from America and the colonies. We were exporting the growing poverty.

Is G.D.P. a Measure of Wealth?

Today they keep telling us that "we've never had it so good". They claim this because the Gross Domestic Product (GDP) keeps rising. But this GDP is no fair measure of well-being. The GDP is the total of all the output of factories, offices and shops in the country. When that goes up the politicians say we are wealthier. If a household produces more cloth the GDP would rise, but if the price of food increases more, so that the greater amount of cloth would in fact buy less food, the household would be poorer even though the GDP had increased.

Primitive societies are warm, well-fed, healthy and long-living – "the original affluent society". Their food, fuel and other necessities of life are free. They have no money. Their GDP is nil. Yet they are affluent. If they are driven off their land and have to get a job, the politicians would say their wealth had increased even though their greater income could buy less food. One wonders how a Mongolian, say, can survive on $100 a year. If most of what he needs is still free, food, fuel, clothes which he weaves himself, he might be quite well off.

Today, if there is a traffic accident, the cost of the police, ambulance and hospital services will increase the GDP but we will be poorer. So a rising GDP is no measure of increasing wealth.

Who are the Consumers?

The myth of economics is that the artisans of the towns make industrial products for the peasants of the countryside in return for the peasants' food. But in fact the peasants are proudly self-sufficient, making nearly everything themselves, buying hardly anything from the towns. In sixteenth century England: "At the base of the social pyramid there was throughout the period a continuous decline in the number of the small peasant farmers, practising a mixed husbandry, whose propensity to purchase the products of industry was notoriously small." (Clay. 2.) For instance: "Countrymen almost universally wore breeches made of home-tanned leather." (Bridenbaugh). In medieval Europe: "Spinning, weaving the wool of their own sheep, processing the hides of their own animals, making their own clothes and shoes at home, hammering and carving their own tools out of such materials as could be found locally or acquired through the petty trade that existed, and many more varied tastes filled much of the idle seasons of the subsistence farmer in the pre-industrial era . . . Medieval settlers in the central European forest regions, by their own efforts, scratched out of the soil practically all their needs." (Dovring.)

So the urban artisans were not making goods for the peasants. It was for themselves that some of their goods were made, for obviously, they could not be self-sufficient. "Since industrial employment was more demanding in time than agriculture, many industrial workers were forced to go to the market for clothes." (Cipolla. 2.) But most of all the artisans were making luxury products for the rich. Of the factories before the industrial revolution in Europe: "Most were concerned with producing either munitions of war or consumer goods for the rich. They were established to make 'fine' cloth or glass ornaments. At least a dozen factories were founded in the eighteenth century to produce Chinese-style porcelain. Nowhere does one find in the pre-Revolutionary era any encouragement for the mass production of coarse, cheap wares suited to the needs and the pockets of the majority of the population." (Pounds. 6.) Whenever the rich got richer, the artisans were able to make more goods for them, and economic growth increased: "monetary recovery and the concentration of wealth in the hands of the powerful, in the context of the sixteenth century, had an almost totally positive influence on the demand for manufactures." (Miskimin. 9.) . . . "While one may lament the inequalities that resulted, it was as a consequence of the inequality of income distribution that the economies of the sixteenth century were able to sustain flourishing industries in spite of the thin nature of the market and the utter failure to generate an economic system based on mass consumption." (Miskimin. 10.)

Town versus countryside

The urban artisans make their products for the rich lords who possess the surplus, and the artisans depend on the lords extracting that surplus because the peasants don't grow a surplus unless they're forced to. "This town-country confrontation is the first and longest class struggle history has known." (Braudel. 4.)

In the Roman Empire: "That the cities in fact depended on the economic exploitation of the peasantry is axiomatic." (Matthews.) "An area of surrounding land would also be attributed to the new foundation (of a town) to provide farms, pasture and arable for the inhabitants." (Wacher.) Galen, writing at the time, says: "The city dwellers, as it was their custom to collect and store enough corn for the whole of the next year immediately after the harvest, carried off all the wheat, barley, beans and lentils, and left to the peasants various kinds of pulse – after taking quite a large proportion of these to the city. After consuming what was left in the course of the winter, the country people had to resort to unhealthy foods in the spring; they ate twigs and shoots of trees and bushes and bulbs and roots of inedible plants." Not surprisingly the peasants sometimes revolted. "Such revolts also took place in Syria, in Asia Minor, where the country people loathed the town dwellers whom they regarded as their exploiters." (Grimal.)

In the Middle Ages hungry or proud peasants fled from their rapacious lords in the villages to the 'free air of the town' where they could earn a living by making luxury goods for the rich who owned the food. But that living was only available as long as the town could control the surrounding countryside and remove its food. "The town did not create or intend to create a regional body, but asserted instead the right of conquest. The relationship between towns and their conquered territories in the thirteenth and fourteenth centuries reminds one more of the relationship between the European states and their colonies in the nineteenth century than of the relationship between a provincial capital and its province in our contemporary society." (Cipolla. 3.) The towns of Europe "ruled their fields autocratically, regarding them as positive colonial worlds before there were such things". (Braudel. 5.)

When the ruling elites lose their power as in the French and Russian revolutions, the urban artisans quickly realised how much they depended on their rulers to remove the crops from the countryside and themselves sent the army into the villages to take them. "Thus during the radical phase of the French Revolution the needs and the aspirations of the urban sans culottes finally came into direct and open conflict with all sections of the countryside. The main symptom was the deterioration of exchanges between the city and the countryside, especially the provisions of the city, a problem that was to have great influence on the course and consequences of the Russian Revolution as well." (Moore. 4.)

Because of lower living costs on the periphery where food, fuel and water are sometimes free, there is pressure on industrialists to take advantage of the consequent lower labour costs and relocate their industries on the periphery. The urban workers fight a constant battle with the rural workers to hold on to their jobs, as the workers of the developed world are fighting the Third World today. The medieval workers used the judicial control by the cities over the surrounding countryside to forbid the jobs to the rural workers. In Flanders: "attempts were made not only to suppress the country industry in favour of the town market but also to limit the freedom of trade of the countryside in favour of the town market for which Staple privileges were jealously sought. Manufacture of cloth was forbidden in districts round Ghent and Bruges and Ypres;" (Dobb. 4.) When this didn't work, they used violence. "Armed craftsmen from the great cities exercised main force to break looms and destroy tenter frames and vats of the fullers of the countryside." (Lopez. 1.)

In the cities the higher cost of living from higher competition for food and from the fact that necessities like water and wood now have to be bought means that wages have to be higher and so labour costs are higher. It becomes necessary to invent labour-saving machinery. "The woollen guild in Florence achieved probably the maximum labour-saving use of water power that could have been found in any medieval textile centre, along with supreme efficiency in standardising quality at a high level." (C.E.H.E.III.)

Regression

In Flanders the high population and landlessness produced the same industry: "the real expansion of industry began in the eleventh century and went forward with very great rapidity in the twelfth and thirteenth centuries. This development was largely due to a rising population . . . Flanders was one of the most densely populated parts of Europe and its agriculture was totally unable to support the surplus population . . . emigrate or industrialize – there was no other choice." (Power. 2.)

As we might expect, if circumstances of population pressure, food supply or land supply improve, industry would diminish. This happened in both Italy and Flanders. "In the case of Italy, Germany and the Netherlands (and to a smaller extent in France) what is remarkable is less the early date compared with England, at which the capitalist production made its appearance, than the failure of the new system to grow much beyond its promising and precocious adolescence." (Dobb. 2.) The 'failure' in Italy and Flanders was caused by a decrease in population and in Flanders probably also by a fairer distribution of land after the Spanish were thrown out. They just weren't so hungry.

The Achievement of Cities

The success of the cities in producing manufactured goods brought great compensations. Specialisation brought greater specialisation. Athens could afford to feed its fine dramatists and their actors. Sculpture reached its first peak with its naturalistic portrayal of the human figure and its emotions. Architecture with its highly sophisticated treatment of the archaic temple forms was the seedbed of architectural ideas for 2000 years. Its philosophers similarly dominated European thought. Yet all these accomplishments were but the side effects of a deteriorating situation, a growing population, dwindling resources and a poverty transferred to the peasants of the Black Sea.

In fact the peaks of cultural achievement have usually taken place against a background of economic or political crisis. Commentators have frequently noticed the connection with surprise. "The cultural history of the Levant during the 16th–13th centuries – the late Bronze Age of the archeologists – seems to disprove the theory that civilisation requires peaceful conditions in which to flourish. Although Syria and Palestine were torn by Imperial contests, the period witnessed remarkable achievements in Art, Architecture and Literature and the general level of material culture was perhaps higher than it would be again in the region for more than a thousand years." (Encyclopaedia Britannica.) It seems that at times of stress, when competition gets fierce, the rich need to be seen to be winning by giving their artists lavish commissions – the Tarzan syndrome. Athens' cultural peak occurred at a time of economic and military collapse, the Peloponnesian Wars.

If things get better then the interest in the Arts declines. After the Black Death in the Middle Ages wages went up and for a short time there was the 'golden age of the peasant'. Pope-Hennessy shows that this golden sociological age produced a debased artistic age. "On the fine arts the impact of these disasters (the Black Death) was immediate and direct. In painting it is manifest through the third quarter of the century in a debasement of quality and a change of style, and in sculpture both factors are also present, though to a less extent. In these years Florence threw up only one major artist, Orcagna." Who?

Then things gradually got worse again, and the worse they got, the better the painters painted until that peak of cultural achievement, the thirty year period of the High Renaissance, which was exactly accompanied by severe economic and military crisis, when the French army was marauding through Italy and the Medici Bank went bankrupt. "Italy, the earliest and most brilliant centre of the artistic Renaissance, felt the impact of the economic recession most heavily. Its condition resembles somewhat that of England after 1718 or that of New England after 1929." (Lopez. 2.)

In Denmark: "The catastrophic economic conditions and the difficult political situation in the first half of the nineteenth century . . . nevertheless formed the background of an unprecedented burgeoning of Danish literature . . . If any period can belie the theory that literature cannot flourish in a period of national collapse it is this epoch of Danish history." (Glyn-Jones)

High Population but no Industry

There are some countries like Indonesia where population is very high but industrialisation doesn't happen. "Indonesia has the dubious distinction of having the highest population density in the world. In some agricultural areas of Java population density already exceeds 2,000 persons per square kilometre . . . it is not difficult to show that neither lack of resources nor the size of the objective risk premiums is the major determinant of peasants' unwillingness to innovate." (Penny)

They don't industrialise simply because they are not hungry enough. In these cases the fairer distribution of land still allowed a high population to feed itself. In the industrialised countries the distribution of land was very unequal, with the aristocracy and the church owning a disproportionate share, and some owning none at all, leaving them with no choice but to enter industry.

The Theory of Comparative Advantage

The Theory of Comparative Advantage is the Theory of Labour applied internationally. It suggests that if each country specialises in what it is best at, then overall the two countries will produce more goods. True. It then says that because more is produced then the workers in both countries get higher wages; "The principle of comparative advantage shows us that both fears (of foreign competition from imports produced by low-paid workers, or produced by more efficient machinery) are unjustified; workers in both countries *will be able to earn higher wages than before* because of the increased productivity that comes about through specialisation." (Baumol and Blinder. (Their italics)). Nonsense. The higher wages are not shared. They all go to the more developed country.

If all the industries of a country have been destroyed and the agriculture is carried out by a few ranch hands in a highly mechanised fashion, how can the income of that country as a whole possibly be higher. It's a sleight of hand. They no longer count the unemployed in the calculation. It's just remotely possible that the few left in employment get higher wages (tell that to the ranch hands on the new plantations). But millions are no longer working at all. We are talking about the country in general; their income has been slashed. A few are perhaps earning more; most are now not working at all but must be included in the calculation.

When the Portuguese king, to keep his crown, was forced by Britain, in return for military support, to allow in British goods without tariffs, Portuguese industry was destroyed by the cheaper British industrialised products. Portugal, with its 'comparative advantage' in sherry-making and agricultural products concentrated in those areas. But the work-

71

ers did *not* get an increase in wages thereby. The wages were forced down by the unemployment in all the other areas. There is no evidence at all that overall, taking the new unemployed into account, Portuguese wages rose. It is quite true that together Britain and Portugal between them produced more crops and manufactured goods. But the benefit all went to Britain. The theory of Comparative Advantage is disproved. That the Third World workers do not get the higher wages which the theory predicts with the overall increase in production is indicated by the falling prices for their agricultural crops. The prices, like wages, are determined by the hungriest. Because they are all hungry they are all producing more crops so the price goes down. "'In 1963' says the government of Tanzania, 'we needed to produce 5 tons of sisal to buy a tractor. In 1970 we had to produce 10 tons to buy the same tractor.' Similarly a rubber exporting nation could buy 6 tractors for 25 tons of rubber in 1960 but today only two for the same effort. A cotton growing Sahelian country had to produce two and a half times as much today ('76) as in 1960 to import the same low-priced French automobile." (George. 3.)

As one might expect the effects of allowing cheap industrial goods into the Third World countries have been disastrous. All their craft-based industries have been destroyed. Before we arrived there was a thriving textile industry in much of Africa. In the sixteenth century "As soon as the Portuguese reached the old kingdom of Kongo, they sent back word on the superb local cloths made from bark and palm fibre – and having a finish comparable to velvet . . . Well into the present century local cottons from the Guinea coast were stronger than Manchester cottons." (Rodney. 2.) We have already seen the effects on the textile industry in Algeria. It was the same throughout Africa. In the same way the iron industry was wiped out. "The abandonment of traditional iron smelting in most parts of Africa is probably the most important instance of technological regression." (Rodney. 3.) Africa was 'undeveloped' by our cheap industrial goods by having to concentrate on equatorial agricultural products. In no way did it benefit from the supposedly higher wages.

In Japan: "Peasant handicrafts, an important supplement to the peasants' meagre resources and a way of using surplus labour power during the black times of the agricultural cycle, suffered severe blows at the hands of the cheap western textiles." (Moore. 3.) In Silesia: "By the 1820s exports of yarn had halted completely, defeated by the murderous competition of English mechanised spinning mills; within the following twenty years, linen export too dropped to nearly nothing. Utterly destitute, cottage workers died by the thousand during the 1840s just as in Ireland." (Lis and Soly)

The capitalist will answer that since they are no longer starving that was just a temporary blip. In fact just as they on the periphery were starved by the core products, they have now themselves industrialised and shifted the starvation even further out onto the periphery in the Third World where our and their industrialisation has caused massive unemployment, hunger and starvation. 800 million are permanently malnourished: up to 30 million die of starvation and allied diseases every year. We have driven them off their land to use it to grow crops for us, and we have destroyed their industry.

The Effects of Industry on Periphery Agriculture

Today in the Third World, in order to feed the developed core, agriculture has been changed from subsistence to cash cropping for export, therefore producing less for consumption within the country. In 1976, "About 55% of the entire Philippine farming acreage is used for export crops – sugar, coconuts, bananas, rubber, pineapples, coffee and cocoa – much of it directly controlled by foreign interests in co-operation with a tiny local elite. Meanwhile, according to FAO figures, the average Filipino is eating just a hundred calories a day more than the average inhabitant of Bangladesh." (George. 2.) Twelve years later the figure had risen from 55% to 75% of land devoted to export crops.

"In Brazil well over 12 million acres, or a fifth of all cultivated land, is used to grow soya for Western Europe ... Brazilians' own protein supplies have dropped by 6% while production of protein has risen by 68%" (Gorz.) "In Ghana cocoa takes up no less than 56% of all cultivated land. Groundnuts in Senegal take up 52%." (ibid.) 78% of Guinea Bissau grows peanuts for our vegetable oil. They starved in '69, '70, '71, and '79.

"Algeria became an 'export enclave' within the French imperial system, chiefly for wine which most Algerians did not drink. In 1870 there were thought to be about 22,500 hectares of vineyard. In 1900 this total had become 154,000 hectares and in 1953 eventually reached an all time high of 378,000 hectares. Nine tenths were in European ownership. As elsewhere – and it is a theme we shall return to – this cut savagely into food resources for local consumption. It could be calculated in the middle of the 1950s that cereal production stood at the same level as in the 1880s although the population had trebled." (Davidson. 4.)

The colonial masters were single minded in their production of crops for cash: "Good examples of Africans literally being forced to grow cash crops by gun and whip were to be found in Tanganyika under German rule, in Portugese colonies and in French Equatorial Africa and the French Sudan in the 1930s." (Rodney. 1.)

The techniques used to produce these crops are those of industrialised agriculture. The effects on the soil of the deforestation and intensive use of agrichemical fertilizer are serious erosion, infertility and desertification.

With the justification of Adam Smith's theories that more cash-cropping will increase trade and industry to make their countries wealthy, the Third World governments, with our guns, are driving the people off their land. The most vulnerable groups are the tribal peoples with no concept of private ownership of land. This means that in the country's law they have no legal claims to the land. They don't 'own' it. They've got nothing down on paper. So, without a legal qualm, governments allocate their legally unowned land to new owners with new papers, to cut down its forests and develop it for cash crops.

There are a few jobs for the dispossessed tribal peoples on the new plantations for starvation wages and where unrestricted use of dangerous pesticides causes frequent illness. But otherwise, with no source of food they are driven into the shanty towns of the burgeoning cities, where they hope there is food to be earned. They have no choice.

Summary
So Does Industry Alleviate Poverty?

The first of cites to industrialise was Athens who, because of her growing population could no longer be fed from her own hinterland. Industrialisation was caused by poverty.

Historically this has been interpreted as an advance and analysed in terms of the advantages of 'specialisation' and 'division of labour'. But we find that in the real world specialists are poor and looked down on, doing the menial jobs which people with the food are unwilling to do.

The elites, no longer able to justify taking the crops from the peasants to feed the nobility simply because it was 'seemly', invented the theory of 'Division of Labour' which said that when jobs are divided up amongst specialists, more is produced more cheaply, which is true. Therefore, they said, the wages of both management and workers are increased, which is not true because the wages of the lowest paid are determined, not by the success of the firm but by the hungrier unemployed outside, prepared to work for even less.

The theory also tries to show how industry created wealth by confusing the uses of wealth (food) with wealth (products), so that they say that the wealthier the consumer in terms of food, the more goods can be produced for him to buy. Therefore wealth creates wealth. Therefore we get the concept of the self-generating engine of economic growth.

This theory justifies driving the peasants off their land which can then grow cash crops to stimulate trade and industry to create wealth which will 'trickle down' back to the peasant. And it creates a landless proletariat to fill the factories making goods for the rich.

In fact we have seen that the building of the cities, its infrastructure, shops, and fine products are not financed by the profits of trade and industry. They are all financed by the peasants' food and other necessities of life. People do not work in factories because of all the industrialised goods that they can buy, but because otherwise they would starve. When they have access to their own land, they refuse to work in the factories and obey the orders of the bosses.

Nor is it true that we are better off in factories. We are having to work longer and harder, and living standards globally are deteriorating.

The effect of importing the industrialised goods from the core is to destroy the craft industries of the periphery. Previously the local peripheries had then industrialised and exported that poverty to wider peripheries. But there are no peripheries now left so the poverty finally rests in the hills of the Third World where the land has been taken over for cash crops and the local craftsmen have been made destitute by the West's goods.

The West justifies this with their theory of 'Comparative Advantage' which says that if two countries specialise in what each does best then more is produced. True. It then says that because of the increased production, the workers of each country get higher wages. Untrue, because like 'division of labour', while the rich of each country benefit, the wages of the lowest-paid are determined by other hungry countries.

In the Middle Ages the countries which industrialised first were those whose large population could no longer be fed from the countries' own resources, or where the distribution of land was unfair. Countries with high populations but fair distribution of land did not industrialise because they were not hungry.

So industry does not alleviate poverty. It is caused by poverty and its effect is to transfer that poverty from the industrialised core to the agricultural periphery.

Chapter 4. Does Industry Reduce Poverty?
References

W.J. Baumol & A.S. Blinder. "Economics". Harcourt Brace Jovanovich. '82.

F. Braudel. "Capitalism and Material Life 1400-1800."Weidenfeld and Nicholson. '67. 2: p.129., 4: p.373., 5: p.396.

C. Bridenbaugh. "The Colonial Craftsman". New York. '50. p.35. Quoted by Wilkinson.

A.R. Burn. "The Lyric Age of Greece". Arnold. '60. 2: p.15.

C.M. Cipolla. "The Industrial Revolution. 1700-1914." Harvester Press/Barnes and Noble. '73. 1: p.131., 2: p.142. "Before the Industrial Revolution." Methuen. '76. 3: p.149.

Cambridge Economic History of Europe. Ed Postan. C.U.P. 1st Edn. Volume II. p.386. Vol. III p.270.

C. Clark. "Population Growth and Land Use'. MacMillan. '67. 2: p.134.

J. Clapham. "A Concise Economic History of Britain". C.U.P. '66. p.14.

C.G.A. Clay. "Economic Expansion and Social Change". C.U.P. '84. 2: p.153., 4: p.101.

B. Davidson. "Africa in Modern History". Allen Lane. '78. 3: p.116., 4: p.119.

A.S. Diamond. "The Evolution of Law and Order". Watts. '51. p.44.

M. Dobb. "Studies in the Development of Capitalism". Routledge Kegan Paul. '46. 4: p.155.

F. Dovring. in "The Cambridge Economic History of Europe" Ed. Postan. Vol. VI. '65. p.666.

Encyclopedia Britannica. History of Syria and Palestine. p.936.

M.I. Finley. 'Early Greece:The Bronze and Archaic Ages". Chatto and Windus. '81. 1: p.65., 2: p.61.

A. French. "The Growth of the Athenian Economy". Routledge Kegan Paul. '64. p.6.

D. Gellner and C. Humphrey. "Ghurka Swords into Ploughshares". New Society. 17.8.78.

S. George. "How the other Half Dies." Penguin. '76. 2: p.172., 3: p.37.

W. Glyn-Jones. "Denmark". Benn. '70. p.48.

A. Gorz. "Paths to Paradise". Pluto Press. '85. p.93

P. Grimal. "The Civilization of Rome". Allen and Unwin. '63. p.236

T. Hobbes. "Leviathan." Chapter 13.

A.G. Hopkins. "An Economic History of West Africa". Longman. p.17.

O.H. Hufton. "Bayeux in the Late Eighteenth Century. A Social Study" quoted by N.J.G. Pounds. Oxford '67. p.322.

C. Lis and H. Soly. "Poverty and Capitalism in Pre-Industrial Europe". Harvester Press. '79. p.159.

R. Lopez. 1: "The Commercial Revolution of the Middle Ages". Prentice Hall. '71. p.98. 2: "Hard Times and Investment in Culture". Metropolitan Museum of Art. p.38.

S.A. Matheson. "The Tigers of Baluchistan". O.U.P. '75. p.18 and 98.

J. Matthews. in "The Roman World". Ed. J. Boardman. O.U.P. '88 p.348.

W.H. McNeill. "A World History". O.U.P. '79. 3: p.115.

H.A. Miskimin. "The Economy of Later Renaissance Europe. 1460-1600". C.U.P. '77. 9: p.84., 10: p.85.

B. Moore Jnr. "The Social Origins of Dictatorship and Democracy". Penguin. '66. 4: p.90., 3: p.218.

D.H. Penny. in "Agricultural Development in Asia". Ed. R.T. Shand. Allen & Unwin. '69. p.253 and 261.

E.H. Phelps. "The Economics of Labour". Newhaven. '62. p.10.

K. Polanyi. "Trade and Market in Early Empires." Free Press. '57. 4: p.77.

Polybius. "The Histories". Loeb Library. London. '60. p.311. quoted by Anne Ross. '86.

J. Pope-Hennessy. "Italian Gothic Sculpture". Phaidon. '55. p.27.

N.J.G. Pounds. "A Historical Geography of Europe". C.U.P. '79. 1: p.119., 4: p.221., 6: p.221.

E. Power "The Wood Trade in Medieval History." O.U.P. '41. 2. p.34.

N. Riasanovski. "A History of Russia". O.U.P. '63. p.13.

W. Rodney. "How Europe Underdeveloped Africa". Bogie-L'Ouverture. '72. 1: p.171., 2: p.50., 3: p.114.

T. Rogers. "Six Centuries of Work and Wages" 1884. 1: p.63., 2: p.79.

M. Sahlins. "Tribalism". Prentice Hall. '68. 3: p.79.

G. Treasure. "The Making of Modern Europe. 1648-1780." Methuen. '85. 3: p.63.

S. Viljoen. "Economic Systems in World History". Longman. '74. 1: p.182.

T. Wacher. "The Roman Empire". Dent. '87. p.99.

C. Ward. in an editorial appendix to "Fields, Factories and Workshops tomorrow". by P. Kropotkin. Freedom Press. '85.

R. Wilkinson. "Poverty and Progress." Methuen. '73. 1: p.157.

Chapter 5
REGRESSION

THE THESIS OF THIS BOOK is that cities and technology are the result of a population being forced by the sword and religion to hand over the crops to an elite. If this is true one must expect, when an elite loses the power or the will to extract the surplus, that the cities and technology would decline. That is what happened at the end of the Roman Empire.

Rome manufactured little. She got her food for her population by straight theft – she got herself an empire. Rome started out, according to tradition, as a colony of Troy, an indigenous Latin population ruled by a foreign elite. Perhaps because it was foreign it had less compunction in taxing the Latins more heavily than the neighbouring Etruscans were taxing their people. So the Romans could afford more and better weapons for more soldiers than the Etruscans. The Etruscans were conquered, the first of many. The Romans had brought their own gods from Troy who formed the basis of the state religion which they imposed on the local population and used as a justification to make the laws which extracted the crops.

For a long time these laws weren't written down, just 'remembered' by the patricians, and as far as the plebs, the urban population, was concerned, the patricians' memories only seemed to remember what was in the patricians' interest. "There followed a long struggle on the part of the plebeians to have the laws of Rome written down so that they would no longer have to trust to patrician memories." (Wells.)

The Roman Empire followed the usual pattern at the core, of deforestation and the subsequent erosion, a stage it reached about 200 AD. "Thus during the four centuries of Roman power (roughly 200 BC. to 200 AD.) many parts of Italy would have lost from six to sixteen inches of topsoil. The direct effect on fertility would have been serious and when we add in the presumable decline in the effective rainfall, through increased run-off (the same process that Plato described in Greece) it is clear that Italian agriculture must indeed have fallen on bad times." (Clayborne.)

So Rome's territorial expansion could well have been caused by its need for timber. The first emperor, Augustus, boasted that he found Rome built of brick and left it built of marble. They were having to build it in brick in the first place because they'd already run out of timber.

Technology in the Roman Empire

The Roman Empire came at the end of a long period of technological stagnation. "Around 2500 BC. technological advance ground almost to a stop and during the next three thousand years rather little progress took place." (Lilley.) Rome knew about the technology but chose not to use it. "Cogs and gears were employed only for creating toys or automata." (Gimpel. 2.) "Engineers of the classical world – men like Hero of Alexandria – knew the use that could be made of the cam, but applied it only to animate toys or gadgets." (Gimpel. 3.)

Around 70 AD. the Emperor Vespasian rewarded an engineer generously for an idea of a labour-saving device to transport marble columns. But he didn't use the idea because it would cause unemployment. He said, "You must let me feed my poor commons." (Suetonius). He was already having to feed the unemployed in Rome. So the food saved by using the labour-saving device would have to have been given out as dole instead. It was no economic benefit to anyone.

The difference between then and the subsequent introduction of technology in the Christian era was that the Christians didn't seem to worry about the hunger that the technology caused. There was no dole. If the merchants and the Church had had to pay dole to those the technology had made unemployed as the Romans did, they would not have introduced the technology because it would not then be profitable.

Nevertheless, although the Romans didn't use labour-saving techniques, they did sometimes use large-scale factory production: "immense quantities of Samian ware were shipped out from the factories of Lezoux and La Graufesenque in Southern France and later from Rheinzabern in the Rhineland, bringing great wealth to the owners of the potteries and employing large numbers of workmen and distributors." (Pounds. 1.) Corn was grown on vast farms, latifundia, in North Africa, using conventionally capitalist production, just as they are farming the Third World today. The corn was then transported to Rome for the urban population and the army.

Roman Supremacy

Until the invention of the cannon the Roman army would have slaughtered anything put into the field before that time and even then nothing on the scale of the Roman army, or navy, was seen perhaps until the Battle of Lepanto in 1571. Technologically the Dome of the Pantheon and Santa Sophia were not matched until the nineteenth century. The Europeans were not able to sculpt the human form like the Romans or Greeks until the fifteenth century. It was only with the invention of printing c. 1450 that Rome began to be overtaken. In c. 180 AD. a full size equestrian bronze statue of Marcus Aurelius was cast. Not till the mid 15th century could Europe build another.

Rome knew about the technology but chose not to exploit it. It was not threatened by a powerful neighbour so it didn't need money from trade to support its army. It was self-sufficient in food and raw materials within its own jurisdiction so it didn't need to trade and use technology to reduce the cost of its exports. Apart from in Rome itself, it had no landless proletariat who needed to find jobs in factories. And it had nowhere to export the poverty created by technology.

Different Empire, Same Result

At the time when the Roman Empire was all-powerful in Europe, China was equally powerful in the East. Rome declined. China developed. During the Tang and Sung dynasties cash taxation, trade, technology and cities all grew.

The growth had started with the Tang with the introduction of taxes paid in cash. From c. 780: "more and more taxes were imposed in the form of money instead of in kind. This pressure forced farmers out of the land and into the cities in order to earn there the cash they needed for their tax payments." (as we saw in South Africa) "These men provided the labour force for industries and this in turn led to strong growth in the cities especially in Central China where trade and industry developed most." (Eberhart.)

During this period of growth China invented gunpowder, paper, printing, paper money, and the compass. It built the first mechanical clock. This process continued until "around 1300 Chinese technology had developed to a point where industrialisation comparable to the 'industrial revolution' in Europe in the eighteenth century was possible. It did not take place because the intensive agriculture of China could keep many more people alive than European agriculture so that there was always an oversupply of human labour which made the use of machines uneconomic." (Block)

The final expression of technological achievement was the voyage of Cheng Ho at the beginning of the fifteenth century, an armada of sixty two 'treasure ships' the largest of which was 1500 tons, six times as big as Vasco da Gama's ship which rounded Africa sixty years later. This spectacular fleet of 40,000 people travelled as far as Africa and the Persian Gulf for reasons which are obscure. Trade was very secondary. All they seem to have wanted was "the collection of drugs and medical knowledge and materials such as rhino horn, and exotic beasts like giraffes and zebras". (Cotterell and Morgan. 1.) The idea was probably sold by Cheng Ho to the emperor by emphasising the glory to China of such an expedition and the tribute that could be demanded from all the territories visited – a sort of protection money. But the colossal expense of the fleet must have eaten any potential profit. On the death of the emperor the voyages were discontinued, and the next emperor forbade the building of any large sea-going ships for good.

So China had the capacity to industrialise. It had the technology and the transport capacity. It also had the incentive of more revenue. It was already taxing trade. During the periods of the Tang and the Sung government income came increasingly from indirect taxation on trade. "Tang also established barriers on the principal trade routes and strictly controlled city market places as a way to tax and regulate trade. Despite this interest in taxes on trade, however, it showed the traditional Chinese scorn for merchants." (Fairbank and Reischauer. 1.) "The system of limiting foreign trade to certain official ports where customs duties could be collected had started in the eighth century, and during the Sung these customs duties became an important source of government income." (ibid. 2.)

So it had the capacity and the incentive. Why then did it not industrialise? The small countries of medieval and renaissance Europe, small in comparison with Rome or China, were in intense competition with each other, each fearful of being invaded. For protection they needed high population and gold to buy arms and soldiers. To get the gold they needed to export crops or goods. This is called Mercantilism. To sell the goods, they had to make their exports cheaper by reducing the labour content by inventing labour-saving machinery. To survive they were forced to industrialise.

China had no need to industrialise because it was not under such pressure. It did not need gold from exports for arms and soldiers because it was so big that it had no competitors. It was not threatened by a powerful neighbour. It had no fear of being invaded except by the low-tech nomads of Central Asia against whom it did not need high tech armaments. In the 1220s Genghis Khan invaded from Mongolia and installed himself as the Celestial Emperor. For the next 400 years Central Asia was a containable threat with no need for high expenditure in military technology. (Japan, in China's shadow, kept level with China's technology. It was only when threatened by superior European technology that it chose to industrialise.) So China didn't need the gold from exports to buy arms.

Since it didn't need the gold, it didn't need to encourage the export of crops, so it didn't need to drive people off the land which could then be used for cash crops for export. The Chinese rulers, because most of their income came from the land, had always tried to ensure that the peasants had enough land so that they could pay the taxes. "In 485 the Northern Wei instituted an 'equal field' system according to which all able-bodied adult peasants were supposed to be assigned agricultural lands of equal dimensions . . . During the Sui and Tang dynasties the equal field system was greatly elaborated. Each able-bodied male between the ages of eighteen and fifty nine was supposed to receive about 13.7 acres." (ibid. 3.) Because of this land policy there wasn't the pressure, as in Italy, Flanders and later Britain, of a large landless proletariat who had to manufacture goods just to eat.

What landless workers there were, were quite capable of providing all the luxuries which the Chinese rulers could desire. There was very little that the outside could offer. Japanese exports to China "consisted mainly of gold, mercury, fans, lacquerware, screens, timber and swords." The main Japanese imports from China were "silk, brocades, perfumes, incense, sandalwood, porcelain, and copper coins, as well as tea." (Cortazzi. 3.) The Chinese rulers had no need of a manufacturing industry to produce goods to exchange for foreign luxuries. There weren't any foreign luxuries.

So while there were no advantages or pressures to industrialise, there were also positive pressures against. The long Pacific coastline was subject to constant Japanese piracy and the cheapest answer was to withdraw from the coast rather than expensive protection. So external trade would need high government expenditure to protect it. Foreign trade was also the source of destabilising ideas from abroad, such as Christianity. One of the major factors in the stability of the Chinese empire was its intellectual consensus, Confucianism modified by Taoism and a little Buddhism. What the rulers didn't need was unsettling new ideas.

So it made the specific decision not to engage in foreign trade and therefore not to industrialise. In 1390 it prohibited trade with foreigners. "In 1500 it become illegal to build a sea-going junk with more than two masts and in 1551 it became treasonable to go to sea in a multiple-masted ship. It was decided that the Chinese lost more than they gained through such maritime contacts and a period of withdrawal from maritime intercourse ensued until the Europeans prised China open." (Cotterell and Morgan. 2.)

China lost all interest in technology. "Although during the Two Sungs the examination questions included technical and scientific questions such as astronomy, engineering and medicine, the curriculum for Ming scholars was confined to orthodox literature and philosophy, a reflection of the passing of Chinese interest in technical invention and science." (Yap and Cotterell.)

There are many, such as the Marxists, who think that economics determines politics; and many who think that you can't hold back the march of progress. China disproves them both. The emperors made a political decision to stop economic growth, and it held for 500 years. For 500 years the march of progress was halted. It only started again because of outside military pressure from overpopulated Europe, desperate to export their manufactured goods in return for the necessities of life.

If the Chinese or Roman emperors had decided not to use technology, couldn't the people nevertheless have used it themselves? Within each empire there was an enormous population of consumers. Even if trade was forbidden abroad couldn't entrepreneurs have made a fortune capitalising on the technological know-how? No, without a landless proletariat, they couldn't. They wouldn't be able to get anyone into the factories.

So China had the capacity to industrialise and chose not to use it because: there was no neighbouring threat which required gold for arms expenditure and soldiers; it was self-sufficient in food and raw materials; it had no landless proletariat. There was simply no need for industry's social turmoil, huge expenditure on infrastructure, ugliness, environmental destruction, pollution and poverty.

The assumptions of later economic theories that technology and trade create wealth was clearly not accepted by either China or Rome. They both knew they were wealthy because of the crops they took from their own peoples. And they were keeping it that way.

Decline and Fall

The Roman Empire, driven by its need for food and raw materials, expanded until its maximum about 120 AD. Then the population started to decline: "The extent of the decline is unknown but contemporary references to labour shortage and to abandoned fields and depopulated towns imply that it was considerable." (Pounds. 3.) The government, as usual, wanted a larger population. "Ever since Augustus' time, the government had taken steps to promote marriage and parentage among Roman citizens." (Lopez. 3.) But it didn't work. Although no reason has been established for the population decline, suggested reasons have included plague or lead from the pipes of the water supply. But it is possible that the lack of religious consensus during the slow growth of Christianity until the fourth century had weakened the usual religious pressure for high population growth. "The adoption of Christian marriage from the fourth century onwards put an end to the voluntary restriction of births that had been common in earlier centuries." (Hodgett. 1.)

With a smaller population to feed it was no longer worth the expense and effort of holding on to all of its empire. It's possible that an empire must keep growing, that its strength is derived from the cheapest raw materials plundered from its new conquests and that continuing exploitation of that same territory, requiring continuing policing, is not nearly so profitable. At any rate the decline of the Roman Empire from its peak was fairly swift.

But it was only the western half that fell; the eastern half with its capital at Constantinople, today's Istanbul, continued for another thousand years. So any explanation of the fall of Rome must be one that does not equally apply to Constantinople.

Though the decline had been building up since the beginning of the third century, the fall was fairly rapid. In 406 the Vandals crossed the Rhine into Gaul, now Northern France. In 410 Rome retreated from Britain and lost the British wheat that fed their legions in Gaul. In 476 the last Roman Emperor in Italy was pensioned off and Odoacer was crowned the first king of Italy.

The reason was the division of the Roman Empire into two parts. The eastern half survived because it had the greater income and could afford a better army: "Yet we also know that of all the eastern provinces, Egypt produced the most in taxes. In the West, Africa headed the list – yet the total of its fiscal receipts was equivalent only to one-third of those derived from Egypt! There can be little doubt, then, that the West was poorer than the East and would therefore have had greater difficulty in finding the wherewithal for defence, as well as being so heavily taxed." (Rouche. 1.) Rome had grown powerful on the wheat from Egypt. And the Levant too. When the wheat, after the division, went instead to Constantinople, Rome died.

It seems that the division became official about 395, but the wheat from Egypt, which belonged, not to the state but to the Emperor personally, had probably been going to Constantinople since about 320. In 381 Ambrose, Bishop of Milan described towns of Central Italy as "semirutarum urbium cadavera" – corpses of half-ruined cities.

The Roman Empire in the west crumbled from the edges. While it held onto the towns on its periphery and the roads connecting them, it lost control of the surrounding countryside; and so it lost the crops. So it could feed fewer soldiers. Its power to collect the taxes weakened. It lost more revenue. It lost more territories and their crops.

Because it had lost control of the land, it could not stop people going back to that land. It started losing labour in the towns. It passed laws to force the sons of potters and other specialists to be potters and bakers etc. themselves. It didn't work. The sons could find land to feed themselves. They didn't need to do the demeaning jobs of the specialist worker. The other people could make their own pots. They could make their own bread. "Even the potter's wheel fell into disuse in Western Europe, pots again being made by hand." (Thomas. 1.) The pottery factories closed, mainly because their customer, the army, had gone.

And the blacksmith went back to the land too. "The decline of Rome and the Roman civilization was marked as much as anything else by the decline of metallurgy." (Thomas. 2.) They also forgot the plane. "The Renaissance also revived the plane, known to Rome but forgotten for centuries." (Thomas. 3.) Agriculturally they regressed too. "The fall of Rome was made manifest in the restoration of a culture not for cultivation but for the exploitation of the natural wilderness." (Duby. 1.)

Beyond its own territories Rome had kept a buffer zone with client kings held in power with Roman arms, ruling over a disarmed population. But the real threat lay beyond these kingdoms where the nomadic peoples had not been disarmed. When they broke through the client kingdoms, there was no opposition left. The Roman population was disarmed and defenceless. The Huns, Goths, Visigoths, Franks and Alans rode through the Roman Empire and delivered the coup de grâce.

Rome grew powerful because it was able to extract more taxes from its population than its neighbours. So it could afford more soldiers and more arms. It could take the food to feed the cities. When it lost its power to extract the crops, or when the crops went somewhere else, the cities died.

Chapter 5. Regression
References

M. Block. "Feudal Society". Routledge Kegan Paul. '61. p.245.

R. Clayborne. "Climate, Man and History". Angus and Robertson. '73. p.336.

H. Cortazzi. "The Japanese Achievement." Sidgewick and Jackson. '90. 3:p.79.

A. Cotterell and D. Morgan. "China". Harrap. '75. 1: p.211., 2: p.213.

C. Duby. "The Early Growth of the European Economy" Weidenfeld and Nicholson. '74. 1: 21.

W. Eberhart. "A History of China". Routledge Kegan Paul. '59. p.209.

Fairbank and Reischauer. "China. Tradition and Transformation". Allen and Unwin. '89. 1: p.105., 2: p.136., 3: p.100.

J. Gimpel. "The Medieval Machine".Arnold Pacey. '74. 2: p.1., 3: p.13.

C. Hodgett. "A Social and Economic History of Medieval Europe." Methuen. '72. 1: p.11.

L. Lilley. "Technological Progress and Industrial Revolution." Vol III. "Fontana Economic History of Europe". London '73. p.188. (quoted by Cipolla.)

R. Lopez. "The Commercial Revolution of the Middle Ages." Prentice Hall. '71. 3: p.11.

N.J.G. Pounds. "A Historical Geography of Europe 450 BC.-AD. 1330". C.U.P. '73. 1: p.164. "An Economic History of Medieval Europe". Longman. '74. 3: p.43.

M. Rouche. in "The Middle Ages". Ed. R. Fossier. C.U.P. '89. 1: p.24.

H. Thomas. "An Unfinished History of the World". Hamish Hamilton '79. 1: p.29., 2: p.271., 3: p.209.

H.G. Wells. "The Outline of History". Penguin. p.261.

Yong Yap and A. Cotterell. "Chinese Civilization from the Ming Revival to Chairman Mao".Weidenfeld and Nicholson. '77. p.33.

Chapter 6
TECHNOLOGICAL PROGRESS

FOR THREE THOUSAND YEARS through to the end of the Roman Empire there had been technological stagnation. Then in the sixth century started the spread of the water mill and the beginning of the technological bandwagon. "A schematic inventory of the main technological developments of the West from the sixth to the eleventh century should include: (a) from the sixth century: diffusion of the water mill, (b) from the seventh century: diffusion in Northern Europe of the heavy plough, (c) from the eighth century: diffusion of the three field system, (d) from the ninth century: diffusion of the horse shoe and a new method of harnessing draught animals." (Cipolla. 2.)

Rome knew all about the water mill but chose not to exploit it because of the technological unemployment it caused. Nor did it need to reduce the price of its goods by reducing the amount of labour in them with labour-saving machinery because it was not in competition with hungrier people.

So what happened in the sixth century to change three thousand years of technical stagnation? The unlikely new factor was monastic Christianity. Surviving literary sources suggest that the monasteries of northern France were the earliest technologists. "Indeed it may be said that until the development of the towns in the eleventh century it is the monasteries who are the pioneers of industry and commerce." (Evans. 1.)

Benedictine Technology

The Benedictine monasteries with their great agricultural estates were in the technological vanguard. "Dotted about the estates of St Germain-des-Prés were 83, perhaps 84 water mills. At Corbie there were water mills driven by three or anything up to six wheels. Irminon boasts of having installed and renovated four. Unfortunately this does not mean that the man-powered mill has disappeared, but merely that efforts were being made to economise on manpower." (Patlagean. 1.)

A twelfth century report on a Cistercian monastery at Clairvaux describes the use of water. "Entering the Abbey under the boundary wall, which like a janitor allows it to pass, the stream first hurls itself impetuously at the mill where in a welter of movement it strains itself, first to crush the wheat beneath the weight of the mill-stones, then to shake the fine sieve which separates flour from bran. Already it has reached the next building; it replenishes the vats and surrenders itself to the flames which heat it up to prepare beer for the monks, their liquor when the vines reward the wine-growers' toil with a barren crop. The stream does not yet consider itself discharged. The fullers established near the mill beckon to it. In the mill it had been occupied in preparing food for the brethren; it is therefore only right that it should now look to their clothing. It never shrinks back or refuses to do anything that is asked for. One by one it lifts and drops the heavy pestles, the fullers' great wooden hammers . . . Leaving it here the water enters the tannery, where in preparing the leather for the shoes of the monks it exercises as much exertion as diligence; then it dissolves in a host of streamlets and proceeds along its appointed course to duties laid down for it, looking out all the time for affairs requiring its attention, whatever they might be, such as cooking, sieving, turning, grinding, watering, or washing." (see Luckhurst)

To understand why the monasteries started to industrialise we have to clear away some misunderstandings. To us 'monastic' sounds like a severe regime of utmost simplicity and equality. It wasn't like that a bit. Most of the monks were aristocrats, inconvenient children consigned to the monasteries to pray for the family's post-mortal wellbeing. These rich men lived in a sort of odd hotel of great size and visual luxury, waited on by lay brothers, working-class monks. Until St. Peter's was built in Rome, Cluny was the biggest, most elaborate church in Christendom. Another, the ninth century Abbey of Corbie, comprised "three basilicas and four oratories; a monastery to hold between three and four hundred monks and a hundred and fifty lay brethren, with refectories, kitchens, cellars, dormitories and chapter houses; a guest house with quarters for bishops, lords, monks, clerks, and beggars, each with its separate oratory; a school; outbuildings to shelter the abbey's vassals in troubled times; and homes and workshops for forty workmen - cobblers, parchment makers, founders, masons, carpenters, wood carvers, brewers, and gardeners." (Evans. 2.) "Benedictine monasticism fostered and developed the arts in an age when the outside world was distraught with warfare and struggle - music for its services, architecture, sculpture and glass for its buildings, frescoes and work in gold, bronze and ivory for their adornment." (Evans. 3.)

Everything but the food and the clothing was of the sort of sumptuous standard maintained only by the imperial courts, but the monasteries were without the taxation that paid for it. They were always short of money in a way that the Roman landowners never were. It is this need for cash that caused technology. They had to save money on labour costs by building labour-saving machinery.

The reason that the Church itself gave, which was partly true, was that it was now responsible for looking after the poor which had not previously been a function of religion. In Constantinople: "in contemporary legislation the connection was made . . . between the delegation to the Church of responsibility for dispensing charity and the fiscal immunities granted to the clergy and to ecclesiastical property . . . Houses of charity staffed by monks then started to multiply especially in the capital during the first half of the fifth century." (Patlagean. 2.) For these houses of charity the first need was money. Help for the poor had become monetised. But the Knights Hospitallers of Southern France, though it was their raison d'être, only spent five per cent of their income on charity and a significant proportion of that was crops, not money. So it is a true, but small, reason for the Church's need for cash and the monasteries' need for labour-saving machinery.

Also, Christianity is an apostolic religion - it is dedicated to making new converts. For monasteries the more money they could make, the more monks they could support. For the Hospitallers "to be rich meant to recruit new brothers." (Duby. 2.)

It is possible that the Christians were less upset by others' poverty than the Romans. For the Christians this life is an overture to the real life - the after-life. So poverty in this life was more likely to lead to an eternal after-life spent in Heavenly Bliss. For the Romans this was the important life, so poverty mattered more. It couldn't be balanced out in the after-life. So it is possible that the Christians were less worried by the technological unemployment caused by the water mills than Rome, or China.

Building water mills is very expensive, only justified if money is saved on labour costs. If the monks had decided to live only on what their own farms could have produced and not bought anything from outside and therefore had no money (a decision some monks made), then there would be no labour costs to save and the mill would not be built, or, if it had already been built, it would not be expensively maintained. It would not be economic. When it broke down, it would stay broken down. There would be technological regression.

The major effect of the monasteries' need for cash was their exploitation of their land. They expended much energy increasing the output of their land, not because they needed the food, but to sell it off for cash. For this they evolved the three field system, the heavy plough, the horse shoe and the new harness for draught animals which used the collar and so no longer put pressure on the animals' throats.

This agricultural revolution had started early in the sixth century, possibly not by monks but by bishops in the towns. In Italy: "More positively, the return of agricultural prosperity enabled bishops to invest their surpluses in new constructions. While the Roman civic monuments fell into decay, the towns of the sixth and seventh centuries witnessed a proliferation of basilicas built with triangular pediments, timber roofs and detached bell towers." (Rouche. 2.)

This quote is presented as evidence of a heavy building programme. But I would disagree with Rouche's argument that agricultural prosperity caused that building. Rather it was the other way round. The building costs caused the agriculture. Also 'agricultural prosperity' implies that everyone is better fed. But as in the Third World today, since the crops were grown for cash, only those with the cash, the rich, were better fed. The poor had no cash and went hungry.

Later when the monastic movement gathered strength, it was the monks who took over leadership of technical change. They were trying to support a far larger number of people at a higher standard of living than the Roman landowner who was only trying to keep his own family at the high standard and who therefore didn't need to use the advanced agricultural techniques. The monks, to maintain their high standards, had to support far more specialists, ivory carvers, gilders, artists, jewellers, who were therefore not available to grow the food. So the peasants, the food-growers, themselves fewer in number, were each having to support a larger number of specialists. The fewer peasants were each being forced to grow more food by heavier taxation and by being forced to use more intensive techniques entailing harder work. The more artisans each peasant has to support, the larger the economic size of a farm has to be. Today that size is about 200 acres.

As they've found in the Third World today, advanced agricultural techniques only benefit the rich. A self-sufficient peasant doesn't need to increase his output. He and his family can only eat so many strawberries. It would not be sensible to spend money on a machine to produce more potatoes which he couldn't eat and which, in a small community, it would be anti-social to sell.

The small cash-crop farmer has to have a high enough output to justify the capital expenditure of the more advanced technology. To produce insufficient crops through a new technology would increase their cost, not reduce it. Therefore the larger farmer can reduce his costs where the smaller cannot. So the higher technology only benefits the richer farmer who can then produce the crops more cheaply and undercut and destroy the smaller farmer.

The wage labourer gains nothing from the 'labour-saving' technology. The labour is saved in the product, not for the labourers. With a machine the labourer can produce a good in a shorter time. As long as he works as long as before, more goods are produced more cheaply. *He* still has to work as long. Historically, as we have seen, he works longer.

The new agricultural techniques, introduced by the monasteries, to produce more crops with less labour, benefited the rich, not the poor. They were forced on the population. Had they the choice, they would have reverted to their more primitive technology.

The Forges of the Cistercians

So the cause of the growth of agricultural technology in the first millennium was the Benedictine monks' extravagant building programme and its ornate decoration which required a large cash income from increased agricultural productivity and reduced labour costs.

The aristocrats, who gave these monasteries their lands and their children, looked on a little nervously at such a parade of wealth. They'd given their land to the monks because the monks were supposed to be extra specially religious and so would be able, by singing to the Lord, to ensure the salvation of the souls of the rich aristocrat and his family. He was beginning to wonder just how religious these monks really were. Was his soul safe? Was God still listening to them?

So in the twelfth century when a new order of monks, the Cistercians, came along promising to be even more extra specially religious, the aristocrats gave their endowments to the Cistercians instead. To prove how good they were, they promised not to use many of the Benedictines' more dubious fund-raising methods. They rejected "churches, altar dues, burial rights, the tithes from the work or nourishment of other men, manors, dependent labourers, land rents, revenues from ovens and mills and similar (property), which is not in accord with monastic purity." (see Platt. 1.)

Very praiseworthy. But the Cistercians were still competing with the Benedictines and each other to build the longest, the highest, the most impressive abbeys for which they still needed more and more cash. Because they had rejected the Benedictines' use of tithes etc., they had to find a different way of raising money. It was this which led directly to technological progress.

To show how religious they were, they had set up their monasteries far out in the wild places which turned out to be extremely useful for agricultural exploitation. Their Rule allowed them to use their own working class monks to work the land. It did not allow them to use other people. So they cleared everyone else off the land and worked it themselves with every possible efficiency. "Far more common was the destruction of villages, and the sight of hamlets disappearing within the ring-fences of the white monks (the Cistercians wore unbleached woollen robes), especially when the latter were becoming wealthy, and the arable was converted into pasture for sheep, caused widespread and adverse comment." (Knowles. 1.) But to finance their ambitious building programmes the income from their efficient agriculture was not nearly enough.

At this time there was a great technological spurt in Europe. Carus-Wilson called it the First Industrial Revolution. The Cistercians weren't just up there amongst the front runners. They created it, alone, to pay for their building programme. "Thus the Abbey of Foigny, to take only one example, had fourteen wheat mills, a fulling mill, two cable twisting machines, three furnaces, three forges, a brewery, three wine presses, and a glass works." (Gille. 1.)

The Cistercians almost single-handedly created the iron industry because they needed the iron to build their abbeys and grow their cash crops. "The Abbey of Clairvaux, situated in the centre of one of the great iron ore areas of France (the Plateau de Langres), gradually took over a large number of the iron ore mines of the neighbouring regions. It went on acquiring iron ore deposits and forges - either by donations or purchases - until the eighteenth century. From 1250 to the seventeenth century the Cistercians were the leading iron producers of the Champagne region and by the end of the eighteenth century owned half of the industrial iron and steel complex of the 'Plateau de Langres'." (Gimpel. 5.)

And because their monasteries spread all over Europe, the technology went with them. "There are hundreds of documents referring to the Cistercians working iron ore deposits all over Europe." (Gimpel. 6.) "The first iron mills mentioned in Germany, Denmark, England, and Southern Italy are all Cistercian establishments." (Gille. 2.)

In order to procure cash to build a bigger church than the next monastery, and later to keep themselves in the luxury they'd got used to, the Cistercians had to produce more crops and to reduce their labour costs by introducing labour-saving techniques and machinery. They also increased their cash income by getting into trade, selling their surplus wool, iron, glass, wheat, wine. What they were selling was not just an incidental surplus but grown or made specifically to be traded. The technology and trade didn't develop with an effortless inevitability. The Cistercians were driven into commerce and industry, and all to pay for their building works.

Nobody liked the noise, the dirt, the pollution, the ugliness of industry. But once the Cistercians had started building, nobody had a choice. For the city poor it was industry or starve. For the rich Cistercians it was industry or bankruptcy.

If the Cistercians had not extravagantly built their monasteries, if they had not driven the peasants off their land into the cities and concentrated all their crops into one abbey, the first industrial revolution would not have happened; it could not have happened because the cash expenditure on the machinery could not have been paid for by sufficient output. The cost of the processed crops would have been increased by the machine, not reduced. There's nothing inevitable about technological progress. It depends on the religious obedience to the law which drove the peasants off their land, or the gathering together of that land into a single, large enough unit to justify the investment in labour-saving technology. Revolution could give the peasants back their land. Land reform could break up the large units and reverse the technological process. It always does.

The Church as Banker

In spite of the medieval church's fulminations against usury, it is beginning to look as though they took the lead in the development of banking. Because the Church at Rome was demanding taxes, tithes and every other form of money-raising device from the churches all across Europe, it was Rome which needed to develop safe ways to transport bullion or to transfer credit.

The Crusades, the Church's attempt to take Jerusalem back from the Moslems, led at the beginning of the twelfth century to the formation of a new religious category, the soldier monk, dedicated to chastity, frugality, prayer, and fighting. These contradictory characteristics made one order, the Knights Templar, very useful heavies as security men for the transport of monastic bullion.

Soon the Templars were extending their operation, providing secure accommodation for treasure - ie. bank deposit - at a price, presumably. "In the three Italian cities where banking activities developed in the late twelfth century the Templars had already been established by mid-century; in Sienna, Lucca (the Church of San Pietro) and Florence (S. Giacomo). It seems likely that the Templars were involved in the great improvements in credit and payment techniques that took place in the twelfth and thirteenth centuries." (Burman. 1.) Rome and its financial needs caused this development. "It was the relationship between Florence and the Holy See, increasingly close in the second half of the thirteenth century, which helped to develop Florentine banking, for the firms of that city obtained most of the business of collecting papal taxes and it was the danger of transporting bullion which caused bankers to devise safer methods of credit transfer." (Hodgett. 6.)

We don't seem to know how much the Templars were leading in the Italian field. But it could not have been inconsiderable because at the same time in France the Templars were in almost total financial control: "The Paris Temple was literally the centre of financial administration in France. It offered a complete financial service, administering finances and collecting taxes, transmitting money, controlling debts and paying pensions." (Burman. 2.)

There were very strict religious laws against usury, lending money and charging interest, which was the reason that Jews, unimpressed by Christian laws, became moneylenders. The Knights Templar lent money and charged interest but carefully called it commission or bank charge or gift or other euphemism.

But there's a lot we don't know. The Champagne Fairs flourished in France at this time; they were the centre of international trading. And yet there's little mention of any church involvement even though they took place in the middle of monastic territory; the monasteries were providing most of the goods and the monks were the major French bankers.

In 1307 the Knights Templar came to a very sudden and sticky end. Their contradictory characteristics had produced a group much like some modern right wing security groups. They were aggressive, sancti monious, arrogant and secretive. The French king, perhaps with an eye to their supposed vast wealth, organised an overnight, country-wide operation against them. They were arrested and charged with witchcraft, homosexuality and heresy amongst other things. Many died rather nastily including their leader, an aged nobleman who was slowly roasted to death. With their demise ended the church's banking activities which were taken over by merchants, mainly Italian.

So banking developed, not as a benefit to the general population, but as a financial service to the very rich. Nor did anyone at the time suggest that banking in any way created or helped to create wealth.

Banking is not neutral. It helps those-who-have against those-who-have-not. Banks would claim that they help to create wealth. As we have seen, wealth is not created, only moved around. If the banks are helping those-who-have have more, then those-who-have-not have less. Banks harm the poor.

Nor is credit neutral. Those given credit are put in a stronger competitive position than those without. It is the rich, because they have security, who get the credit. So credit helps the rich against the poor. Also credit creates inflation and inflation helps the rich who can borrow and pay less back because of inflation. If two people each have a hundred thousand pounds, they can bid for a house up to that price. If one also has ten thousand pounds credit, he can bid up to a hundred and ten thousand. The credit has increased the price of the house. There's more buying power chasing the same amount of goods.

That only applies, of course, if the lender's loan has not reduced the lender's own buying power. With bank loans it does not. The bank has deposits of say a million pounds. Because it does not think that everyone is going to come for their money all at once, it lends out more than a million pounds. It is that extra which is inflationary.

The Effects of Higher Labour Costs

When paper arrived in Europe its production was immediately mechanised. "Paper which was manufactured by hand and foot for a thousand years or so following its invention by the Chinese and adoption by the Arabs, was manufactured mechanically as soon as it reached medieval Europe in the thirteenth century." (Gimpel. 7.) Did this take place simply because technology, the mills, just happened to be there, or were there other factors?

Since the technology did not immediately return to the Arab world, the situation was particular to western Europe. The difference had to be higher labour costs. Presumably a far higher proportion of the population lived in cities where the cost of living must be higher, where even water has to be bought, and where everything has to be transported into the city, which costs money.

Increasing labour costs will cause increasing mechanisation, poverty and unemployment on the periphery where the cheaper core goods are sold to buy the crops. Beyond the periphery in other economic spheres such as Islam or China there will be little effect. For instance there was no impact on China for five hundred years.

Population

It has been persuasively suggested, particularly by Richard G. Wilkinson, that economic and technological growth is caused, not by religious and governmental clearances from the land, but by population pressure, which causes a shortage of resources and therefore an advance in technology to replace them. For instance, as the population increased and ran out of timber and firewood, it became necessary to mine deeper for coal which requires engines for drainage to be invented.

To a certain extent this is true. But if it was the whole truth than one would expect to see a considerable regression of technology when Europe lost a third of its population at the time of the Black Death. As we shall see, there was no regression. So to what extent is a growing population the cause of economic growth and to what extent is it caused by the need the cut labour costs when the rich want more money?

The population in Europe started growing strongly about 1000 AD at 42 million and in three centuries nearly doubled to 73 million. This coincided with a period of climatic warmth. And it coincided with a strengthening of religious influence. "The French population grew to more than 20 million (in 1940 the population of France was just double that of medieval France). This suggests why France played such an important role in the medieval period in the agricultural and industrial revolutions. Her population was nearly one third of the whole of Europe." (Gimpel. 8.) (Presumably the climatic effect was the same all over Europe. But France had many more monasteries. So if the French population went up more than the others, then it's religion and not the climate that is to blame.) Certainly, if a population increases, then food production must increase. But the techniques of such an increase differ in a monetary and non-monetary economy.

As we have seen in Ethiopia today, increasing cash-crop production doesn't help poverty because the poor have no cash to buy that production. So an advance in technology of cash crop production would not be caused by a population increase unless it had the cash as well. As we have seen, the monasteries weren't growing their crops to feed their poor but to sell to the rich for cash to build their abbeys. Their major agricultural innovations were the three field system, the horse shoe, the horse collar and the heavy plough. None of these techniques have any relevance to the self-sufficient farmer. They apply only to the large cash-crop farmer and the production of corn which is grown by the rich because it is not perishable and can be stored and used as a source of power. Grain in a granary is as powerful as money in a bank.

The self-sufficient peasant depends far less, if at all, on corn. For food he needs pasture for his animals, an orchard for his fruit and a piece of land the size of a large allotment for his vegetables. He certainly does not need a horse-drawn heavy plough on an allotment. A three-field system is a total irrelevance.

The techniques used by self-sufficient peasants to increase food production are just the opposite of the monasteries. They are labour-intensive, not labour-saving; intercropping, multiple cropping, composting, carefully using every inch of ground which is a lot of work.

So the advance in agricultural techniques was caused not by a need for more food for a growing population, but by the monasteries' need for more money by cutting labour costs.

The Weaving Towns

In the tenth century the population started growing. "In general these estimates indicate at least a doubling of the population during the three centuries between 1000 and 1300." (Miskimin. 2.) The major population densities were in northern Italy, northern France and Flanders. And it was in these areas that the towns grew into cities, and industry and technology developed. "Certain areas very early developed such a pre-eminence in the manufacture of fine luxury cloths that the products of their looms and dyeshops found a market all over Europe and the Near East. Such was the case with the cloth manufacture of Flanders and Italy and to a lesser extent with the linen manufacture of the north of France and silk manufacture of Lucca." (Power. 1.)

Cities do not grow by natural fertility. Their fertility is much lower than the rural areas; and the people die earlier because of the urban squalor. Cities grow because of immigration. So what caused people to migrate to northern Italy, northern France and Flanders? What attracted people to these areas?

We know that northern France was the centre of the monastic movement. We also know that northern Italy had probably the second major concentration of monasteries. In the eighth century: "nowhere were bishops more numerous and more powerful than south of the Alps." (Pirenne. 5.) "Churches and monasteries were built in great numbers." (Bautier. 7.) These two monastic centres coincided exactly with the later growth of manufacturing cities. There were monasteries in Flanders but I don't know how many.

The monasteries owned vast acres of land. Unlike the princes, the monasteries were very heavy spenders. That is to say they could offer employment to immigrants. The produce of their often distant estates was transported, itself or as cash, to the core monasteries which could therefore employ considerable numbers of immigrant builders, weavers, artists etc.

Was it the monasteries' requirement for fine cloth for vestments and church decoration that created the cloth industries that later flourished in those same areas? Means, motive, opportunity. The evidence is circumstantial but it all points to the monasteries as culprit.

The migrant population did not see working in the cloth industry as a great advance in human endeavour. They did it because they were hungry. They'd lost their land to the monasteries. There was nothing inevitable about that industrial growth, no natural progress. As we have seen in Indonesia a high population does not mean more towns or technology. The alternative is more labour-intensive agriculture. This did not happen in Medieval Europe because of the unequal distribution of land caused, or condoned by Christianity. In Britain the church owned a quarter of the land, which it was using, not to feed the people but to grow crops for export to raise cash.

There was another alternative too, that taken by China. She had reached the same stage of technological development, but from now on she developed no further because the rulers got their income by taxing the farmers' produce rather than by taxes on trade, so the rulers made sure that the farmers had enough land to produce those crops and the farmers therefore didn't need to go to the cities as artisans.

But the peasants of Europe's densely populated areas had no such support from their rulers, so they were forced to go to the cities, were forced into manufacturing. For those peasants industrialisation and urbanisation were not an advance in human achievement but a desperate attempt to find food and shelter. "Later in the Middle Ages, i.e. from the middle of the twelfth century onwards, the regions of the northwest littoral, Flanders, Brabant and Holland, maintained an industrial population which they could not feed out of their own agricultural production." (C.E.H.E.II.) "The real expansion of industry began in the eleventh century and went forward with very great rapidity in the twelfth and thirteenth centuries. This development was largely due to a rising population . . . Flanders was one of the most densely populated parts of Europe and its agriculture was totally unable to support the surplus population . . . emigrate or industrialise - there was no other choice." (Power. 2.) Well, yes, they had no other choice since they had no land. If the Church had given them back their land, they could instead have cultivated it intensively as in Asia.

The Expanding Periphery

As the core landless population of Flanders grew, the rings of its periphery and hinterland expanded. The innermost ring of the hinterland, dairy cattle and market garden crops, now encompassed the whole country. And it wasn't wealth that caused it. "It has been said that in the home of intensified husbandry, the Low Countries, the origins of innovation are to be found not in wealth but in poverty; in the need to make a living for a growing and dense population out of relatively low incomes. Something of the same kind happened in England too." (C. Wilson. 1.)

The further hinterland of beef cattle and grain moved outwards to include Britain and Germany. But though they were now in different countries they were still part of the single economic unit - the core and the periphery. To decide whether trade and industry create wealth and jobs one has to look at both the core and the periphery together.

Just as in the nineteenth century, when the Europeans invaded Africa and America and turned the hunter-gatherer societies into crop producers for Europe, so in the Middle Ages the Germans invaded the Slav countries of Eastern Europe to feed Western Europe. "On the eastern border the German eastward movement (*Drang nach Osten*) unfolded. This movement was already under way early in the tenth century . . . and reached its height in the first half of the thirteenth century . . . In most of the conquered territories, the Slav economy was largely based on fishing, fowling, hunting and stock rearing. Agriculture was poorly developed. The German immigrants possessed more advanced agricultural technology as well as more abundant and better capital; they moved into the new territories with the heavy wheeled plough and with the heavy felling axes which enabled them to clear the thicker forest and cultivate the heavier soils." (Cipolla. 5.)

The cheap grain from the expanded periphery forced the inner grain producers to move into crops which made more profit but which entailed more work. "Increasingly in the fourteenth and fifteenth centuries Western European farmers turned to the cultivation of wine, hops, oil-bearing seeds, flax and dye stuffs, profiting from the relatively high prices of industrial products." (Lis and Soly. 3.)

As usual with grain production on the periphery it was achieved by serfdom which the countries had not known before. "Not surprisingly the peasants, despite hopeless outbursts of violence, ultimately succumbed to seigniorial reaction and the imposition of serfdom. For the first time in history a true manorial economy arose in the East." (Lis and Soly. 4.)

"By the sixteenth century the demand for Baltic grain from Western European towns was such that German 'junkers' ruling non-German peasants found it profitable to tie them to the land - to create in effect plantations with coerced serf labour. This coincided with the emergence of slave plantations beyond Europe. The rise of cities in Western Europe would very largely depend on both these developments while the German and Polish towns in the East went into decline. What has been called 'the development of underdevelopment' had begun." (Calder. 1.) This underdevelopment caused the usual migration from the periphery to the core for unskilled jobs. In Amsterdam c. 1650: "The latter (menial) tasks were generally allotted to German immigrants, poor wretches who seem to have become more numerous after 1650 and who were known generically as the *Hollandgänger*, those who go to Holland, usually to work on the earthworks of the polders. Nearby Germany was a pool of cheap labour." (Braudel. 16.)

Flanders' furthest periphery was now the Baltic and Russia to which they sent their fine cloth in exchange for the crops. But while it was the peasants who produced them, it was the lords who owned them, so it was the lords for whom the weavers wove their cloth. "The demand (for these luxuries) was limited to the fairly small numbers of people who could appreciate and afford them. Far more important was the flow of raw materials from Russia, Poland and the new and old German hinterland: rye, grain, timber, pitch, tar, honey, wax and furs. More timber, pitch and tar came from Scandinavia. Bohemia and

Hungary sent some of their precious and non-precious metals; England, her wool and hides. The odour of salted herring, less sweet but more substantial than that of spices, dominated the scene." (Lopez. 4.)

Core Meets Core

Industrial development came a little later in Italy. To solve their food shortage they started by trading, which is much less unpleasant than manufacturing, but an option only open to towns on the coast. "Almost none of the other French regions suffered from the dramatic food shortages that almost forced the Italians to become merchants." (Lopez. 5.)

"The Italian ports which pioneered this revival (in trade) were small cities such as Amalfi, Gaeta, Salerno and Bari which had been forced into trade two centuries earlier. The ravages of the Lombards had compelled those districts still under Byzantine control to trade in order to make a livelihood." (Hodgett. 2.) The most successful town was Venice, set on a muddy shore with no cultivable land. It depended totally on obtaining food from inland or from abroad. "Venice, however, did not rely exclusively on Italian sources of supply but also drew quite large amounts from abroad, sometimes from Crete and Egypt, more often from the Balkan peninsular (Upper and Lower Romania) and the Black Sea ports. Altogether the yearly corn imports were so considerable that it must have needed dozens and dozens of small and medium sized ships to carry them." (Luzzatto. 3.)

But all these grain-producing lands were part of the Byzantine Empire, the eastern remnant of the Roman Empire. For a thousand years it had survived the fall of Rome and mostly prospered. For a thousand years it had been the core of Europe. But now it was getting old and losing crop-producing territory to a virile Islam. Venice, to protect its sea-going trade, had developed a strong navy. The rulers of Byzantium, the ageing core, needed military help to hold on to the throne and were, as usual in such conditions, prepared to sell out their own people to get such help. Venice, the growing core, demanded the control and profits of all Byzantine external trade. "The Byzantine Empire, pressed simultaneously by the Turks in the East and the Normans in the West, bought massive naval assistance from the Venetians at the heavy price of exempting them from all duties still paid by his own subjects in a whole row of Mediterranean sea-ports . . . The treaty between Venice and Alexius Commenius . . . made the native Byzantine merchants underprivileged in their own land." (Lopez. 1.) The Byzantine rulers gave the Venetians "many exemptions and privileges. The treaty of 992, the first of a series that was to make Venice's fortune in the East, allowed Venetian merchants considerable reductions in import and export duty payable at the Dardanelles as well as guarantees against molestation by the Byzantine officials. The treaty of 1082 renewed, confirmed and amplified during the twelfth century, increased these privileges . . . Thenceforth Venetian merchants could buy and sell in every part of the Empire free of duty or customs examination . . . Their vessels sailed into the Black Sea, to the Crimea, to fetch wheat from South Russia . . . even ships' companies of the imperial fleet were full of Venetian seamen." (Diehl.)

Without having to pay duty the Venetian merchants could undercut the Byzantine merchants in all international trade. So the Venetians took over all the Byzantine trade. "Thus, whereas Byzantine nationals had to pay the duty of 10%, the privileged Italians could export and import free of duty. The result was that the carrying trade passed almost entirely into Italian hands." (Viljoen. 2.) The profits from that trade went to Venice and not to Constantinople which was gradually bled dry and finally couldn't afford a large enough army to confront the Turks. In 1453 Constantinople fell.

The Islamic conquerors had no need for Venetian protection, so Venice could no longer demand the trading privileges which had created its wealth. It was gradually forced out of the Black Sea and the Eastern Mediterranean. Venice declined to a small town, reduced to manufacturing. "Venice at the beginning of the sixteenth century was still nursing its incipient cloth industry, largely created in order to compensate for the revenues no longer forthcoming from its centuries-old Mediterranean commerce." (Miskimin. 3.)

The Ottoman Turks changed the name of Constantinople to Istanbul and built up a thriving, though short-lived, core. For this it needed a strong army and therefore the grain that had previously been exported. When the grain exports to the Mediterranean finally stopped after the Battle of Lepanto, Poland had to feed not only north-western Europe but the Mediterranean as well: "Grain from Poland and the Baltic inevitably proved essential for the survival of Mediterranean cities." (Miskimin. 8.)

Italian Industry

The hungry inland towns of Italy, without the option of overseas trading, were forced very early on into manufacturing. Because of the high cost of living in cities they were compelled to develop a technology to reduce the amount of high-cost labour, otherwise they would not be able to sell their products in the low-cost periphery which was where the crops that they needed came from. "Whenever labour is dear, it must be supplemented by machines; this is the only way to compete with those countries where it is cheap." ('Encyclopedie'. See Braudel. 10) "The cities could increase their agricultural supply only through international trade. Florence for example, imported nearly two thirds of her grain supply from lands beyond her territorial jurisdiction during the fourteenth century." (Miskimin. 9.)

Italy obtained her food from the Balkans, Sicily and Sardinia where the peasantry unwillingly grew the grain and livestock: "Rising urban demand had repercussions as far away as Hungary where central European magnates repressed the peasantry in order to gain control of the burgeoning export trade in livestock." (Miskimin. 4.)

The beginning of European industry depended on an expanding periphery in which the peasants could be forced to produce the crops. "Thus in the fourteenth century in the two sectors of Europe - Hanseatic and Mediterranean - vast areas were put under cereal cultivation; they flooded the western markets with their massive output, obtained from enslaved dependencies. (Bautier. 1.)

Un-Development on the Periphery

The effect on a country which becomes a bread basket for other countries is to un-develop it. Its craftsmen are made unemployed by the cheaper products imported to pay for the exported grain, and the craft disappears. "The strong Dutch demand for grain on the Polish market in the sixteenth and seventeenth centuries, the Dutch, English and French demand for oil and silk on the Italian market in the seventeenth century favoured the involution of the economies of Poland and Italy along feudal agricultural lines and created the preconditions for the long term stagnation of these countries." (Cipolla. 4.)

The rulers of the periphery countries deliberately encouraged this stagnation. In Spain: "manufacturers were heavily taxed and local raw materials (mostly wool) freely sold abroad - even with subsidy payments." (Wilson. 2.) In the British Empire: "India was eventually in the nineteenth century de-industrialised, reduced to the role of a major producer of raw materials." (Braudel. 15.)

"In Poland and Central Europe, where the nobility crushed industrial development and drove merchants and artisans back to the fields, internal demand for products of local manufacture, with the exception of some military supplies, virtually collapsed, but the nobles' requirements for quality goods imported from Western Europe grew sharply." (Miskimin. 7.) "Out of self-interest the nobles successfully contrived to crush Polish economic development in order to reserve for themselves the rich grain trade and to assure adequate supplies of agricultural labour for maximum exploitation of their estates . . . Had Poland developed large cities and supported a substantial non-agricultural population engaged in trade and manufacturing, it is highly likely that Amsterdam and many other cities of the West would have starved . . . Amsterdam could not have survived without access to the 70,000 square miles of grain fields in the Vistula Basin." (Miskimin. 6.) "It is only too clear how Gdansk, cocooned in her egotism and comfort, exploited and betrayed the great Polish hinterland." (Braudel. 11.)

The Spanish Road to De-Industrialisation

Present economic theory says that economic growth is encouraged by reducing protection of manufacturing. History disproves it. The comparison between the actions taken by the Spanish government and those of the English government shows how one country, England, made a conscious decision to protect industry, sacrifice agriculture and become a core country, and how the other country, Spain, deliberately sacrificed industry in favour of agriculture and became de-industrialised.

From the Norman Conquest up to the beginning of the fourteenth century England, by government decision, was a periphery country supplying raw materials, mostly wool, to the industrialised core, Flanders. "the English weaving industry was sacrificed in favour of exporting wool to the Low Countries." (Bautier. 8.) Because the king needed loans from English manufacturers to pay for his wars, the English government started to restrict sales of wool abroad to help the English weaving industry. "in 1463 foreigners were forbidden to export wool." (Pirenne. 6.) Finally the export of wool was forbidden altogether. "By 1614 the export of wool was formally prohibited." (Wallerstein. 1.)

Spain, in contrast, because the king was getting his loans from the land owners, encouraged the export of wool at the expense of her weaving industry. In the fourteenth century the decision was in the balance – whether to become an industrialised core or an agricultural periphery. The Mesta, the sheep-owning aristocracy, won the first round by rejecting "the proposal of the Cortez of 1348, held in Madrigal, requesting a ban on imports of foreign cloth and on exports of Castilian wool. This decidedly protectionist policy was not accepted by John II because of the firm intervention of the Mesta and those who were profiting from the wool trade." (Vicens-Vives.) The Castilian cloth industry therefore got neither the cheap Spanish wool nor the protection from imported cloth. The battle raged for a hundred years but the result was confirmed at the Cortez of Toledo in 1462 which decided that only a quarter of Spanish wool could be retained for the Castilian cloth industry.

Then silver started arriving from the new mines in America. This confirmed Spain's direction towards periphery status, as the monarch got his income from the periphery silver mining rather than taxation on trade as in England.

Although Spain invested heavily in arms, they were bought with American bullion and not indirect taxation on the Spanish people, so the cost of living and labour costs did not increase sufficiently to require labour-saving technology. Spain had become a core country for a short while, not because of a high cost of living from indirect taxes but because of her military strength bought with the American bullion. What technology she needed she bought from abroad with her silver (rather like Russia this century). So the import of manufactured goods destroyed all her previous manufacturing capacity for which the Spanish government offered no protection, and in fact penalised it.

De-industrialisation was inevitable. By about 1620: "It was not only the textile industry that declined, but the metallurgical industries and shipbuilding as well . . . Thus in this era of stagnation Spain suffered not only the agricultural involution of the peripheral areas but also de-industrialization." (Wallerstein. 3.) By the end of the eighteenth century Spain was fully peripheralised with her government being decided by core countries in the War of the Spanish Succession.

British military strength, bought by indirect taxation, was soon greater than Spain's. Britain continued its encouragement of industry by heavy protection. In 1722: "The import of some foreign manufacturers was banned altogether, and high duties were set on others." (Calder. 8.)

The Pattern

A charismatic leader and his companions impose their control over the group which they disarm and force to hand over a proportion of the crops to the leader. The companions derive their wealth from the generosity of the leader in distributing the crops and arms. This situation is unstable and usually collapses at the death of the leader.

Kingship

To preserve their wealth and privilege the companions make the leadership hereditary by stating that the leader's family is descended from the gods. The companions' continuing wealth thus depends on an influential religion which has to be imposed with cruelty on the whole disarmed population. A system of 'justice' is imposed to enforce this religion, and to reinforce the removal of the crops, the taxation. This taxation is imposed by the ruler's law, enforced by the rulers 'justice' and religion. The priests were the first tax collectors. Final Appeal is to the ruler's judges.

Society is now divided into three groups, "those who work, those who pray and those who fight." The workers, in case they might object, are not allowed to bear arms or fight. The rich, to preserve their position, are the only ones allowed to bear arms and fight, about 5% of the population, the nobility, the rich farmers and their henchmen.

Towns grow round the courts of the rulers where the food, brought to the ruler, provides jobs for artisans, servants and soldiers. The larger the hinterland providing the food, the larger the town. The roads, walls, buildings and manufactures of the towns are all financed by the peasants' food. Towns create no wealth. The workers at the core depend for their living on the exploitation of the periphery.

By expropriating more crops, increasing taxation, the rulers are able to feed more soldiers and artisans making arms, so that the rulers can take control of neighbouring territories, disarming the people, making laws to remove the crops and imposing 'justice'. Final Appeal is to the rulers' judges at the core.

Money

With the introduction of money the ruler finds another way of removing the peasants' crops. Money is the rulers' IOUs, promising to exchange it for crops etc.

These IOUs are demanded as taxes forcing the population to work for the ruler, or his companions or contractors, the only source of the money, to obtain the money to hand back as taxes. Or they are forced to grow crops to sell for the money, cash cropping, to pay the taxes.

Money allows the ruler to remove more crops in another way, a half-hidden tax on trade. A sales tax is imposed on all transactions. Because the trader pays the tax to the ruler, the consumer doesn't notice that the cost of the product has increased correspondingly, so the consumer pays the tax. The trader, not the priest, is now the tax collector.

Towns

This tax was so successful and trouble-free (because it was half-hidden), that the rulers put great effort into enforcing and encouraging trade which was providing an increasing proportion of their income and power. All trade was restricted to the towns, where it could be taxed. So the rulers needed towns within half a day's walk of as many people as possible. The more towns they could build, the more income for the rulers. And so the less income for the people. Trade and towns cause poverty. To encourage trade (and get the crops into the towns and the soldiers out to control the villages), roads, bridges and harbours were built, still financed by the peasants' food. The only reason for towns and roads is government control and tax-raising.

Technology

To increase trade the peasants were driven off their land so that it might be used to grow cash crops, like sheep for wool. The landless peasants had no choice but to take work manufacturing luxury products for the rich, such as fine cloth or pottery. Because living costs in the city are higher (wood for fuel, and water etc. must be bought), wages in cities must be higher. Therefore labour costs are higher and it becomes necessary to invent labour-saving technology. The higher the taxation, the higher the labour costs, the higher the technology. But the high cost of the machines must be recouped by high quantity of production. Given such quantity the price of the core product must always be cheaper than the periphery product.

Because cheap goods from the core destroy employment on the periphery, any attempt by the periphery to put a tax or tariff on goods from the core is suppressed by laws from the core. This is called 'Free Trade'.

Core rulers bribe rulers on their periphery with money and the core's superior arms to take the crops from their own people and sell them off to the core. The core ruler, the trader and the periphery ruler form a 'triangle of corruption' to exploit the periphery people. This is why the Third World starves.

The core currency and credit is made freely convertible with the periphery currency so that the core can remove the natural resources, the job-creation in exchange for its IOUs. By issuing more of them it creates inflation so the core rulers have to redeem their IOUs with less natural wealth. The more cash and credit which is issued, the richer is the core, the poorer the periphery.

Chapter 6. Technological Progress
References

R-H. Bautier. "The Economic Development of Medieval Europe". Thames and Hudson. '71. 7: p.39., 1: p.194., 8: p.199.

F. Braudel. "The Perspective of the World". Collins. '84. 11: p.256., 15: p.522., 16: p.186. "The Wheels of Commerce". Collins. '82. 10: p.304. quoted from Diderot's Encyclopedie." 1751-80.

E. Burman. "The Templars. Knights of God". The Aquarian Press. '86. 1: p.75., 2: p.88.

A. Calder. "Revolutionary Empire". Jonathan Cape. '81. 1: p.6., 8: p.442.

Cambridge Economic History of Europe. Vol II. p.120.

E.M. Carus Wilson. "An Industrial Revolution of the thirteenth century." Edward Arnold Ltd. '54

C.M. Cipolla. "Before the Industrial Revolution". Methuen '76. 2: p.168., 4: p.63., 5: p.205-7.

C. Diehl. "The Economic Decay of Byzantium". quoted by C. Cipolla in "The Economic Decline of Empires". p.94.

G. Duby. "The Chivalrous Society". Edward Arnold. '77. 2: p.214.

J. Evans. "Life in Medieval France." Phaidon. '25. 1: p.56., 2: p.57., 3: p.56.

B. Gille. in "A History of Technology". Ed. M.Dumas. John Murray. '69. 1: p.560., 2: p.560.

J. Gimpel. "The Medieval Machine". Gollanz. '74. 5: p.67., 6: p.67., 7: p.14., 8: p.57.

C. Hodgett. "A Social and Economic History of Medieval Europe". Methuen. '72. 2: p.50., 6: p.68.

D. Knowles. "The Monastic Order in England". C.U.P. '40. 1: p.351.

C. Lis and H. Soly. "Poverty and Capitalism in Pre-Industrial Europe". Harvester Press. '79. 3: p.33., 4: p.30.

R. Lopez. "The Commercial Revolution of the Middle Ages". C.U.P. 1: p.65., 4: p.119., 5: p.120.

D. Luckhurst. quoted in "Monastic Water Mills". Society for the Protection of Ancient Buildings". No 8. (London) n.d.6.

G. Luzzatto. "An Economic History of Italy". Routledge Kegan Paul. '61. 3: p.89.

H.A. Miskimin. "The Economy of Early Renaissance Europe". Prentice Hall. '69. 2: p.20., 9: p.23. "The Economies of Later Renaissance Europe". C.U.P. '77. 3:p.87., 8:p.142., 4:p.75., 7:p.85., 6:pp.60, 63 and 64.

E. Patlagean. in "The Middle Ages" Ed R. Fossier. C.U.P. '89 1: p.500., 2: p.145.

H. Pirenne. "Economic and Social History of Medieval Europe". Routledge Kegan Paul. '36. 5: p.28., 6: p.221.

C. Platt. quoted in his "The Abbeys and Priories of Medieval England." Secker and Warburg. '84. p.47.

E. Power. "The Wool Trade of English Medieval History." O.U.P. '41. 1: p.2., 2: p.9.

M. Rouche. in "The Middle Ages". Ed. R. Fossier. C.U.P. '89. 2: p.73.

S. Viljoen. "Economic Systems in World History". Longman, '74. 2: p.94.

J. Vicens-Vives. "An Economic History of Spain". 69. quoted by Wallerstein.

I. Wallerstein. "The Modern World System". Vol I. Academic Press Inc. '74. 1: p.228., 3: p.181.

C. Wilson. "England's Apprenticeship, 1603-1763". Longman. '65. 1: p.262., 2: p.269.

Chapter 7
THE PATTERN IN BRITAIN

HAVING ESTABLISHED the general thesis, we can now reverse the process and see what light the new model throws on the development of Britain.

About 4500 BC. the pollen record indicates a sharp decline in the number of elm trees, the Elm Decline. It's thought that this shows the beginning of cattle and sheep rearing. Elm branches are used as fodder. Pollen records also indicate cereals are starting to be grown. "It was some time in the Mesolithic period, so far as we can ascertain, that the population of England had risen to nearly 15,000, beyond the safe limit. It was becoming clear that the country was overpopulated . . . But agriculture eventually had to be adopted, with, we can imagine, how much resistance, because increased pressure of population simply left no alternative. For some generations however – as in some parts of the world now – the men still regarded agricultural work as so degrading that it could only be performed by women." (Clark. 3.)

The great stone circles and barrows of Southern England make it clear that by 2500 BC. the population had been disarmed and cowed into submission to authority. Britain had already passed through the Heroic Age into the Archaic age of institutionalised authority backed by religious terror. By 2000 BC. the priest kings and their companions were wielding enough power to extract the crops to feed workers for two to thirty million man-hours, building the final great stage of Stonehenge. "During the early period (2000 BC. – 1400 BC.) a rich gold-using aristocracy flourished in the South West – the Wessex culture . . . It was during this time that the monument of Stonehenge as we think of it today was completed." (Laing.)

Then the fever seems to have abated and they stopped building their threatening religious constructs. After that there is 500 years of little activity and an increase in forest cover. Is it too much to hope that at least on the periphery the peasants were able to rearm and live in undisturbed peace, leaving little in the archaeological record?

About 1000 BC. times were getting rough again. Settlements were defended and the hill forts appear. These fortified citadels with considerable grain storage capacity imply an elite again extracting the produce from a disarmed peasantry. Possibly the wider use of the new iron weapons was creating the instability.

By the end of that millennium Britain was divided into about twenty major tribal territories. The power of the elite was backed by the Druids who inspired the necessary religious terror by human sacrifice. They built large wicker, man-shaped cages which they filled with criminals and others, and burned. "The skilled craftsmanship of the Belgic blacksmith can be seen . . . in the slave chains with elaborate neck shackles which enabled captives to be controlled on the estate or for the foreign slave market." (Frere. 1.)

But while the south of England was becoming 'civilised', it seems the north was still untouched. Julius Caesar reports: "The people of the interior for the most part do not sow corn but live on milk and meat and dress in skins." Archaeologists come to the same conclusion: "beyond the Gloucester-Lincoln line a different economy seems to have been practised, that of pastoralism eked out by garden cultivation." (Frere. 2.)

The Romans at first maintained the petty kings as clients. But as the Roman power got established, the services of the client kings were dispensed with. The companions of these kings quickly changed their allegiance to Rome. The British elite assumed Roman culture; they gave themselves Roman names, wore Roman clothes, spoke Latin, built villas in the Roman style, however inappropriate to the British climate. And they exploited the British peasants just as enthusiastically as their Roman masters.

The British peasants were much worse off. They were now having to support Rome and the Romano-British elite at a much higher standard of living. They were also having to feed the Roman legions, the bureaucrats, the builders, the potters and all the other craftsmen and hangers-on of a more 'advanced' society, to say nothing of the legions in Gaul and Rome itself.

So when the Romans legions finally left Britain to defend Rome, the British elite was seriously worried, to put it politely. The British peasantry was of course disarmed, but without a militia even a pitchfork can be lethal to the rich.

So the British upper classes invited Angle and Saxon mercenaries to help them 'keep the peace'. It was a pretty silly thing to do. The Anglo-Saxons themselves attacked the British upper classes and drove them into the hills of Wales. The disarmed peasantry watched from behind their haystacks as their masters beat hell out of each other. The peasants would probably not have fled. They had their land and their crops. They would just have to pay out a proportion of those crops to different masters. And in fact they were much better off.

Back to the Heroic Age

The new Anglo-Saxon masters were not the sophisticated rulers of an urban society, or even an archaic one, but our old friends, the gang of thugs, a leader and his companions, the heroes. They had none of the experience of their predecessors' highly efficient methods of taxation. Nor was the peasantry likely to tell them. All that heroes like Beowulf need is a roof, food, women, someone to plunder to keep the companions sweet, and plenty of beer. The British peasant must have been delighted to be let off so lightly.

Taxation was in the form of 'feorm' or food rent, enough to feed the king's retinue for 24 hours once a year. For a particular group of villages this was: "two tuns of clear ale, one 'cumb' of mild ale, one 'cumb' full of British ale, seven oxen, six wethers, forty cheeses, thirty 'ambers' of rye corn and four 'ambers' of meal." (Stenton. 1.) The heroes and their women, servants, blacksmiths and musicians went round their territory feeding where the food was. They must have fed very well, but there wasn't any left over to feed any cities.

Conventional wisdom would have us believe that the peasants, no longer having to support the Roman Empire, would exchange their food for the products of the craftsmen in the cities. It didn't happen. The peasants obeyed the Law of Least Effort. There was no demand for the craftsmen's products. The pottery factories closed, and even the potter's wheel disappeared from use. What little pottery was used was made by hand. "Pottery did not return to plentiful use on ordinary open-country farming sites until the 12th century or later." (Morris. 1.) "Cities disappeared, the market economy collapsed, literacy became a rare accomplishment, imported consumer goods such as Rhenish glassware were rare." (Collins). From the fifth century to the seventh there are no coins. Given the choice peasants don't send their food to the cities.

It was inevitable, since cities produce no wealth, if the level of taxation went down, there would be a decline of the cities and a regression of technology. Gildas, writing about AD550. says, "not even at the present day are the cities of our country inhabited as formerly; deserted and dismantled they lie neglected." And that applied to the biggest and the smallest cities alike. "In Cirencester, the second city of Roman Britain . . . unburied bodies were found in the streets and the town seems to have contracted to a few wooden huts inside the amphitheatre." (Whitelock. 1.)

In London: "there is no evidence for urban occupation or function between the abandonment of London ante-450 until there was again occupation along the River Thames in the form of a number of farms in the seventh century." (C.J. Arnold)

As the cities disappeared, the network of Roman roads which brought the food to those cities disappeared too. "Burials cut into the metalling of the Watling Street at Cestover in Warwickshire and elsewhere are proof enough that roads were out of use and grass-grown." (Morris. 2.)

For heroes, power lies not in an institutionalised authority backed by religious fiat but in the sword. So the heroes had no use for the church. The Christian church of the late Roman Empire vanished: "Urban society had collapsed completely, and with it had gone all those concerned with local administration, nearly all manufacturers and traders and the whole apparatus of the Christian Church." (Myers).

The Archaic Age

But our heroes were not slow to learn. Between 450 AD. and 900 AD. the Anglo-Saxon kings went through a crash course in the art of tyranny, covering at high speed a process which had previously taken millennia. By 900 AD. they were top of the European class. (But Britain would still not reach the Roman level of political and cultural development until the 16th century).

The king's companions quickly learned the advantages of an inherited kingship. To recap, when a heroic leader is replaced, the companions of the new leader get all the goodies. The companions of the old leader lose them. To avoid this, companions need an inherited leadership, preserving the status quo. Therefore, the king's family had to be seen as something special, requiring the son to be the new king. So the companions said that the king's family was descended from the gods. The Anglo-Saxon College of Heralds was suddenly working overtime. "Publicists and poets, operating to clear-cut conventions, quickly set to work to establish or to fabricate a genealogy for the most successful of the princely houses. A genealogy, accurate if possible, would be attached to descent from a recognised kin of Germanic heroes. In turn this would be attached to a further set of figures, largely supernatural. The vast majority of English princely houses looked back to Woden, the war god, as their ultimate progenitor." (Loyn. 1.) Thus, with an inherited kingship, the companions were able to keep their wealth and privileges.

But the companions soon found that the religion, which gave them a hereditary king, had many other uses as well. It enabled them to force the people to obey in all sorts of areas, all of which benefited the elite, forced labour on their estates, an enforced preservation of privilege by a caste system which forbade people even to attempt to improve their position at the expense of the elite, and it legitimised terror. An elite which had been disinterested, suddenly found religion.

110

At about this time Rome started sending missionaries to Britain to convert the pagan Anglo-Saxons. The Christian dogma was slightly more coherent nonsense than the pagan nonsense. And it legitimised taxation at an annual 10%! Now for kings that's convincing. One after another the Anglo-Saxon kings converted.

Having rejected their pagan gods, their genealogies and sagas became a bit of an embarrassment. For a time they tried to hitch their genealogies onto Adam. Then they tried the Pope. Alfred got himself adopted as son of the pope; anything to get religious credibility. Finally the genealogies and sagas were ditched. Their excuse for ruling was now: "A Christian king is Christ's deputy amongst Christian people." (11th cent.).

The peasants' new Anglo-Saxon masters had said that they were kings because they were descended from the gods. This might not impress a peasant who did not believe in those gods. He might not be so willing to hand over the crops. So a strong campaign had been necessary to 'convince' unbelievers. And now they weren't the correct gods after all. This was all very confusing for an honest peasant. They'd only just converted back to paganism. But swords are very persuasive, so Christianity it was.

The king's companions, macho musclemen, whose criteria of the good life were fighting, women and beer, must have been a bit put out to realize how much they now depended on the priests, a clique of religious wimps. But they needed each other: "even in the early eighth century the bishops and abbots attending a king's court seem incongruous members of an assembly that was still essentially a war band." (Stenton. 2.)

There are many who still think that Anglo-Saxon England was basically a society of free men. This was Elizabethan wishful thinking. It's not so. "Evidence which cannot be gainsaid obliges us to think of the English countryside in the seventh century as largely dominated by an aristocratic, slave-owning class, with demesnes cultivated for them partly by slaves, partly by tenants with servile antecedents. For positive evidence of independent and self-governing villages we search in vain." (Finberg.)

The popular assembly, the folk moot, isn't mentioned till the ninth century and then it's only for people to be taxed and accept 'justice'. As in present courts, you were forced to attend.

After the Romans had left, the Britons had dropped religion. At the same time the population fell. When the Saxons got interested in religion again, the population started rising again. Is there a connection?

When they arrived, they were just small war bands who took over small territories. Fighting amongst themselves, the stronger bands took over the smaller territories. The larger the territory, the more crops could be expropriated, the more soldiers and arms could be afforded. By about 600 AD. England was called the Heptarchy – the rule by seven kings. Hundreds of territories had coalesced into seven, and the king of each was trying to continue the process.

Kings have to keep a very fine balance between having as few of the people armed as necessary to keep the peasants under control and reduce costs, and having enough armed men to withstand attack from outside. That balance seems to lie around 5% of the population armed, the elite, the wealthier peasants and their henchmen/soldiers.

Having established their religious credentials, the kings were now more easily able to extort the crops from their peasants. The appearance of town names in the literature makes it clear that they were now extracting sufficient crops to afford permanent fortified headquarters. While nearly all the Roman towns, without taxation to support them, had fallen into ruin, a few, such as Canterbury, Lincoln, York and Dorchester, were used as these fortress/courts for the Anglo-Saxon kings, who could now feed a growing number of soldiers, servants and artisans. Canterbury was not only the court of the king of Kent but of the Archbishop of Canterbury who also extracted the crops by tithes, various religious con-tricks and land-owning, so providing more jobs in the town – created by the peasants' food.

Other towns appeared on the coast as trading centres – Southampton, London, Fordwich, Sandwich. A letter from the Merovingian king in France complains to King Offa about the quality of English woollen cloaks exported to France. So already the land is being used to grow cash crops, wool, and being exported for the benefit of the Anglo-Saxon landowners, and at the expense of the peasantry, whose land is no longer growing their food. The coastal trading towns would be exchanging the woollen goods for luxury goods from the continent for the Anglo-Saxon landowners. Presumably the kings would by now have realised that they could increase their income by quietly taxing both the exports and imports.

After 150 years without coinage King Offa now mints a new high quality currency. The Merovingians had also issued new coins, so they were probably paying coins for the English exports and not sending the desirable goods in exchange. And Offa would be losing taxation on the imported goods. By using the English coins to pay for the French imports the balance was redressed. The introduction of coinage also allowed for much more efficient tax-gathering.

Offa did not mint his coins because he thought that the people would benefit, but that he would benefit at the expense of the people, or the French, and he was right. His rich friends benefited too, for a king depends on rewarding his supporters. And the townspeople benefited because all their work came from the rich. It was the peasants, who were the losers from the coinage.

"Edward the Elder and Althelstan had attempted to confine all buying and selling to the boroughs." (Saylles. 1.) King Athelstan ordained that "no goods over 20 pence are to be bought outside a town, but they are to be brought there in the witness of the town reeve or of another trustworthy man, or, again in the witness of the reeves in a public meeting." (R. Arnold. 1.)

That means that the kings were already getting a significant proportion of their income by the hidden taxation on trade. If the trade is not taking place in the towns, it's very difficult to tax it. It also means that to increase their income they would want to increase the number of towns, increase the amount of trade and build the necessary infrastructure – mainly the roads. "The idea that the highway was the king's is as old as the highway itself, and the law codes give plentiful evidence of the basic function of the king to maintain full royal control of communications within his kingdom." (Loyn. 2.) When the king was maintaining the roads, as the government still does, he wasn't ensuring that the peasants could go on their hols but that his soldiers could keep control and that the produce could get to his towns to be consumed or traded. All the early charters recording transactions of land include duties to maintain roads and bridges.

So the growth of towns and their linking network of roads was not a natural process but a highly artificial means of increasing the king's income only achieved by heavy law. "The trouble was that there were no ready-made towns in Britain that could be made into administrative centres – no towns, that is to say, that the Romans would have recognised as towns.

"The solution that was adopted was to set up a few models of 'military colonies' or *coloniae*, and *municipia* or chartered towns." (R. Arnold. 2.) Asser, boasting for Alfred the Great, "tells of the cities and towns which he built where none had stood before." (Loyn. 3.)

And so the process continued. "The recovery of urban life in England in the tenth century was the result of deliberate royal planning rather than organic growth, the conscious creation of towns and centres for refuge, defence and commercial life." (Whitelock. 2.)

It's usually thought that Britain started growing with the Norman Conquest, but it's clear that the whole system of tyranny was in place long before. "The Anglo-Saxons were also responsible for introducing the first system of national taxation in Western Europe that was consistently levied and collected." (R. Arnold. 3.) "a co-ordinated system of administration had been formed (before the Conquest) which had no peer in Western Europe, and England was comparatively a much-governed country." (Saylles. 2.) "it is no coincidence that the well-taxed English should produce the most advanced currency in the Europe of its day." (Loyn. 4.) "by the eleventh century Anglo-Saxon England possessed the most elaborate peace keeping machinery of any western kingdom." (R. Arnold. 4.)

The Norman Conquest

When William invaded, the whole system for creating poverty and wealth was already in place, religion, justice, towns, roads, coinage, cash-cropping and international trade. The seed which was to grow into the Industrial Revolution had already been sown. The only factor missing is the land enclosures. All William did was to tighten the screw, and even that begins to look uncertain.

By the time William invaded Britain, it had reached the stage of development which Greece had reached in their early classical period, about 600 BC., and Rome in its republican period, about 300 BC. It had a disarmed obedient population producing a small surplus; it had built small fortified towns; it had imposed a state religion and a unified system of 'justice' and it had writing. But the amount of taxation it collected was tiny compared even to the republican period of Rome. Though its temple building was impressive, its art was primitive and it had no urban culture to produce a theatre and drama.

In fact William's arrival led to a short regression. He was only two generations from the Viking Heroes who had invaded and settled in France. So we get the re-appearance of saga writing and feudalism. His Domesday Book was an attempt to understand the far more sophisticated systems of taxation than he was used to in Normandy. It is really quite difficult to understand why 1066 is considered so important. His ruthless brutality in putting down a revolt laid waste vast areas of the North, so that would have cut his income from forthcoming crops. His inexperience would also have allowed many to have escaped taxation. After 20 years on the throne he presumably realised, finally, that he wasn't getting so much taxation as his predecessors, so instigated the Domesday Book to try to find how they did it.

Before William arrived, town building was in full swing: "In England the first renaissance of town life came in the late ninth and tenth centuries, directly and self-consciously fostered by King Alfred and his son. Again in the twelfth and thirteenth centuries over a hundred new towns were founded by the English kings." (Brooke. 1.) Town building happened before William arrived, stopped during the Norman period and then took off again. So the Normans were not extracting so much wealth which could support the towns.

114

The Regression to Feudalism

The way the heroes increase their wealth is by fighting, plundering the next door territory of its baubles and crops. If that territory increases in strength by its own plundering, the leader must increase his own strength by more plundering or by extracting more from his own peasants. As his territory increases in size, he is able to be generous not only with arms, food and beer but also land, on condition that the companions provide a specified number of armed men to the leader. This is called feudalism. The object of the feudal system is to raise an army for the king. Feudalism is a direct extension of the leader/companion relationship. The king gives great estates to his companions on condition they provide him with the troops and armour, in proportion to the estates, when he needs them. The companions sublet their estates and include in the lease the condition of providing those troops. Although in British history medieval feudalism came after the Roman Empire, the system predates urban empires. In Britain after the collapse of the Roman Empire, we went right back to square one and the Age of Heroes, Beowulf etc.

English feudalism developed from that. Not till the Renaissance did we catch up with the Roman Empire again. A feudal system is impossible in an urban society. The king then raises his own troops from taxation.

(Some societies are called 'feudal' when the original intention of raising armies for the king is thwarted because the vassals, the companions, become so strong that they no longer need the support of the king and become war lords in their own right. This happened in Japan but it is not typical of the feudal stage in the development of government which would normally happen in the pre-literate or early literate stage.)

The Private Ownership of Land

William took the vast estates from the Anglo-Saxon lords and gave them to his Norman companions in return for their armed services. "Something like a quarter of the landed wealth of England was held by no more than twelve men, most of whom were bound to the king by close bonds of blood or personal loyalty or both." (Loyn. 5.) He did not give it to them as private ownership of the land. They couldn't sell it off. What they got was the ownership of a proportion of the crops. Some land, 'book land', it is thought, was already privately owned, which could be bought and sold, and this book land is the first real private ownership of land.

If the lord of a vast estate misbehaved in a big way, was treacherous for instance, the king might reclaim the estate. All the land except the book land belonged legally to the king, 'terra regis'. And that became, and still remains, the legal basis for the private ownership of land. Gradually the estates came to be considered as privately owned and alienable. Bits of them could be sold off as private land. And so we get the private ownership of land.

There's nothing natural or normal about it. It didn't happen in India until the eighteenth century when Britain forced it on the population to ease tax collection. In Nigeria there is still no privately owned land. It is still tribally 'owned', though they're trying to get round that.

Britain as Periphery

At this time Britain was providing the raw materials, wool, for the industrialised core, Flanders. William had brought with him monks to whom he gave great estates. In the classic tradition of rulers in periphery countries the people were driven off their land and replaced with exportable crops, in this case sheep. "Because they had no use for tenants, whether servile or free, they sometimes destroyed existing villages to make way for granges, and evicted the peasant occupiers, who were settled elsewhere. Investigation of the Cistercian settlements in the north of England has verified the charge of the twelfth century satirist, Walter Map: "they raze villages and churches and drive people from the land." (Lawrence.) "the sheep which were wont to be so meek and tame and so small eaters now, as I hear say, be become so great devourers and so wild that they eat up and swallow down the very men themselves. They consume, destroy and devour whole fields, houses and cities." (see Brooke. 2.) "for a time the white monks (the Cistercians) were the most considerable body of producers of wool in England." (Knowles. 2.)

The Cistercians needed the wool to sell to finance their ambitious building programme, Rievaulx, Fountains Abbey etc. They built them on credit. "At the death of that great financier, Aaron of Lincoln, in 1186, no less than nine Cistercian abbeys, and among them Rievaulx, were in debt to him for the gross sum of more than 6400 marks." (Knowles. 3.) To pay off the debt they had to raise more sheep.

To build Ely, Lincoln and Peterborough Cathedrals the monks faced different problems. They had much better land which could grow more profitable crops. But to increase production needed drainage. "Whereas in 1086 the uplands of Lincolnshire had been many times more prosperous than the fens, subsequent reclamations of waterlogged land had reversed the position by 1334 being very largely the work of monks . . . Indeed each of the three principal regions of growth during the period coincided strikingly with areas of known monastic investment." (Platt. 2.)

Thus economic growth was directed exclusively to benefit the rich, not the poor. The English land, the periphery, was being used to grow crops for the core, Flanders. The English peasants derived no benefit whatsoever. The only benefit was to the few English artisans who were employed with the money from the sales to build the abbeys.

Planted Towns

There's no evidence that shows that William understood the advantages to him of indirect taxation on trade. There are no surviving charters to towns to hold markets. Though he built an awful lot of castles, there's no evidence of attempts to found towns for other than military purposes. But by the time of Henry I, his third son, the kings were beginning to catch on. There is a surviving charter from Henry I to Lincoln which says that all 'stranger traders' of Lincolnshire should trade at Lincoln alone "so that my reeves may not lose my royal customs." He was now aware that the more towns there were, the richer was the king.

In the 12th and 13th centuries the British kings started planting new towns (particularly in Wales, though that was probably for military purposes). Liverpool, Portsmouth, Salisbury, Chelmsford, Chepstow, Bury and Harwich were all new planted towns. In 1296 Edward I issued an edict "to elect men from among your wisest and ablest who know best how to devise, order and array a new town to the greatest profit of ourselves and of merchants." Edward's profit came from the market dues, the tolls, the fines imposed at his courts and the higher rent on the townspeople. What Edward could offer to persuade country people to come and live in his towns and pay the higher taxes was freedom, freedom from working for the local landowner.

It was not just the king who was planting towns. Local landowners could also augment their income by planting towns. If a lord had a bit of waste ground on the edge of his land, near a road or a ford which might attract passing trade, he could charge a higher rent on burgesses than on his peasants working the same land. He could also collect the tolls, dues, booth rents, court fines. Bridgetown with only 23 burgesses contributed £7 2s. 11d to the Pomeroy family's purse. The land on their manor contributed £26 10s. 6½d a year. Bridgetown had increased the Pomeroys' income by 27%. If the lords were richer from their towns, then someone is poorer, the peasants, who were forced to take their goods to the town market, where they probably paid an entrance fee to get in and received a lower price for their goods because of the monopoly rights granted to the wholesalers by the king or the lord in return for collecting the taxation.

The lords were also increasing their income at the peasants' expense in many other ways such as building corn-grinding mills and making

117

it illegal for peasants to grind their own corn, forcing them to pay the lord to grind it for them. They built fulling mills for felting cloth too, which the peasants had to use. "For like the corn mill, the oven, the wine press, the dye pan, or any other such equipment erected by the lord, it could be made a manorial monopoly to which the tenant owed suit." (Carus-Wilson. 1.)

Flanders at the time had already outgrown its food supply. Presumably that was where Britain's exports were going: "for much of the twelfth and thirteenth centuries, when many at home knew what hunger was, a significant amount of foodstuffs grown in England was sent overseas." (Miller and Hatcher) The monasteries were also using their land to grow cash crops, wool, again for the Flemish weavers. At that time we were a periphery country exporting crops to the core in Flanders. But as usual the first thing to go is the timber. "Moreover landlords, stimulated by the high speculative profits of marketing wood, moved to limit or even to prohibit admission to forestlands in the early thirteenth century. Smallholders lost not only fuel, construction material and a little extra food, such as berries and small game, but also a place to pasture the few livestock." (Lis and Soly. 2.)

The towns were already trying to keep the jobs from the countryside. "The first great measure of government control of the English cloth industry was the Assize of Cloth in 1197 which confined the manufacture of dyed cloth to the towns." (E. Miller. 2.) "At Winchester in 1402 clothmakers of the town were forbidden to employ either fullers or weavers outside the town." (Carus-Wilson. 2.) To reduce the cost of living in the towns, laws controlled the prices paid to the peasants for their goods. "In the first place there were the Assizes of Bread and of Ale and Wine which were contrived to cheapen the supply of commodities of which the town figured as a consumer . . . Sometimes things like wood, coal, hides, wool, tallow and candles were subjected to regulation as well." (Dobb. 5.)

The reality of cheapening the supply of commodities to the townsmen was to reduce the price the peasant received for his crops. The peasant was subsidising the town.

So the towns were not a natural development of progress. They were built to increase the income of the rich by taking more from the poor. They grew because the countryside was forbidden to compete with them. They impoverished the peasants.

Conditions for the Peasants

"The population of England and Wales doubled between 1100 and 1300," (Clapham. 2.) So at the least they were having to work harder to produce more food and their lords were taking an increasing percentage. "By the end of the thirteenth century the money dues of a villein tenant siphoned off about 50 per cent or more of his gross output." (Lis and Soly. 5.) Nevertheless by later standards the peasants weren't too badly off. "the condition and means of persons who entered into hired service on annual wages and allowances with the lord's bailiff were far better than anything of which our modern experience informs us as to the condition of farm labourers in our time, or indeed within recorded memory." (Rogers. 3.)

They weren't working too hard either. "At Thaxted a virgater had worked 137 days in winter and summer and thirty eight during the harvest, on a basis of a five day week, four weeks holiday at Christmas, Easter and Whitsun and 61 Saints days in winter and summer and four in the harvest season." (Kenyon.)

The position of the specialist, as we might expect, was not an honoured one. "In the older arable-centred villages, the status of the individual craftsman had not, it would seem, stood high. Such a man would be outclassed by the land-holding villein, and his skills, although they might keep his family in the village for a generation or two, seldom promoted them to permanent residence. Those for example, who at Warboys in Huntingdonshire, occupied themselves as artisans, did so because they could not have made a living for themselves on the land. They were smallholders at best, and migrants, taking their trades to whatever community might offer them a temporary market." (Platt. 3.)

The Wool Trade

England was the major source of high quality wool for the weavers of Flanders and Italy. From the export of this wool the English rulers derived an important part of their income by taxing it. So it was in their interest to encourage sheep walks for wool production instead of using the land to grow food. To collect the tax they insisted that only certain ports, the staple towns, should be allowed to export wool. The tax was collected at those ports. "The main object of this restriction on the free trade in wool was to facilitate the collection of the export duty; but the effect of it would be to give the English merchants of the few larger towns thus selected an advantage over those of the numerous small market towns that dealt in wool." (Unwin. 1.) Just as the towns had grown when villages were refused markets, so larger towns grew because smaller towns were refused markets for wool by the government. So the larger towns grew, not because it was natural for some towns to get larger but because of government law.

As the king created the large towns, so he created the individuals of great wealth. "The government conferred upon a small and exclusively privileged body of wool exporters a monopoly of the export trade in consideration of their services in the collection of customs, the furnishing of loans and the payment of large subsidies to continental powers." (Unwin. 2.)

Conventional economics would say that England benefited from this trade. The Gross Domestic Product had increased because of the export wool trade. There were larger towns. There were some very wealthy merchants whose wealth would 'trickle down' to the poorest peasants. The transport infrastructure was being improved particularly at the ports and the roads leading out of England. The economists would deny that the growing hunger was anything to do with this export trade. But: "The progress made by the upper reaches of the economy and the increase in economic potential were paid for by the hardship of the mass of the people." (Braudel. 17.)

The rulers and a few wealthy men had benefited, and the landowners, particularly the church, owned 15% of the land. But nearly all of the population of England was worse off. Much of the land was now devoted to sheep instead of growing food for the peasants. They were therefore forced to work harder producing food more intensively on a smaller land area. Because of foreign competition wool prices increased to the peasants. The poorest of the peasants who had been forced by poverty into weaving were hit by the cheaper imports from the technologically more advanced weavers of Flanders. Growing hunger forcefully indicates the growing poverty.

The peasants were being forced to produce a surplus by the laws of their Norman lords. Would they have done so without that pressure?

Some authors have seen population growth as the cause of economic growth and would therefore think that, yes, they would have produced the surplus since the population was increasing sharply. But the example of Indonesia would contradict that.

From 1100 to 1300 the population probably doubled. If the land had been fairly distributed, that would have caused an intensification of agricultural techniques and consequently harder work. But it would not cause more trade, industrialisation or the growth of towns. If everyone had enough land, and there was quite enough land to go round, there would have been no specialisation caused by poverty. If the lords had been unable to force the peasants to use their mills for grinding corn, fulling etc., the mill would not have been built.

The Mill

The thirteenth century has been called "the first industrial revolution". (Carus-Wilson) The mechanization of fulling was "as decisive an event as the mechanization of spinning and weaving in the eighteenth century." (Carus-Wilson. 3.)

The mills were used for malting, tanning, and paper-making, but most importantly for corn-grinding and fulling (cleaning and felting cloth). They were built to make money by renting it out to a miller. The king received his cut too. The Domesday Book was particularly required to list all the mills which were regarded as an important source of revenue. The mills benefited the landowners who built them, the king and the consumers because mill-ground corn was cheaper than hand-ground – the economics of scale.

The mills only made a profit if they ground enough to cover the capital outlay and the operating costs; but they could only get enough corn to grind by forbidding the peasants to grind their own and instead make them pay to have it ground at the mill. This applied to the fulling mills too. Clearly, if it had been in the peasants' interests, they would not have needed to use force. In fact the peasants and the townspeople were very angry indeed, what we would call totally Luddite about it.

In 1326 the monastery of St Albans, after being besieged by angry townspeople twice, searched all the houses and seized their grindstones. The Abbot then used the grindstones to pave his court-yard. The townspeople protested to the Queen. But that didn't do any good. All that was left to them to do was to rip up that courtyard during the Peasants' Revolt.

They protested against the fulling mills too. Whereas before they had been able to full the cloth themselves they were now compelled to take the cloth to the lord's mill and pay to have it fulled. The fulling mills were much more efficient than human labour so the cost of the cloth was cheaper to the consumer. The fullers were made unemployed. The lords benefited, the king benefited from the revenue from the mill, the consumers, the rich, benefited. The poor paid out to have their cloth fulled and were made unemployed.

So this major technological innovation made the rich richer and the poor poorer. It did not create wealth. It made a profit by taking a portion of the peasants' corn in return for grinding it, or a piece of the cloth.

The export of timber, wheat and wool would not have happened if the peasants had not been driven off their land or had owned their own produce.

So it was not the population growth, in this case, which caused the economic growth but the maldistribution of land and government taxation.

Chapter 7. The Pattern in Britain
References

C.J. Arnold. "Roman Britain to Saxon England." Croom Helm. '84. p.34.

R. Arnold. "A Social History of England. 55 BC. – 1215 AD.". Constable. '67. 1: p.255., 2: p.63., 3: p.112., 4: p.125.

F. Braudel. "The Perspective of the World". Collins. '84. 17: p.87.

C. Brooke. "The Structure of Medieval Society".Thames and Hudson. '71. 1: p.91., 2: p.84.

E.M. Carus-Wilson. "An Industrial Revolution of the Thirteenth Century" in "Essays in Economic History". Economic History Society. Edward Arnold Ltd. '54. 1: p.52., 2: p.59., 3: "The Woollen Industry" in "The Cambridge Economic History of Europe". Ed Postan. C.U.P. Vol. II. p.409.

J. Clapham. "A Concise Economic History of Britain". C.U.P. '66. 2: p.77.

C. Clark. "Population Growth and Land Use". MacMillan. '67. 3: p.57.

D. Collins. "The Origins of Europe." George Allen and Unwin. '75. p.296.

M. Dobb. "Studies in the Development of Capitalism". Routledge Kegan Paul. '46. 5: p.90.

H.P.R. Finberg. "The Formation of England". Hart Davis McGibbon. '74. p.73.

S. Frere. "Britannia. A History of Roman Britain." Routledge Kegan Paul. '78. 1: p.39., 2: p.17.

N. Kenyon. "Labour Conditions in Essex" in "Essays in Economic History". Ed. E.M. Carus-Wilson. '62. p.94.

D. Knowles. "The Monastic Order in England." C.U.P. '40. 2: p.352., 3: p.353.

L. and J. Laing. "The Origins of Britain". Routledge Kegan Paul. '80. p.148.

C.H. Lawrence. "Medieval Monasticism". Longman. '84. p.162.

C. Lis and H. Soly. "Poverty and Capitalism in Pre-Industrial Europe". Harvester Press. '79. 2: p.29., 5: p.6.

H.R. Loyn. "The Governance of Anglo-Saxon England. 500–1087." Edward Arnold. '84. 1: p.13., 2: p.33., 3: p.73., 4: p.122., 5: p.179.

E. Miller in "The Cambridge Economic History of Europe". Vol. III. 2: p.307.

E. Miller and J. Hatcher. "Medieval England". Longman. '78. p.82.

J. Morris. "The Age of Arthur". Weidenfeld and Nicholson. '73. 1: p.30., 2: p.442.

J.N.L. Myers. "The English Settlements". Clarendon. '86. p.213.

C. Platt. "The Abbeys and Priories of Medieval England". Secker and Warburg. '84. 2: p.73. "Medieval England". Routledge Kegan Paul. '78. 3: p.118.

T. Rogers. "Six centuries of Work and Wages". 1884. 3: p.94.

G.O. Saylles. "Medieval Foundations of England". Methuen. '48. 1: p.187., 2: p.190.

F. Stenton. "Anglo-Saxon England". Clarendon. '71. 1: p.287., 2: p.302.

G. Unwin. "Studies in Economic History". Ed. Tawney. Cass. '66. 1: p.140., 2: p.145.

D. Whitelock. "The Beginnings of English Society". Penguin. '52. 1: p.45. 2: p.119.

Chapter 8
STAGNATION

FOR THREE CENTURIES the economy had been growing strongly; that is to say that poverty had been increasing, urban squalor had been increasing, landlessness had been increasing and starvation and serf-dom on the periphery had been increasing. "The period of economic boom was a period of increased poverty and hardship for many, prob-ably the majority of the population." (Hodgett. 3.) And the rich were getting richer.

A century and a half later the same thing would happen again, and continue to the present day. But that century and a half from about 1320 to 1470 saw stagnation. In 1348 the plague struck Europe and killed perhaps a third of the population, so it is a useful period to test whether economic growth are caused by population pressure or gov-ernment action. If technological progress and economic growth are caused by population pressure then the Black Death should presage considerable regression.

To start with the stagnation started about 30 years before the Black Death. The price of grain fell. There was "a general lowering of grain prices which has been noted in all the western European markets from about 1315." (Bautier. 3.) The princes and priests, who had borrowed vast sums from the Italian merchants and bankers, depended on their sales and rents to pay their debts. With less cash coming in for the crops and lower rents they could not repay their bankers. The bankers, unable to repay the money they had borrowed to lend on to the princes and priests, went bankrupt. "In Italy the majority of the large banks which had for so long dominated the trade in money, foundered in a series of sensational bankruptcies; in 1327, the Scali failed; in 1341, the Bonnaccorci, the Usani, the Corsini and many others; in 1343, the Bardi, the Peruzzi and Acciajuoli." (Pirenne. 1.)

The fall in the grain price was caused by the extensive new planting in eastern Europe. We have already seen that: "in the fourteenth century in the two sectors of Europe – Hanseatic and Mediterranean – vast areas were put under cereal cultivation; they flooded the western mar-kets with their massive output obtained from enslaved dependants. No other explanation is required for the fall in cereal prices in the countries of western Europe." (Bautier. 1.) It started about 1250: "Flanders, which had relied on grain supplies from northern France or from southern Germany switched over to Baltic sources of supply at least between 1250 and 1350." (Hodgett. 4.)

In the early years of the fourteenth century grain exports from the east suddenly expanded considerably. "It is true that it was precisely then that countries which had hitherto been unaffected by the general movement, like Poland and especially Bohemia, began to take a more active part in it." (Pirenne. 2.)

A depression, after a fall in grain prices from a sudden opening up of a new grain-growing periphery, has twice since reappeared: first in the period 1860–1890 when the grain from the American mid-west arrived in Europe causing the Great Depression; and the great increase in crop production in Africa, Australia and South America after the First World War causing the Depression of the 1930s. Because the price of grain falls, the workers have to produce fewer goods to exchange for their grain, so production falls. Also, because of the bank failures, everyone puts their money back under the bed and there is a shortage of credit. Again production falls. The effects are unevenly felt. Those still in jobs enjoy lower prices. The others get the poverty of unemployment. And bankers jump from high windows.

In the Middle Ages it was the new grain-growing periphery of eastern Europe which felt the worst effects. Corrupted by western merchants, the eastern landowners, to hold up their income, did everything to increase their exports of grain, like the Third World today. The peasants were tied to the land and enserfed which had never been so before. That serfdom was caused by the economic growth in the West.

The merchants bought the grain from the east because it was cheaper; land prices were lower, the cost of living was lower so labour costs were lower. The effect of the cheap grain was to make grain production closer to the core unprofitable. The grain farmers were forced to change to cattle and sheep farming. This needs more land and more capital but less labour. Whereas grain-growing peripheries need to tie the peasant to the land, the circle of cattle country needs to evict them.

England and Spain were two countries who changed from arable to pasture. England had to increase its growth of fodder for cattle and sheep: "consequently from this time on in spite of a fall in production, England was largely dependent on the outside world, mainly the Hanseatics, for its supplies of wheat and rye." (Bautier. 4.) Spain concentrated on sheep-rearing. "As a result in the later Middle Ages and the Renaissance Spain became largely dependent for its food supplies on Baltic and Mediterranean corn." (Bautier. 5.)

Just like the cheap grain the new cattle growing areas undercut the previous cattle country closer to the core which was forced to grow more expensive crops requiring higher capital and harder work. "Increasingly in the fourteenth and fifteenth centuries, western European farmers turned to the cultivation of wine, hops, oil-bearing seeds, flax and dyestuffs, profiting from the relatively high prices of industrial products." (Lis and Soly. 3.) As the periphery expanded, the circles of the hinterland expanded within them.

For the rich it was not a good time. Those in debt were badly hit. The monks who had borrowed heavily to build their abbeys could not pay their debts because of the lower prices for their crops and their lower rents. Nor could they borrow because the bankers were not lending. The monks and the clergy had to stop their extravagant and competitive building. The grain arrived from Poland and the grain prices collapsed in the 1320s. The last abbey was built in 1325, more than twenty years before the Black Death. "City raced city and abbey raced abbey: in 1163 Notre Dame of Paris had the highest roof, 103 feet; in 1194 Chartres built up to 108 feet; in 1212 Rheims reached 113 feet, and nine years later Amiens topped them with 128 feet. Finally in 1225 Beauvais beat the record with 157 feet." (Weber.) Abbeys can still be seen with their two front towers, one climbing magnificently to the sky, its brother cut off in its prime when the price of its abbey's grain collapsed.

The kings suffered hard too. Edward III reneged on his debts to his Italian bankers, the Peruzzi, driving them into bankruptcy.

To get more money he invaded France to increase his possessions there and so increase his income. The plunder would come in handy too. That was the start of a war which devastated France for a hundred years. For this war the kings demanded high taxes from the poor, a poll tax which was just as unpopular then as now. It sparked the Peasants' Revolt in 1381.

So the economic crisis, caused by a drop in grain prices, produced an advance in farming patterns, a move to the cities by peasants evicted from the land and a banking collapse. The economic crisis was not caused by a drop in the population.

The Black Death

The plague struck Europe in 1348 and a third of the population died. The cities were the hardest hit. "At Florence for example credible sources relate that three quarters of the people died." (Luzzatto. 4.)

The main effect was a rise in wages because so many of the urban workers died that there was a labour shortage. Although the price of grain had already dropped (and didn't drop further because of the Black

Death) food prices stayed level in general. But wages doubled. So it was thought that the people were much better off; it was called 'the golden age of the peasant' and 'the golden age of the artisan'. But it is not nearly as simple as that.

With the drop in the grain prices the results were fairly straightforward. But with the advent of the Black Death things get a bit complicated, very complicated. Sometimes the effects of the two events coincide and add to each other. Sometimes they contradict and cancel each other out. So working out whether the people were better off or not, or whether there was regression or not gets a bit difficult.

Agriculture was affected by the two trends which conflicted. The fall in grain prices caused a move to cattle production, a move closer to the core in the core/periphery pattern. But the amount of vacant land caused by the Black Death, and the reduced need of food for the cities for the same reason allowed a return to subsistence farming for those richer peasants who could afford to buy the vacant land – a move outwards in the core/periphery pattern – regression. But in one way the effects coincided. The landowners wanted to evict their peasants to clear their land for cattle. The Black Death did the job for them.

The large landowners, farming for cash, went into cattle and sheep. In contrast, peasants, able to buy empty plots, had enough land for subsistence farming. So for some there was an "increase of self-sufficiency and decline in food production for the market." (Gould. 2.) The poorest, without money to buy the vacant land, went to the cities. In Britain the remains of 1500 villages which were deserted at this time have been identified.

The effects on the cities of the two events cancelled each other out to an extent. Although the populations of the cities fell because of the high death rate, this was countered by the high immigration to the cities caused by the change to pastoral farming.

With technology the two events again produced opposite effects. The fall in grain prices would reduce the cost of living and therefore labour costs and the need for technology. But the Black Death, because of labour shortage, increased wages and labour costs and so caused a need for labour-saving technology. The pursuit of inventions continued. After the Black Death "the blast furnace made its appearance at the very end of the century." (Bautier. 6.) "The municipal clock appeared about 1330 and in less than half a century spread to all the urban areas in northern Italy, southern Germany, the Rhineland, the Low Countries, France, especially Provence, and Catalonia." (Bautier. 7.) In Britain "between 1340 and 1474 it is clear that there was a great increase in the number of mills pushing up into the dale country right away from the home abbeys." (Raistrick.) In Holland there was "the invention of the herring cask in 1380." (Pirenne. 3.) "In 1402 the managers of the *Fabrica del Duomo* in Milan studied the proposals for a stone cutting machine which with the help of a horse (costing three shillings a day) would do the work for which four men (at a cost of $13^1/_2$ shillings per man day) would otherwise be needed. A few years later the same managers studied the plans for another machine – this for the transport of marble – which would reduce the labour force normally required." (Cipolla. 6.) And in the 1440s printing was invented and quickly spread across Europe. The cannon was invented at this time too. That doesn't sound like a regression of technology.

Commerce seems to have stagnated. But one wonders why it didn't drop. If grain prices were lower, fewer products were needed to exchange for it; a third of the population had died; credit had dried up; some of the population had gone back to subsistence farming. And yet commerce only stagnated.

As we have seen it is government which caused trade. In contrast to Poland and Spain, Britain changed its policy and started to protect and encourage its weaving industry. "In the first half of the fourteenth century Edward II tried to prohibit the import of foreign cloth except such as was destined for the use of the nobility". (Pirenne. 4.) It sounds as if he failed. But Edward III tried harder. "The export of wool sank from an average 32,000 sacks a year in the 1350s to 19,000 in the last decade of the century; in the same period the cloth exports rose from 5000 cloths a year to 37,000." (Hindley.) Perhaps Edward III was successful because after he had destroyed his banker, Peruzzi, he had to rely on English traders for loans. And they could get more added value from cloth than from wool. So if he wanted the loan, he had to protect English cloth. He had no choice. If that's true, it was the turning point which decided that Britain would be an industrial country. Poland and Spain went the other way.

So one reason why trade only stagnated was that the king needed the duty on exports. Another possibility is that the rich suffered less from the effects of the plague, and it is the rich who buy the consumer goods. Or else there was just a general increase in the monetisation of the economy. At any rate "the impression that we gain is that the reduction in the production of commodities was slight." (Hodgett. 5.)

Summary

So the century and a half of economic stagnation was initiated, not by the Black Death but by the cheap grain from an expanding periphery. This caused an advance in the farming patterns, immigration to the cities and enserfment on the periphery.

The Black Death produced different effects some of which conflicted and some of which coincided. Because of vacant land some richer peasants were able to regress to self-sufficiency. It was not the fall in population that allowed this but the availability of land. If the cattle had not taken over the land many more could have returned to self-sufficiency. Technology continued its advance but more slowly. The cheap grain meant lower labour costs but the Black Death meant higher labour costs which predominated, so continuing the advance in technology. So population pressure is not a cause of technological advance.

The loss of city population by the Black Death was to an extent modified by the move to the cities with a change to cattle farming. In general "socio-economic inequality remained a constant factor after the Black Death in both town and country and considerable evidence points towards an increasingly distorted distribution of wealth." (Lis and Soly. 6.)

The great reduction in population did not cause a regression in technology or a reduction in the number of cities. So technology and urbanisation are not caused by population pressure. It is a common precondition but not a cause.

Chapter 8. Stagnation
References

R.H. Bautier. "The Economic Development of Medieval Europe". Thames and Hudson. '71. 1: p.194., 3: p.192., 4: p.200., 5: p.200., 6: p.223., 7: p.225.

C.M. Cipolla. "Before the Industrial Revolution". Methuen. '81. 6: p.182.

J.D. Gould. "Economic Growth in History". Methuen. '72. 2: p.399.

G. Hindley. "England in the Age of Caxton". Granada. '79. p.203.

C. Hodgett. "A Social and Economic History of Medieval Europe". Methuen. '72. 3: p.99., 4: p.84., 5: p.213.

C. Lis and H. Soly. "Poverty and Capitalism in Pre-Industrial Europe". Harvester Press. '79. 3: p.33., 6: p.47.

G. Luzzatto. "An Economic History of Italy". Routledge Kegan Paul. '61. 4: p.138.

H. Pirenne. "Economic and Social History of Medieval Europe". Routledge Kegan Paul. '36. 1: p.194., 2: p.193., 3: p.222., 4: p.221.

A. Raistrick. "The Role of Yorkshire Cistercian Monasteries in the history of the Wool Trade in England". International Wool Secretariat. '53. p.8.

E. Weber. "A Modern History of Europe". Robert Hale & Co. '71. p.30.

Chapter 9
ECONOMIC GROWTH AND ITS POVERTY

FOR THREE CENTURIES throughout western Europe economic growth gradually increased in momentum. Trade increased, technology increased, institutions and infrastructure increased, knowledge increased. And poverty increased. "From the late fifteenth century until well into the beginning of the eighteenth century the standard of living in Europe progressively declined" (Braudel. 24)

As the rich at the core got richer, the poor, particularly on the expanding periphery, Russia, the Balkans, the Caribbean and South America, got poorer, and de-industrialised. China in her own economic fastness with her own core and periphery and no external threats, yet, carried on oblivious, disinterested in the technological antics of the western barbarians.

After the Black Death and its long depression and stagnation, there came the economic growth of 'the long sixteenth century'. And with it the poverty. In sixteenth century France "there was increased toil, hardships, impoverishment and dejection of the majority...The Sieur de Gouberville wrote in his diary in 1560, 'In my father's time there was meat every day, food was plentiful, men drank wine as though it was water , , , the food of the most prosperous peasants is much poorer than the food which the servants used to eat.'" (Braudel. 25).

As the grain growing periphery expanded into Eastern Europe vast acres exported their crops and left the peasants destitute and enserfed to feed western Europe. Within that widening periphery the cattle band expanded. "In Denmark the nobility increasingly concentrated on livestock with an eye on export." (Lis and Soly. 7.) And within that cattle band the industrial core expanded into central Europe: "in Electoral Saxony where between 1550 and 1750, while the population doubled, the proportion of farmers fell and that of the peasants who made most of their living by industry rose from 5 to 30 per cent of the population. (Treasure. 1.)

Mercantilism

During this period three countries of the core, Britain, France and Holland slugged it out to control world trade and its wealth. Britain won because it was able to screw more taxes out of its people to build more ships and guns.

Each of the nation-states struggled for survival, needing cash to buy armies and weapons to ward off predatory neighbours. Each nation tried to restrict the export of gold and silver and the export of raw materials that it needed for its war machine. And they tried to encourage the export of manufactured goods to earn money, and to restrict imports of manufactured goods which spent money. They subsidised exports, even grain, and put tariffs on imports.

This 'mercantilism' was later derided by Adam Smith. But it now seems to be agreed that it was intelligent policy. But if it was intelligent, it implies, contrary to economic wisdom, that the amount of trade was restricted. If another bought your cloth, then they weren't buying someone else's. It implies that there was only so much consumer demand. Correct. The demand is determined by how much food and other necessities of life are in the market to be earned by the makers of the manufactured goods. The workers work to eat. It's no good making thousands of cuckoo clocks if there's no food out there to exchange for them. And if someone has food, or tokens for food, money, and he exchanges that food for your cuckoo clock, that food is not available for other clockmakers or weavers etc. You eat; they do not. Consumer demand can only be increased by bringing more food and other necessities of life onto the market by extending the periphery and its enserfment. So mercantilism was a correct appreciation that international trade is a dog-eat-dog exercise, a zero sum game; one succeeds because the other fails.

Trade Wars

The glittering prize of trade was the spice of Indonesia, controlled by Venice with its overland routed through the Middle East. (The people of the Spice Islands didn't choose to grow the spices. They had to be forced. The Dutch "had to resort to warfare, to peddling supplies of arms, to exactions of 'contingencies' and forced deliveries from the native rulers whom they maintained in authority." (E.E. Rich))

In 1492 Christopher Columbus, working for Spain, threatened by France, discovered America, looking for the western route to the Spice Islands. In 1487 Bartholomew Diaz, working for Portugal, threatened by Spain, rounded the Cape of Good Hope, looking for the eastern sea route to the Spice Islands. In 1498 Vasco da Gama reached Calicut in India and

Venice's monopoly of spice was broken. In 1504 Venice's fleet of galleys found no pepper waiting for it at Alexandria in Egypt.

Within fifteen years Portugal's superior ships had driven the Arab ships out of the Indian Ocean. The West now controlled nearly all the seas of the world. But Portugal with a small population could not raise enough taxation to remain a leading player, and she herself was driven out of the Indian Ocean by the Dutch with even better, more expensive, ships and guns.

Holland, threatened by France, was already a strong contender. She achieved her naval superiority by taxing her population to build the ships. "The main fiscal burden fell under indirect taxes . . . The consumer came under a continuous fiscal barrage. Observers all agree that no other state, in the seventeenth or eighteenth century, laboured under such a weight of taxation." (Braudel. 14.) Holland's problem was that it only had eleven million people and however hard it taxed them it couldn't raise so much taxation as Britain and France.

Holland had the highest cost of living in Europe; therefore her wages were highest. Therefore to remain competitive she was forced to take the lead in inventing labour-saving techniques. She didn't choose to; she was forced to. Her merchant ships, the fluyts, used the fewest crew and were the worst fed, therefore her transport costs were lower, so she captured the Baltic carrying trade. "their rates were ruthlessly competitive, undercutting the English for example, by nearly half." (Maland. 1.) Up till then the Baltic trade had been almost totally in the hands of the Hanseatic traders of the north German cities. But no longer. "by 1560 the Dutch had succeeded in attracting 70% of the heavy Baltic trade." (Braudel. 15.)

She continued to increase her trade until about 1720. After that Britain began to replace her, not because Britain had more competitive rates, but because she had better guns. Then Holland's population declined. It is possible not that there were fewer births but that there was more emigration. There had already been considerable population movement from Antwerp to Amsterdam a century before. If the jobs from trading were no longer there, without the dole there was no point in hanging around. As we shall see neighbouring Belgium was the first to follow Britain's industrial example. This needed a large landless proletariat. Perhaps the Dutch had gone to Belgium.

France had the biggest population of the three and taxed it enthusiastically, but its wages were lower than in Holland and Britain so it did not have the need to invent labour-saving technology and it lost out in the commercial race. Nor did it have as large a landless proletariat. The king, as in China, got more of his income from the peasants. "The relatively great extent of peasant proprietors in France can be ascribed mainly to the protective role of the monarchy, which saw therein possibilities of broadening its power. Peasant production, through non-parliamentary taxation" (i.e. taxes levied by the king) "functioned as a direct source of the income needed by the Crown to strengthen its autonomy." (Lis and Soly. 8.) Because France did not have as large a landless proletariat, her cost of living was lower, so the pressure to invent labour-saving technology was lower. Germany got behind in the industrial race for the same reason. "The western German princes carried out a conscious policy, *Bauernschutzpolitic*, protection for peasant proprietors with the goal of providing an independent tax base for themselves." (Lis and Soly. 8.) Louis XIV spent his vast taxes on extending the territory of France at the expense of western Germany, leaving Britain and Holland to concentrate on world trade.

Britain

In Britain for centuries the king, the aristocracy and commerce had been driving the peasantry off the land. "The property rights of the English peasantry, in contrast, were extremely limited. The English monarchy evolved from the fifteenth century onwards in close association with landlords, as seen in the contemporaneous growth of parliamentary institutions, while they decayed in France. Therefore English landlords frequently succeeded in seizing peasants' holdings vacated during the fourteenth century crisis." (Lis and Soly. 8.)

Britain's economic growth started gathering momentum in the sixteenth century when she became Europe's leading cloth manufacturer: "by the time of the Tudors England had superseded Flanders as the leading centre of cloth manufacture in Europe." (Viljoen. 3.) So there were many more landless in Britain than the rest of Europe.

Increasing economic growth was accompanied by increasing poverty; "the long sixteenth century was a time of secular economic expansion" accompanied by "an absolute impoverishment of the rural masses." (Lis and Soly. 9.); "the poorest and most numerous sections of society, the peasantry and the industrial artisans, became still poorer." (Maland. 2.) "Between 1500 and 1600 grain prices rose sixfold while wages rose only threefold." (Lis and Soly. 10.) The poverty was increased by a spurt in the population growth, "rapid population growth – estimated at 60% in the course of the sixteenth century." (Braudel. 16.) The new pastoral agriculture needed less labour and more land. This was a period of extensive enclosures. The peasants were driven off their land and forced to earn their food by spinning and weaving. They didn't choose to go into industry; they were forced. Enclosure "was a massive violence exercised by the upper classes against the lower." (Moore. 1.) And weaving was harder work: "by working harder, as did the peasants and smallholders who took up industrial employments." (Clay. 5.) Industrial work was unpleasant, dirty and much harder work and only happened in areas of greatest poverty. "Contemporaries sometimes commented, with reference to a variety of industrial areas as far apart as Derbyshire, Suffolk, Kent and Cornwall, that villages where industrial employment was available were not only unusually populous but that the condition of the people in them was unusually wretched." (Clay. 6.)

In contrast with France, which only allowed exports of grain when there was an obvious surplus, the British government, to increase its income, encouraged and even subsidised grain exports even though its population went hungry. This went on right up to the middle of the eighteenth century. "Yet in the middle decades of the eighteenth century Britain was an important exporter of grain reaching a peak of almost 1,000,000 quarters in 1750 ... in the years such as 1727-9 there is some evidence to indicate that severe malnutrition provoked the fevers which carried off large numbers of the population." (Holderness. 1.)

From the sixteenth century the power of the British government started to increase as their tax income grew. "In England the revenues of the Crown grew from about 140,000 pounds a year around 1510 to about 860,000 pounds a year around 1640." (Cipolla. 7.) But at this time this was way behind the incomes of the French and Dutch governments. The English Parliament who controlled taxation would not grant Charles I more taxes. Then in 1649 they took his head off. Cromwell was now able to persuade Parliament to raise more taxes. This was England's breakthrough. It was now able to build the navy that drove Holland and France off the seas. It was able to get itself an empire, its own private periphery, paid for by the poverty of a heavily taxed population; "by the 1690s Gregory King reckoned that the burden of taxes per head in England was roughly equal to that in France although still lighter than that in the United Provinces (Holland). By the early eighteenth century however the burden was heavier than in France." (Clay. 7.) "The British themselves were at this time the most heavily taxed people in Europe, apart from the Dutch. About 1765 they paid an average of 26 shillings per head per year ... For Pennsylvania and Maryland the figure was one shilling." (Calder. 2.) "Thus by the period of the Napoleonic war, despite a population of less than half that of France, Britain was for the first time ever raising more revenue from taxes each year in *absolute* terms than its larger neighbour." (Kennedy. 1.)

The function of taxation was, as usual, to take from the poor to deliver to the rich. "The tax system helped rich individuals grow richer, transferring money to them from the poor. The money needed to fight war after war was chiefly raised by indirect taxes on commodities used by everyone – alcoholic drinks, bricks, salt, glass, tea, sugar and tobacco. It was handed over to holders of government bonds, to contractors, to shipbuilders, and to ironmasters. The profits and capital of business was virtually untaxed." (Calder. 3.)

At the beginning of the eighteenth century Holland, unable to raise enough taxation to build even better ships, dropped out of the race. "Eventually – but not until the eighteenth century – England secured by competition in armaments a commercial predominance which it had formerly failed to achieve in competition over transport costs." (Parry.) Britain and France were left to battle it out. Britain won in 1763 with the Treaty of Paris after the Seven Years War. France lost Canada and India to Britain and the pattern was set for the British Empire. The fighting continued until Napoleon's defeat in 1815, but although Britain lost America, the balance didn't change.

Colonialism

Britain now had her own periphery which could deliver over the raw materials at lowest prices because there was no competition from other countries. Britain as the monopoly buyer could determine the price, or even just take the raw materials. Britain could also exclude the manufactured goods of other countries to its colonies. The other manufacturing countries, excluded from this new empire, needed to ensure their own supply of raw materials and safe markets for their own products. There was a rush to build empires. The German Chancellor, Bülow, said, "The question is not whether we want to colonise or not, but that we *must* colonise whether we want to or not." But they'd started too late. By that time the world had already been divided up between the other core countries. In 1905 France and Britain signed the 'Entente Cordiale' to carve up Africa between them and exclude Germany. The First World War was a fight by Germany to take Britain's empire away from it. It failed, and the Second World War was a rerun of the first.

Ireland

Britain's first and most important colony was Ireland: throughout the eighteenth century, trade to Ireland was the most important branch of English overseas trade, i.e. it made the English rich richer and its raw materials created employment for the English poor, and fed them as well. The exploitation started with the English need for timber. In about 1600, since Ireland was covered with forests, she became a supplier of timber to England and developed, again for her masters, an iron industry which collapsed of itself when the island had been completely deforested after a hundred years.

Following the normal course of the periphery, after the trees had been cut down the land was used to grow grain for the core, and then cattle. The Irish themselves were forced to eat potatoes. "In fact, of the total cultivated land in Ireland at the time of the Famine, eight million acres were set aside for grazing, four million for grain growing and

134

only two and a half million for potatoes." (Kelley.) "Irish tenants almost everywhere were the most vulnerable rural class in western Europe." (Calder. 4.) The Irish "are only able to export because the great majority of them do not consume it; it is not the surplus that leaves the country, it is what anywhere else would be the vital necessity." (Braudel. 17.) When the famine came, the export of food continued. The English lords owned the land and sold their crops to England as usual. The starving Irish had no money to buy the wheat when their potatoes were destroyed by blight. As usual the periphery starved to feed the core.

There was great publicity about the Famine and dockers in Liverpool refused to unload the ships of wheat coming from Ireland. It made no difference. The ships went to other ports. The British government said the Irish should learn to feed themselves and therefore shouldn't be helped – the survival of the fittest. They carefully forgot that the Irish were feeding the English instead. And that it was the English who had driven them off their land in the first place.

Ireland had its own parliament of English landlords, creatures kept in power with English soldiers. But the English demands were too much even for them to take. England's answer was democracy, a cynical confidence trick. The Irish would be given a hundred members in the English Parliament in London. In 1799 an English under-secretary wrote to Pitt, the Prime Minister, "By giving the Irish a hundred members in an assembly of six hundred and fifty, they will be impotent to operate on that assembly, but it will be invested with the Irish assent to its authority . . . The Union is the only answer to preventing Ireland becoming too great and Powerful."

As usual the periphery suffered a deliberate policy of de-industrialisation. "Prohibition of wool export was followed by a cold blooded attack made in 1699 on the woollen industry of Ireland. All export from Ireland of wool or yarn or cloth was forbidden – except to England. She was to have no part in the markets that England supplied or coveted." (Clapham. 1.) Nevertheless since its cost of living would be lower and therefore its wages lower, it would not have needed labour-saving technology, so would have been de-industrialised by England's technology anyway.

Britains next most important colonies were the sugar islands of the Caribbean. About 1770 "the tiny islands of Monserrat and Nevis combined were a better market for British exports than the giant colony of Pennsylvania. Imports from Monserrat alone were three times higher than those from Pennsylvania and imports from Nevis almost double those from New York. As a consumer of British goods Jamaica equalled New England, and it exported to Britain six times as much as all the northern and middle colonies on the mainland put together." (Calder.

5.) As one would expect on the periphery the work to produce this great wealth was done by force – this time by negro slaves.

Britain, to hold on to these colonial peripheries which provided the food and other raw materials, needed guns to keep the colonies. So it needed money. So it needed to export manufactured goods. So it needed to protect its markets. So it needed to suppress colonial manufacture. And if it didn't it was going to have some pretty unhappy merchants to say nothing of a mutinous, hungry proletariat on its hands. "Steps were taken to prohibit the colonial manufacture of commodities which competed with the exportable products of English industry and to forbid the export of enumerated colonial products to other markets than England. Thereby, it was hoped, England would be given the pick of the colonial trade. For example the American colonies were forbidden to export woollen goods by an act of 1699 while tobacco and sugar were "enumerated" and could only be exported to England or to other colonies." (Dobb. 6.) "In order to break the English dependence on supplies from northern Europe, colonial smelters were given a free market for their products in Britain (in 1750). Colonial ironmongers, however, were forbidden to manufacture iron goods because that would reduce the demand for English hardware." (Viljoen. 4.) Rules protect the rulers, not the ruled!

All colonial empires found themselves forced to protect their own manufacturers against the lower labour costs of their colonies. In 1786 the Queen of Portugal said, "I deem it well to order that all the factories, manufacturers of shops or ships, of textiles, of gold and silver-smithing . . . or of any kind of silk or any kind of cotton or linen . . . or other kind of woollen cloth shall be extinguished and abolished in any place in which they may be found in my dominions in Brazil." But in this case she was attacking the wrong problem. The King of Portugal back in 1703, to save his skin from Spain, had signed a treaty with Britain, in exchange for protection, to open Portugal's market to Britain's cheaper goods. It was Britain, not Brazil, which was destroying Portugal's manufacturers. And then Portugal did it again. "The invasion of Portugal by Napoleon forced the Regent, Dom João VI, in 1808 to transfer his court to Brazil under British protection and at British expense – and then seek still more protection from Great Britain. For this Portugal naturally had to pay a price . . . He signed a commercial treaty with Great Britain which did away with almost all restrictions to trade and opened all the ports of Portugal and Brazil to economic liberalism." (Frank. 2.) 'Economic liberalism' means allowing in cheaper goods by ending all tariffs against them and letting your own manufacturers be destroyed. This 'Free Trade' only benefits the core countries with higher labour costs and technology. Dom João VI justified this, as they always do, by saying that competition would encourage local manufacturers to improve. They couldn't. The local labour costs were too low to make higher technol-

136

ogy profitable. The higher technology could only be profitable with greater output, which meant protecting local manufacturers against imports. But the commercial treaty forbade this. Portuguese and Brazilian manufacturers were destroyed and Britain grew rich: "Between 1731 and 1745 18 per cent of British exported manufactures went there." (Doyle.) Thus do periphery governments, to save their skins, betray their people to the core.

Agricultural 'Improvement'

As the periphery expanded into eastern Europe both grain and wool prices declined, relatively. Cheaper grain had driven the English farmers out of grain and into cattle and sheep. Now cheap wool was coming from central Europe. In Britain: "Wool-growing probably lost its competitive lead over other products by the late sixteenth century and a hundred years later the returns upon wool production were almost always lower than upon any other agricultural enterprise." (Holderness. 2.) English farmers were forced out of cattle-farming too. They had to look for new ways to make farming profitable. They didn't choose to increase yield per acre or improve animal breeding. They were forced to. And it meant harder work. "Enterprising farmers were faced with the need to increase their profit margins by greater specialisation, by a more intensive use of the land and by increasing yield per acre. The goad pricked harder because labour costs did not fall to the same extent as commodity prices." (Holderness. 3.) "Improvement was therefore not merely a gentlemanly hobby amongst landowners. It was a gentlemanly necessity." (Wilson. 3.)

The farmers had to use the more intensive techniques of the core market gardens because the core was expanding. "The factors which encouraged the gradual changeover to new crops and new systems of rotation were many and varied; but it is possible to recognise some which operated in the 'advanced' regions north and west of London, in the West Country especially round Exeter and Bristol and in East Anglia and Kent . . . these areas all had access to the cities." (Wilson. 4.) It was cheaper crops from the periphery which forced the heavy expenditure and harder work of the agricultural 'improvement' of the core. If the supply of cheaper corn and wool had stopped and the price therefore increased, the 'improvements' would have ended and more extensive methods replaced them. They would be less work.

So Britain was forced down the agricultural road of increasing yield, harder work and reduced labour in the product that was to lead to the present monoculture, herbicides, pesticides and soil erosion. In a non-cash economy it would instead have developed labour-intensive agricultural techniques. But that wasn't an option in a cash economy.

Although the standard of living at the core had gone down, the real poverty of economic growth was on the periphery, unseen, unrecorded. In the sugar islands of the Caribbean the original population had been worked to death. Literally. They are no more. To continue sugar production stronger labour was introduced from Africa, the negro slaves. They were worked to death too. But their death took longer. They were expected to last about ten years.

But there were more where they came from, sold by local African chiefs to the European and American merchants. The trade was nearly all directly between Africa and America, it is now thought.

Economic growth depended on the exploitation and early deaths of the African negroes. The growth and the deaths were the two necessary parts of the same system. The building of St Paul's Cathedral and Newton's theory of gravity were paid for by the deaths of the negroes in the Caribbean.

Likewise the deaths of millions of South American Indians paid for the arts of the Spanish Golden Age, Velasquz, El Greco, Murillo. It wasn't an incidental tragedy. The deaths were the price. The starvation of the Hungarians was the price of the Baroque glories of South Germany. The enserfment of the Russian peasantry bought the philosophy of Kant. European civilization was paid for by the starvation of its periphery.

Industrial Squalor

The historians now generally agree that up to the industrial revolution as economic growth increased, so poverty increased. But then they think that something changed, that suddenly industry created, not poverty, but wealth. They might put it differently: that, while in the early stages industrialisation caused more poverty than wealth, the change was that industry, later, created more wealth than poverty.

It's an easy mistake. Clearly, at a most basic level, huge numbers of people in the industrial countries are now living much longer; there is no starvation; nearly everyone is warm, well-fed, well-clothed and housed. Even unemployed single parent families, poor by the standards of the West, live fairly comfortable by the standards of the South. They are not cold and hungry. But that's only at the core.

As has been shown earlier, manufacturing creates no wealth. The change at the time of the industrial revolution was only quantitative, not qualitative; whether a machine is producing ten or a hundred thousand units, still no wealth is created. The quantity is simply a measure of how much poverty is being transferred to the periphery by the destruction of the local industries and by the removal of the crops. The vast increase of production at the core during the Industrial Revolution meant a similar vast increase of poverty on the periphery. But it was now, because of advances in transportation, so far away as to be invisible. People are living longer at the core because they are dying earlier on the periphery. 30 million starve to death every year. 800 million are malnourished.

The Timber Shortage

British manufacturers were driven by two pressures – the cheaper labour costs of their European competitors and a timber shortage. They didn't choose to advance; they were forced to. While everyone has noticed in detail that 'Necessity is the mother of invention', the generalisation has been unrecognised.

"The shortage of firewood and timber for construction – 'the timber famine' – became acute during the population rise of the sixteenth and early seventeenth centuries." (Wilkinson. 3.) So timber had to be replaced by coal, which no one liked. It smelt and made much more smoke and at the beginning was only used by the poor. Chimneys at great expense had to be built. "The spread of coal as a domestic fuel during the late sixteenth century and early seventeenth centuries was paralleled by the spread of chimneys as the smoke forced people to abandon the traditional custom of having fires in the centre of the room with a hole in the roof . . . the rich were able to delay using coal longer than the poor." (Wilkinson. 4.)

As more coal was used so they had to dig deeper for it. The deeper the mines, the more difficult it became to stop them filling with water. To solve this problem Newcomen invented the steam engine, which was used to pump out the flood water. It was expensive, i.e. harder work, but inevitable, necessary. The steam engine was not needed until the timber shortage. "The invention of the steam engine was a direct result of the new technical problems posed by deep mines." (Wilkinson. 5.) If the supply of the cheap timber had increased, the steam engines would no longer be needed. They would be too expensive and unprofitable.

The timber shortage changed iron smelting techniques. For technical reasons it was not possible to replace the timber, as charcoal, with coal until they turned the coal into coke, an extra process which is more expensive, more work. "Thus techniques permitting the use of coke rather than charcoal in smelting and working iron were devised to combat the growing shortage and therefore costliness of suitable timber in the eighteenth century." (Gould. 3.) If the price of timber went down, charcoal would be used instead of coke again because it would be cheaper.

The steam engine was expensive and although this new source of motive energy could be applied to replace human energy in all sorts of ways, it did not do so until the cost of human energy, wage costs, increased sufficiently to make the steam engine profitable. "Rotary steam power appeared as late as it did, not because of the difficulties of invention, but because it was not needed earlier." (Wilkinson. 6.) If the price of labour decreased, this expensive rotary steam power would be unprofitable and abandoned.

The coal had to be transported to the cities. Most of it went by sea. But inland transport was also obviously necessary. Horses and carts were used. Then they built the canals at colossal expense. Canals are not a new technology. China had built them two millennia before. Canals became necessary because the cost of feeding the horses increased. "Undoubtedly one of the most important reasons for the commercial success of the canals was the high price of horse feed. Only when competition for land had forced the price of horse feed sufficiently high was it worth expending labour and construction of the canals which allowed larger loads to be drawn by fewer horses." (Wilkinson. 7.)

Steam engines were invented, smelting techniques changed, chimneys built, canals built all because of the shortage of timber. If timber had become more available and therefore cheaper, the new techniques would have become unprofitable and been discontinued.

The Goad of Labour Costs

"In the mid sixteenth century, the British Isles were still, industrially speaking, far behind Italy, Spain and the Netherlands, Germany and France. A hundred years later the situation had been miraculously reversed and the speed of the transformation had been so fast that there is no parallel before the equivalent wave of change in the late eighteenth and early nineteenth century." (Braudel. 8.) And this same period saw increasing poverty especially in the countryside where industry was now concentrated. "In the course of the later sixteenth century the impoverishment process reached ever greater proportions in the English countryside. Before 1560 scarcely 11 per cent of rural labourers disposed of only a cottage and garden; after 1640 their numbers amounted to 40 per cent and the proportion without livestock of their own rose from 5 to 13 per cent . . . Between 1500 and 1600 prices rose sixfold while wages rose only threefold." (Lis and Soly. 11.)

So Britain could reduce the relative cost of its cloth. "English entrepreneurs lowered their prices after the Restoration (1660) to a point where Holland and most other continental producers could no longer compete." (Lis and Soly. 12.) The reason for Britain's commercial success was the poverty of its producers. The British spinners and weavers were producing expensive cloth for rich Europeans because otherwise they would starve.

Part of the reason for Britain's success was the political turmoil in Flanders, which enabled Britain to take Flanders' markets; but more importantly while Britain's real wages were diminishing, those on the continent were not. "While in England the level of real wages at the beginning of the seventeenth century was noticeably lower than a hundred years earlier, in Italy the real wages did not show any substantial deterioration in the course of the sixteenth century." (Cipolla. 8.)

Economics is a zero sum game. If Britain's labour costs are lower, people will wear British cloth and not Italian cloth. The Italian wool industry declined. "By 1700 the number of wool weavers in Venice, Milan and Como dropped to scarcely 5 per cent of their sixteenth century total." (Lis and Soly. 13.)

Turnaround

Cromwell's dramatic increase in military expenditure was paid for by an increase in indirect taxation which therefore increased the cost of living, so wages had to be increased, turning Britain from a low wage economy to a high wage economy. By the eighteenth century England "was the country where one had to pay the highest daily expenses; renting a house or a carriage, eating or staying in a hotel was ruinous for foreigners." (Braudel. 19.) Britain had "high domestic prices and labour costs which made her the most expensive country in Europe." (Braudel. 20.) But high wages don't mean less poverty if the cost of living is even higher: "even in the 'smiling forties' of the eighteenth century real wages had almost certainly not regained the level of the late fifteenth century." (Holderness. 4.)

Britain had now changed from a periphery country to the core country because of the high indirect taxation. Because of the high consequent labour costs, to maintain her exports of cloth, she was forced to invent technology that reduced the labour content in the product. "It appears that the wages of industrial workers in France, Flanders and central Europe were lower than in England, so that these areas had a competitive advantage which could only be overcome by structural innovation – mechanization." (Lis and Soly. 14.) The British manufacturers didn't choose to mechanise, they were forced to.

Because of the high cost of the new machines, they had to be kept running as long as possible. Life was no fun in the new factories. "Their progress in the (seventeen) sixties owed a great deal to the hard times and high food prices which sent employers in search of mechanised means of reducing labour costs and at the same time forced the poor to face the hated prospects of disciplined work in an institution." (Wilson. 5.) At first the factories were worked by orphans handed over on contract from the orphanages. "In 1771 Richard Arkwright created a cotton spinning mill where he was soon employing about 600 workers, most of them children." (Calder. 6.) Then the poorest women came, and only finally, driven by starvation, the men. The working hours demanded by the machines influenced the hours worked by the whole population. In the Cornish tin mines: "From the four hours which were customary in Elizabethan times, cores of six, eight or even twelve hours had been substituted in the eighteenth century." (Hamilton-Jenkin.)

If the peasants had got back their land, the factories would have emptied. Whenever there is land reform, there is labour shortage and a reduction of produce for market.

Capital Accumulation

It has been attempted here to show that economic growth is the result of poverty and competitors' lower labour costs. Another suggestion has been the ability to accumulate capital. But it seems to be an insignificant factor. Nearly all the great enterprises were started by small men gradually increasing the size of their businesses out of profits, not out of credit or other people's capital. "Starting from the smallest beginnings, he financed his expansion step by step out of his proceeds, starving himself into greatness." (Stern.) "In 1850 manual skill was still of paramount importance in the heavy trades. The capital required was small. John Brown started in business with a loan of £500." (Pollard.) Disraeli wrote about the railway boom, "what is remarkable in this vast movement, is that the great leaders of the financial world took no part in it." As for the whole industrial revolution, "the city was involved only at one remove; indeed it took place almost independently of the city." (Cairncross and McRae. 1.) "Even in the years shortly before the First World War only about a tenth of real investment in Britain was financed by new issues on the London Stock Exchange." (Cairncross and McRae. 2.) Economic growth was achieved, not by capital accumulation but by high indirect taxation.

Capitalism really isn't a very useful word. No-one agrees what it means. In the eighteenth century a man called himself a capitalist when he was a successful businessman. Marx, though he used 'Capital' as the title for this book, never used the word 'capitalism' apparently. Today more than half the world calls itself 'capitalist' meaning a free market economy rather than a planned economy. It's certainly impossible to isolate a capitalist mode of production that wasn't in operation two thousand years before, unless it just means high technology which doesn't explain anything, or factories which doesn't explain anything either.

The Effects of Technology

From Britain's merchants' point of view the Industrial Revolution was a triumphant success. For the rest of the world it was a disaster. The machines made the cloth much cheaper, so everyone bought English cloth and foreign producers were destroyed. By 1820 the Silesian linen yarn spinning business had been wiped out; "within the following twenty years linen export too dropped to nearly nothing. Utterly destitute cottage workers died by the thousand during the 1840s just as in Ireland." (Lis and Soly. 15.) "European machine-made goods had begun from about 1830 to reduce traditional artisan communities of the Moslem world to penury." (McNeill. 4.) "it was really only the flood of English textiles after the industrial revolution, in the nineteenth century, which eventually brought about their (the Turkish textile trades) almost total collapse." (Braudel. 22.) For centuries India had been a leading cloth producer. "India in the seventeenth and early eighteenth centuries might justifiably be described as the industrial workshop of the world." Then the cheap machine-made cloth arrived. "The advancement of production techniques in England permitted manufacturers there to undersell Indian products and the artificial restriction of imports into England ruined the industry irreparably." (Edward.) "It was the very development of industry in Britain which generated the underdevelopment and de-industrialization of India." (Frank. 5.)

It is just horribly untrue that technology benefits everyone. It benefits the core. It destroys the periphery.

Once the technology has been invented by the core, there is a strong incentive for industrialists to transfer that technology to the periphery where the labour costs are lower, which is what is happening today in the Third World. There is also a strong incentive for the core to stop it. Angry unemployed workers in the core cities can be very destructive. In the end the core will always protect its technology by quotas, tariffs, 'voluntary' restrictive agreements and any other trick it can think up. Ultimately the periphery rulers depend for their power and wealth on their collusion with the core rulers and their guns, so in the end they accept the core's monopoly of technology.

The Great Depression

Halfway through the nineteenth century the decline in living standards which had lasted for at least four hundred years was halted. The reason for this was the arrival of cheap corn from the American periphery of the Mid-West: "between the 70s and 90s there occurred a considerable cheapening of foodstuffs relatively to manufactures as a result of the opening up of America." (Dobb. 7.) At the same time: "What has been known as the Great Depression which started in 1873 and, broken by bursts of recovery in 1880 and 1888, continued into the middle nineties," (Dobb. 8.) The cheap corn caused a depression for two inter-related reasons as it had done in the 1330s. Because the corn was cheaper, fewer goods had to be made to exchange for the corn. And loans by banks to corn producers could not be paid back because of the low prices. Banks went bankrupt and everyone put their money back under the bed. The shortage of credit meant less money to buy manufactured goods.

The Standard of Living

In general everyone at the core seemed to think they were better off, just. "The mass of English workmen are far better off now (1884) than they were two generations ago, though the population has greatly increased. But relatively speaking the working man of today is not so well off as he was in the fifteenth century." (Rogers. 3.)

It really is very difficult to know whether the worker at the core is better off or not. Or which worker. Obviously the rich and their middle classes are much better off. The migrant workers who keep the system going are much worse off. So, in the middle some of the workers may be better off, the skilled ones perhaps, some worse. In the seventeenth century the Dutch at their most powerful seem to have fed well. "The Dutchman was renowned for his fine physique: it was attributed to his great eating of cheese." (Treasure. 2.) In eighteenth century Britain: "For all her poverty, England seemed to herself and to foreigners a fat country where men ate beef, white bread and cheese, and drank strong beer." But by the end of the nineteenth century things seem to have deteriorated. The establishment was deeply concerned at the lack of fitness in its recruits to the army in the Boer War.

Today Americans seem well fed and well built, and yet kwashiorkor, a disease of malnutrition, is found among the migrant workers of the South West. "The U.S. Bureau of Census itself stated in 1972 that at least 10 or 12 million American are starving or sick because they have too little to spend on food." (George. 4.)

Working class Consumer Demand

Originally the urban artisans made only luxury products for the rich, while the peasants proudly made their own. But the artisans, if they were weavers living in towns, couldn't make their own pots or their own shoes. They didn't have either the time, the raw materials or the facilities. So an industry grew not only to manufacture luxury products for the rich, but also necessary products for the urban poor, the mass consumer industry. As the proportion of the population which lived in cities increased so that mass production industry had to increase too.

The fact that industry is now producing for the artisans does not mean that the artisans are wealthy but that they do not have the time or facilities to make the products themselves. Many of the products which seem like luxuries are almost necessities. For instance, television. When you are old and alone because your children have had to leave to find jobs in other towns, television is not a luxury. It is very difficult in a city to find a way of talking to other people that does not cost money. The poorest in cities do not have that money to spend. Television is a cheap form of social interaction. Perhaps that's why soap operas are popular. Television keeps away the loneliness and the boredom.

A cooker is a necessity too. You can't light a fire in the middle of the floor. When a housewife is also working all day in a factory, a vacuum cleaner or convenience foods can hardly be called luxuries. Income which is not spent on the necessities of life is called 'discretionary' income. On average about 5 per cent of our income is discretionary. Migrant workers would have hardly any. Skilled workers might have more. But the mass consumer industries depend not on our 5 per cent discretionary income but on the 95 per cent of our income which is spent on necessities.

The Effects on the Periphery

For the first time we see the change of effect on the periphery caused by mechanisation. Previously serfs or slaves had been necessary to work the land. They had been chained to the soil. They were forbidden to leave the villages. But with the coming of mechanisation they became redundant and were left to starve. The aborigines in Tasmania were hunted to death. Tribes all over Africa were driven off the best, the watered land, and left to subsist far from water. When the drought came they died.

To the extent they had industry it was destroyed by the cheaper manufactured goods from Europe. The weavers took the brunt of this but it also destroyed the iron and copper industry and the pottery, leather and basket industries. The periphery was de-industrialised. The only industries which were allowed were mining and agriculture; and even then all further refining was forbidden, such activities being necessary to provide work for the core.

Some effects on the periphery depend on the distance from the core. So that those periphery countries closest to the core and about to be incorporated as the core expands, find it in their interests to sacrifice what was left of the peasant agriculture to support their industry by importing cheap food from the periphery and subsidies, quotas, tariffs and expenditure on infrastructure.

Further out agricultural countries would have to drop cattle and grain farming and concentrate on higher value, more laborious crops as the cheaper grain, cattle and wool became available from the expanding periphery beyond. The peasants would find, as the cost of living and

145

taxation increased, that their plots were too small to provide a living and the drift to the cities would begin.

Previously highly developed cores like India were de-developed, their industries closed down and their cities emptied. When Britain arrived in India, it was a highly cultivated and industrialised society. "Medieval Indian society had already developed manufacturing skills equal to the best that Europe had to offer at the time and it had a flourishing export trade in textiles." (Alavi. 4.) At first the East India Company had bought Indian products for export to Britain with gold imported from Britain. So there was an exchange between the two countries. But then the British took the land revenue that the peasants had handed over to the Indian rulers and used that to buy the Indian products. So there was no longer any exchange between the two countries and the Indian rulers didn't get their income. "Diversion of the flow of land revenue from the hands of the indigenous ruling class took away the foundations on which India's urban society has rested. There was a dramatic decline in the urban population and cities were laid waste. For example Sir Charles Trevelyan reported that the population of Dacca, the "Manchester" of India, declined from 150,000 to a mere 30,000. Old cities declined, decayed and many disappeared altogether." (Alavi. 5.)

Having de-industrialised India, Britain forced it to produce crops for export, opium. The terrible famine of the 1770s was caused by Britain forbidding the Indians to grow food for themselves, but instead, opium for export to China to pay for the Chinese tea, drunk by fashionable ladies in London, on which the East India Company made its profit. The lands of the periphery are used, not necessarily for crops needed for survival, but crops needed for profit. The profit can then buy the crops needed for survival.

The attitude of colonial cores to starvation is that the peoples of the periphery are too uneducated and lazy to grow enough food for themselves or save some for the lean years. This attitude drew the following comment in 1932 from a French colonial inspector in Upper Volta: "One can only wonder how it happens that populations who always had on hand three harvests in reserve and to whom it was unacceptable to eat grain that had been less than three years in the granary, have suddenly become improvident. They managed to get through the terrible drought of 1912-14 without hardships ... now these people once accustomed to food abundance are living from hand to mouth. I feel morally bound to point out that the policy of giving priority to industrial cash crops has coincided with an increase in the frequency of food scarcity." (See: "Links")

Slow Down

Around 1870 Britain's share of world trade started to fall. She was being overtaken by Germany and America. Britain, because of her high cost of living and high wages. to keep her products cheap enough to sell abroad, had had to reduce labour costs with the extra effort of labour-saving machinery. But now Germany had not only the same machinery but a larger population to buy more goods, making them cheaper by the economies of scale. And Germany was even hungrier.

In America Britain faced the competition of higher labour costs and therefore more labour-saving machinery. America was hungrier too.

Nor did Britain invest nearly so heavily in education and research as Germany and America. It was still greatly influenced by the idea that a good government is that which governs least. It thought that education and research should be provided by the free market. It wasn't. Britain was overtaken by Germany and America. But the underlying reason for the lack of urgency was that Britain just wasn't so hungry. Cheap wheat had begun to arrive from America and Russia and food prices were going down.

Check List

We now have a check list of disadvantages necessary for economic growth: a high population which cannot feed itself; a large landless proletariat to provide factory fodder; a large internal demand and a large tax base; a protected home industry; untaxed imports of food and raw materials; high indirect taxes; high government expenditure on 'defence', and threatening neighbours.

So British industry grew, not because it had found a way for machines to create wealth, but because its labour costs were higher than Europe's, and it was forced into the extra work of producing machines which reduced labour in the product. It saved the workers no labour. They had to work harder. Britain grew rich, not because its machines created wealth, but because it moved the crops from its empire to Britain. With more food, they could feed more workers to produce more luxuries. The unemployment caused by the machines was exported to the periphery where the small craftsmen were put out of business.

References

H. Alavi "South Asia". MacMillan. '89. 4: p.6., 5: p.10.

F. Braudel. "Prices in Europe from 1450–1750" in "The Cambridge Economic History of Europe". Ed. Postan. Vol IV. 24: p.429., 25: p.428. "The Perspective of the World". Collins. '84. 8: p.552., 14: p.200., 15: p.207., 16: p.554., 17: p.374., quoting a French consul in Dublin in 1789. 20: p.575., 22: p.474. "The Wheels of Commerce." Collins. '82. 19:p.171.

Cairncross and McCrae. "Capital City". Eyre-Methuen. '73. 1: p.2., 2: p.12.

A. Calder. "Revolutionary Empire". Jonathan Cape. '81. 2: p.635., 3: p.789., 4: p.31., 5: p.473., 6: p.779.

C.M. Cipolla. "Before the Industrial Revolution". Methuen. '76. 7: p.47., 8: p.261.

J. Clapham. "A Concise Economic History of England." C.U.P. '66. 1: p.238.

C.G.A. Clay. "Economic Expansion and Social Change". C.U.P. '84. 5: p.23., 6: p.92., 7: p.253.

M. Dobb. "Studies in the Development of Capitalism". Routledge Kegan Paul. '46. 6: p.205., 7: p.304., 8: p.300.

W. Doyle. "The Old European Order 1600–1800". O.U.P. '78. p.63.

M. Edward. "A History of India". Thames and Hudson. '61. p.225 and p.224.

A.G. Frank. "Capitalism and Under-development in Latin America". Monthly Review Press. '67. 2: p.162. 5: p.89.

S. George. "How the Other Half Dies". Penguin. '76. 4: p.30.

J.D. Gould. "Economic Growth in History". Methuen. '72. 3: p.355.

A.S. Hamilton-Jenkin. "The Cornish Miner" David and Charles. '72. p.142.

B.A. Holderness. "Pre-Industrial England. Economy and Society from 1500–1750." J.M. Dent. '76. 1: p.9., 2: p.71., 3: p.75., 4: p.204.

K. Kelley. "The Longest War". Z Books. '82. p.16.

P. Kennedy. "The Rise and Fall of the Great Powers." Unwin. '88. 1: p.80.

'Links'. A 'Third World First' pamphlet. No.22.

C. Lis and H. Soly. "Poverty and Capitalism in Pre-Industrial Europe". Harvester Press. '79. 7: p.60., 8: p.55., 9: p.54., 10: p.72., 11: p.72., 12: p.105., 13: p.105., 14: p.155., 15: p.159.

D. Maland. "Europe in the Sixteenth Century". MacMillan. '73. 1: p.182., 2: p.167.

W.H. McNeill. "A World History". O.U.P. '79. 4: p.396.

B. Moore Jnr. "Social Origins of Dictatorship and Democracy." Penguin. '67. 1: p.29.

J.H. Parry. "Transport and Trade Routes" in "The Cambridge Economic HIstory of Europe". Ed. Postan. Vol IV. p.181.

S. Pollard. "The History of Labour in Sheffield". University of Liverpool. '59. p.79.

E.E. Rich. Preface to "The Cambridge Economic History of Europe". Ed. Postan. Vol IV. p.xxiv.

T. Rogers. "Six Centuries of Work and Wages". 1884. 3: p.355.

W.M. Stern. "Britain Yesterday and Today". Longman. p.194.

G. Treasure. "The Making of Modern Europe. 1648–1780". Methuen. '85. 1: p.76., 2: p.38.

S. Viljoen. "Economic Systems in World History". Longman. '74. 3: p.127., 4: p.170.

R. Wilkinson. "Poverty and Progress". Methuen. '73. 3: p.114., 4: p.117., 5: p.118., 6: p.121., 7: p.124.

C. Wilson. "England's Apprenticeship. 1603–1763". Longman. '65. 3: p.159., 4: p.146., 5: p.351.

Chapter 10
THE MODERN WORLD

BRITAIN HAD BEEN FORCED TO INDUSTRIALISE because its labour costs were higher than its competitors in the rest of Europe. But the new industrial techniques made the products considerably cheaper (as long as a much greater number were sold). So the rest of Europe faced bankruptcy. Europe was forced to industrialise too.

Belgium

Belgium was the first to be hit by Britain's cheaper products. And the first to follow Britain's example. It had the same high population density and so was unable to feed itself, and it had the same advanced agricultural techniques as in Britain. But it didn't have the same high labour costs, so the new technology, imported from Britain, put it in a good competitive position. Britain had tried to stop the export of its technology. In 1781 it outlawed the export of textile machinery. The attempt failed. The machinery was smuggled out and English technicians hired to install and teach its use.

Belgium also joined the race to ensure its supplies of raw materials and markets for the extra goods that the machines had to produce to make them economic. It established colonies in Africa and de-developed them by sending them the cheap Belgian products, destroying the local craft industries. The African colonies were impoverished to 'create' the wealth for Belgium. The raw materials had to be produced by force and Belgium didn't hesitate to use forced labour in its colonies.

Germany

Britain 'took off' industrially about 1780. Germany had to wait another 70 years until about 1850 when it produced its 'great spurt'. Why did it wait so long, and why did it suddenly forge ahead of all the others?

It was held back by the lack of a large internal market and a common currency. Germany was composed of more than three hundred autonomous dukedoms, principalities, archbishoprics, electorates and kingdoms, the biggest of which was Prussia. Each had its own currency and tariffs to protect its own industry and agriculture. To protect Hanoverian manufacturers the goods of a manufacturer in Saxony were taxed in Hanover making them more expensive. So no manufacturer could find a large enough market to justify the expenditure on the new machinery which could only be profitable with much higher output.

Germany also lacked a large enough, hungry enough, landless proletariat. The princes got their income from the peasants and not from taxation on trade, so it was in their interest that the peasants should have just enough land.

Frederick the Great of Prussia had already seen that the first requirement for independent survival was a strong army. Prussia has been called less a state with an army than an army with a state. He also saw, like Japan later, that he needed all the military technology he could get, and so used the state to try to build the technology. To the same purpose he encouraged education and research. But because he lacked the landless proletariat, he had few willing to work in the factories, or an urban population which was not self-sufficient and needed mass-produced goods.

The first step to creating a landless proletariat came with the agricultural reforms in the 1810s. The peasants working larger holdings were enabled to buy them from the landowners. But those with smaller holdings, considered uneconomic, got nothing and were forced out. "Propertyless, uprooted, homeless, belonging neither to the state nor an estate, almost half the inhabitants of the German territories lived in poverty and misery." (Böhme.)

After Napoleon's defeat in 1815, his 'continental system', which tried to keep British products out of Europe, broke down. The cheap goods flooded in, causing destitution amongst the manufacturing workers. In Silesia: "By the 1820s export of yarn had halted completely, defeated by the murderous competition of English mechanised spinning mills; within the following twenty years linen export too dropped to nearly nothing. Utterly destitute, cottage workers died by the thousands during the 1840s just as in Ireland." (Lis and Soly. 14.)

Those still in work were little better off. To keep down the price of their goods to compete with the English they had to work harder and harder. "While at the turn of the century in Prussia the average working day was twelve hours, with night shifts and Sunday work being very exceptional, that had changed profoundly by the mid 1820s . . . They worked 16 or 17 hours a day, six days a week." (Koch.)

Napoleon's defeat was crucial to Germany's survival and growth. Otherwise large parts of Germany would have been incorporated into France to increase its internal market and tax base, and the rest apportioned to other countries like Austria and Russia, for services rendered.

Germany would have been dismembered as a threat to French growth. Germany survived because of Prussia's military strength which, with Britain, defeated Napoleon at Waterloo. And it was Prussia's army which defeated Austria in 1868 and France in 1870, completing Germany's unification and enlargement.

The German rulers and intellectuals had long realized that unless they could create a unified Germany, the statelets would be absorbed into the neighbouring states where they would remain exploited, foreign-speaking minorities. And they also realized that unless they could create a large enough internal market to make industrialization profitable, they were destined to the agricultural fate of Italy, Spain and the Balkans. "If we don't want to become a purely agricultural nation, with our products replaced by English goods, and we ourselves subject to direct plunder, then we must have Schleswig-Holstein, and the customs Union must be identical with Prussia." (Siemens, director of the German Bank.)

So Germany circa 1830 could not succeed industrially because, although it had military strength, threatening neighbours and a hungry landless proletariat, it did not have a large protected internal market for which to manufacture on a large enough scale to make the new technology profitable. Nor did it have a timber shortage. "Plentiful supplies of wood fuel and water power encouraged prolonged commitment to the old technologies." (Trebilock. 1.) "The reluctance to adopt coke smelting for iron on the continent, initially anyway, was not due to inertia but was a proper reaction to the fact that it was an expensive process, producing poorcr iron than made with charcoal and only worth while when the supply of wood or the labour to process the wood, was very expensive to come by." (Milward and Saul. 1.)

The Great Spurt

In 1834 Prussia initiated the Zollverein, a customs union of north German states. This was followed by gradual monetary union. "In 1838 the Prussian thaler became the standard unit of all the northern states and the relation between the northern and southern units was fixed. By 1850s Prussian banknotes had become a method of payment preferred over the whole Zollverein, even in Bavaria." (Milward and Saul. 2.)

Basically, by the customs unions and common currency, Prussia's currency, Prussia was absorbing the smaller German states. "The disappearance of the customs gates meant the gradual merging of the state into Prussia, for such states retained an independence of action which was more judicial than actual." (Milward and Saul. 3.) Prussia was printing the money, exporting it to the smaller German states in return for their crops and goods. The other states got the paper money. Berlin got the crops and the goods.

151

Germany now had everything required for industrialisation, a starving population without land to be forced into the factories, a large internal market of non-self sufficient urban workers, a common currency to transmit the natural wealth from the periphery to the core, military strength and threatening neighbours.

It also, like America and Japan later, invested heavily in education and research. "After the middle of the 1830s, Germans made more major discoveries in energy, magnetism and optical research than did Frenchmen or Englishmen . . . By 1890 there were twice as many academic scientists in Germany as in Britain." (James.)

The first effect of the currency union was to widen the core/periphery effect. Previously each little state had been its own core and periphery. "The previous local Prussian tariffs had acknowledged the reality of commercial life in a state where each town was a separate local market and the countryside around it was subjected to its commercial domination." (Milward and Saul. 4.) The Zollverein, by removing local tariffs, opened up the whole country to a single domination by Berlin. Smaller cores, unprotected, became peripheries to the larger centres and they were de-industrialized. "de-industrialisation proved entirely possible, and so too did the emergence of deprived economic regions characteristic of the dual economy. Tipton argues that in Germany the evolution of industrial growth was 'competitive rather than complementary.'" (Trebilock. 2.)

As the population of the industrial core of Europe grew, the periphery, the agricultural countries which fed it, expanded: "in ever widening circles of mutual dependence the whole of industrialized Europe was being fed by an ever widening ring of agricultural producers whom it had itself encouraged and financed . . . In Russia, the end of serfdom in the 1860s allowed landlords and tax gatherers to press more heavily on the peasants so that an even larger proportion of the products was turned into cash by being sent abroad, overtaking early this century the exports of the USA. Even India and the Danube basin developed a grain surplus which was sent into industrial Europe." (Pollard.)

Germany did not choose to industrialise; it was forced to. To survive politically it needed the military technology. To survive economically it had to produce goods as cheaply as its competitors. It succeeded better than others because it had a larger population and therefore a larger internal market, and it invested more in education and research.

Russia

After the revolution of 1917 the peasants thought for a short time that they had achieved freedom. So they stopped sending their crops to the cities, and they refused to have their trees cut down. "Peasant control was established by the imposition of both blanket and partial prohibitions on access to the timber on the part of everyone who was not a member of the local peasant community. In imposing such bans the peasants rejected established defence requirements, commercial contracts and city and railway's needs for fuel as well, as in many cases, the requirements, of private landowners." (Gill.) So Lenin sent in the army and took the crops and the timber by force.

After Lenin's death Stalin took Russia on a crash course to industrialisation. Like Germany and Japan before them he realized that Russia was militarily vulnerable without high technology. The revolutionary regime had been under constant threat from the West and was so forced to build up a heavy war machine, financed both by indirect taxation and by direct food requisitions from the peasants as in the late Roman Empire. This was the 'mistake'. It did not increase the cost of living and therefore labour costs. So labour-saving machinery was not so necessary.

At the end of the Second World War Russia was able to extend its empire into the satellite states of Eastern Europe where it installed its own puppets, kept in power with Russian tanks. In this case the core, Russia, was less developed than its east European satellite periphery. Russia undertook the normal periphery function of the supply of raw materials while the satellites specialised in the core function of industry. It was an unstable situation. The core, to control its periphery, must have military superiority which derives from its industry. In the end a technologically more advanced periphery, because it has more money and technology, must be able to get free from the less advanced core. To keep control Russia would have to have gradually de-industrialised its satellites, transferring the industries to Russia, giving it the money and technology to maintain its power.

In the end Russia did not have enough money and lost control of Eastern Europe.

Mainly for military survival Stalin had determined to industrialise Russia. He started with certain advantages; and he did certain things right. Russia had a large population providing potential high internal demand and tax source; and it had plenty of natural resources including oil. Stalin had rightly built up the military strength. He rightly invested heavily in education and research, and he rightly, for his purposes, exploited the peasants unmercifully to produce the crop surplus.

But, instead of taxing the peasants to hand over the crops, he collectivised the farms, giving each farm directions on what and how much to produce to feed the army and the workers of the new industries. The quotas were so high and constantly increasing that there was little left for the peasants. "For example in 1946 in the midst of the drought, Ukrainian collective farmers were forced to deliver 400 million poods .

153

. . After that hunger and death inevitably awaited the Ukrainian peasants. They began to die by the thousand." (Heller and Neckrich.) Once again the industrialisation of the core is paid for by the starvation of the periphery.

Areas of Russia's periphery in the south were turned over almost completely to monocrop production such as cotton. Food was almost forbidden to be grown. They starved, and the overuse of herbicides, pesticides and chemical fertilizers have produced vast ecological disaster areas.

Stalin was also correct to cut Russia off from the rest of the financial world by making the rouble non-convertible. This gave protection to Russia's infant industries and it stopped the removal of Russia's natural wealth by other countries printing money. But Russia failed to establish the rouble as the common currency in its satellites of Eastern Europe. It was thus unable by printing roubles to remove significant wealth from them. It tried other methods: "The U.S.S.R. extracted from Eastern Europe more value than she provided in return (via reparations or excessively low prices paid, for example, for Polish coal.)" (Hutchings.) Russia was in the process of introducing the Transferable Rouble, issued by a bank in Moscow. But the satellites weren't using it. Given time and tanks, Russia might have succeeded but it's too late now.

Although the government revenue came mainly from indirect taxation, raised at factory and wholesale level, it was not enough to raise wages. Nor did the cowed population have the industrial muscle to demand higher wages through strikes. So Stalin failed to increase the cost of living and wages to make high technology profitable and necessary. Instead he reduced food prices and rents with subsidies.

Russia's failure is often ascribed to its command economy, that is to say one in which the government decides what should be produced rather than the consumer. Perhaps the command economy is inefficient, but Russia's failure was due much more to low labour costs that the command economy. Even if a free market replaced the command economy, without higher labour costs no greater success could have been achieved.

Gorbachev, aware of Russia's technological failure, introduced 'perestroika' – reconstruction – to try to catch up. He tried to reduce subsidies on food as a step towards the market economy. If he had had Stalin's ruthlessness it might have worked, but he ran out of time.

Because the USSR renounced religion, it had lost the justification of obedience to the government's laws. After that it could only maintain the obedience by the KGB's force. It has now also renounced that force and the constituent republics are therefore demanding back their power, and sometimes absolute independence. Some are sending less of their taxation to the centre, reducing the centre's power. They are sending less of their food to the centre, leaving Moscow's shelves empty.

But once they have achieved independence the republics will have to face the problem of their own smaller peripheries also demanding independence. To hold their republics together it is possible to see them reverting to religion again. One could foresee the Russian empire breaking up into four parts based on the four religions, catholic, uniate, orthodox and moslem.

America

So there's a pattern of one country forced by high labour costs to take the industrial lead by high expenditure on technology and therefore harder work. Other countries with lower labour costs are then forced by the cheaper products to follow suit. After Britain, America, with even higher labour costs, took over the lead, dragging the rest of the world unwillingly into high technology.

When settlers first went to America there was plenty of land; at least there was after they'd killed or driven the Indians off with their guns. As we have already seen, agriculturally they regressed because they didn't need the intensive techniques of European cultivation. But some regressed even further. The Appalachian Mountains blocked off the vast interior to the English settlers. But this mountain range stopped short of Canada so the French were not separated from the American interior as the English were. With access to the vast wilderness the French regressed, not to slash and burn agriculture, but even further to hunting and gathering. "While some became farmers many others followed the rich fur trade over thousands of miles They became creatures of the wood who lived (and thought) more like Indians than Europeans. The English, blocked from easy penetration inland in most areas, had to settle down to farming." (Garraty. 1.)

Because everyone could get land it was very difficult to find people who would work for other people. "Where grants of land were made to settlers in small lots at a nominal price or on easy credit terms, the society that developed was one of small cultivators, where few were inclined to work for wages." (Dobb. 9.) "The unskilled worker could command two or three shillings a day, compared to a shilling in England, while artisans and craftsmen could ask as much as eight shillings and sixpence." (Calder. 7.)

In the southern states the land was not allocated in small plots. "By contrast the sale of land in large blocks tended to create an economic society of large proprietors with a sharply defined class division between proprietors and propertyless." (Dobb. 10.)

So, although there were more landless workers, there were still jobs to be had on the land along with the negro slaves, and labour-saving technology was expensive and unnecessary. Therefore the north east of America became the industrial core and the south became the periphery.

In New England wages had to be high to attract labour, so labour costs were high and it was necessary to invent technology to reduce labour content in the product. "The comparative shortage of labour and the relatively high wages of the country encouraged the use of mechanical means of production." (Viljoen. 6.) They didn't choose to. They were forced to. "The introduction of agricultural machinery was the response to the challenge of conditions in America. The westward and urban drift of population made agricultural labour scarce and expensive at a time when the price of agricultural produce was falling. The farmer had to raise his labour productivity or go out of business." (Viljoen. 7.)

And that applied to their ships as well. "It was said that American ships operated even more economically than those of the Dutch." (Braudel. 23.) If an American shipper wanted to get business, his rates had to be as low or lower than the Dutch, so he was forced to spend money, i.e. work harder, to utilise technology that would reduce manpower on his ship, or carry a larger load per man. He didn't choose to; he was forced to. If foreign competition was reduced, there would be no need for the high expenditure. Technology would regress.

America put off using the new technologies as long as possible. Although steam engines had been known for decades, they still used the water power as long as it was cheaper, i.e. less work. "Until the second quarter of the (nineteenth) century, power from running water still predominated industrially over power from steam in Great Britain, and was still the main source for American manufacturing until the 1860s." (Roberts.)

For a society to become industrial there has to be a large landless proletariat, who can be forced into the factories. Although in America there was plenty of land, the high labour costs and necessary machinery forced the farmers to get rid of labour and send men back to the cities. Also New England farmers were under-cut by the cheaper grain of the Mid-West periphery and had to find work in the factories. And there was massive immigration: "growth in the United States population (rose) from approximately 31,000,000 in 1860 to 91,000,000 in 1910." (North). So there was a burgeoning landless proletariat ready for the factories.

"By 1860 Irish immigrants alone made up more than 50 per cent of the labour force in the New England mills. The influx of immigrants does not entirely explain the wretched state of industrial workers during this period. Low wages and the crowding that resulted from the swift expansion of city populations produced slums that would make

156

the most noisome modern ghetto seem a paradise . . . Yet within this rich, confident nation there existed a class of miserably underpaid and depressed unskilled workers, mostly immigrants who were worse off materially than nearly any southern slave." (Garraty. 4.)

America didn't join in the race for a colonial empire. She wasn't forced to, as the others were, because she had her own periphery which could supply all her necessary raw materials. "On the North American continent, indeed until the first decade of the present century, there was something that can be called 'internal colonialism' which goes far to explain the tardiness with which the USA turned attention to the spoils of the new Imperialism." (Dobb. 11.) The only difference was that with the new technology the core traders from the north eastern seaboard didn't need the aboriginal inhabitants to work the grain lands of the mid west. The Indians were superfluous and were killed or herded into reservations. In the southern states it was the pattern as before; the land owned by large landowners and worked by serfs, in this case negro slaves.

In 1857 there was an economic crisis caused by a sudden fall in grain prices, which is the recurring pattern: "During the summer of 1857 a panic struck the New York stock market heralding a sharp downturn in the economy . . . The return of Russian wheat to the world market after the Crimean War caused grain prices to fall. This checked agricultural expansion which hurt the railways and cut down on the demand for manufactures. People called this abrupt downturn the Panic of 1857." (Garraty. 2.)

In 1861 the southern states of America tried to secede. It was the same as this century's wars of independence against colonial masters, the periphery against the core. But in the American Civil War the southern states failed to get their independence. The South was the cotton-producing periphery for the core in the north. A periphery elite wants high prices for its crops and cheap industrial goods in return. The periphery makes its money on the crops, not industrial goods, so it doesn't like tariffs on imported manufactured goods to protect home industries. When one country has both core and periphery within it, there is a very strong conflict of interest. In America the South wanted low tariffs on imported products to keep them cheap. The North wanted high tariffs to protect their new industries. That was the underlying issue of the war, but it was complicated by the highly charged issue of slavery. The Southern periphery required cheap labour to grow its cotton. The Mid-west grain-growing periphery, becoming mechanised, did not need cheap labour, so while it would like cheap industrial products and therefore low tariffs and would not like high government expenditure on support for industry such as building a transport infrastructure, and therefore might side with the South, the other periphery area, it did not need the South's slaves and so on this emotional issue finally sided with the North. The North, with a larger taxable population to buy more guns, won.

By this time America had taken over from Britain as world leader in the technological drive, and all the other countries had to spend even more money trying to catch up. Because it now led the field with its cheaper products, it was in its interest to press for free trade to allow its cheaper goods into other countries without tariffs which protected their own industries. Similarly it was in the other countries' interests to maintain their mercantilist policies of protection for their industries against cheap American imports. When Britain had been technological leader, Free Trade had been in her interest. Having lost that lead, protection at least against America and Germany would have been more sensible. It ended up in a real muddle. America increased its protectionist policies and Britain, pressed by the academic Smithian economists continued with Free Trade. Sort of. 'Imperial Preference' muddled it even further.

Because America was both periphery and core, theoretically it had the option to withdraw from the rest of the world as China and Japan had done and as later Russia and her satellites did. But because it was technological leader it was in her greater economic (though not social) interest to trade with other countries. It would have been in the interests of the poor, not to increase trade, but to get back their land with low enough indirect taxation to make a small plot viable. They were given land at first but they faced the economic need for mechanisation; the high indirect taxation and therefore cost of living meant that the size of the viable farm kept increasing. The farmers were driven back to the cities.

After the end of the Great Depression in the 1890s things went well for the American traders, except for the two years of their First World War. And they didn't do too badly out of that either. But in 1929 there was a crash on the stock market and a depression for 10 years. The cause was, again, a drop in the grain price. "Production facilities had been expanded during the war to meet the huge demands and during the twenties there were further steady increases in agricultural productivity both in Europe and the peripheral areas of the world economy. But total demand was stagnant as population in Europe had ceased to grow and industrial output was depressed. Prices of agricultural products therefore began to fall in the second half of the twenties. This in turn was to reduce demand for the products of the industrial economies." (Harrison.) So the farmers couldn't pay back their loans to the banks, the banks went bankrupt and everyone put their money back under the bed again. The shortage of credit meant fewer were buying the factory goods so there was unemployment.

To maintain her position America had to build up her war machine. In international trade the profit is made on trading raw materials. The raw materials have to be produced by force. The local rulers who control these raw materials, and force their production, must feel secure against their exploited population and against predatory neighbours. So a core trading country must be able to provide military protection for a periphery ruler, or else that periphery ruler will start to trade with another core government who can provide stronger protection. The stronger a core country is, the greater number of periphery puppets will trade with that country since their protection is greater. So America built up her military machine. She was able to do this because she had a large population which she could hit with indirect taxes. "In the later nineteenth century the German Empire and the United States were major countries in which trade taxes yielded a substantial part of the revenue of the central government." (Gould. 4.)

Because of her great military strength America was able to attract the trade of many who had previously been British puppets particularly in South America in the nineteenth century. After her devotion to freedom and equality, trumpeted during the War of Independence and the Civil War, she was a bit embarrassed at having to support, for reasons of trade, some fairly insalubrious dictators in South America. But it's only dictators that can force the raw materials to be produced.

After the western world had pretty well exterminated the whale population in its search for whale oil, it was forced to dig for geological oil. Large discoveries in Texas gave America the world lead in oil trading. But when oil was discovered in the Middle East it was American military strength that persuaded the Middle Eastern oil potentates to price their oil in dollars and give America the trading profits. For a while Britain's military strength persuaded Iran and Iraq and the emirates to trade through Britain. But gradually they are transferring to America. The Gulf War will complete the transfer.

A core country's tax-paying population doesn't usually understand that the raw materials on which it depends have to be produced by force. So it doesn't understand why periphery puppets have to be supported, or the need for the consequent military machine. So a military threat, or a trumped up one such as Russia, can be very useful to multinational traders in providing the excuse for the heavy taxation to pay for guns to protect their dubious puppets.

Genuine nationalist reform movements which threatened American profits were labelled 'communist' and put down with American help leaving the dictator to continue exporting the crops and the profits. As an American general said, "He may be a son-of-a-bitch, but at least he's our son-of-a-bitch."

So America became the technological, commercial and military leader, not because it created wealth by its technological inventiveness but because it had a large landless proletariat, a large taxable population, so a large internal demand, a protected industry, high labour costs increased by high indirect taxation and a large military machine.

China

China and Japan offer an interesting contrast. By the 1850s neither was in any doubt about the technological and military threat from the 'western barbarians'. China did nothing. Japan did everything it could to catch up. China had its own periphery to supply its raw materials. Japan did not, so its spur was greater. Nevertheless China's inability to react to the threat was staggering.

The cause was probably the system of values and government which was ideal for producing a continuing stability with its emphasis on not rocking the boat. But these ideals were totally unsuited to a situation which demanded change, with pressure coming from outside. Resistance to change which had produced stability for three thousand years was inappropriate when change was vital. China couldn't change quickly enough.

Most of the Chinese government's income came from the peasants' crops. Only a very small proportion came from indirect taxes on trade, collected and paid over by the merchants. "The Ming and Ch'ing governments got their major sustenance from the land tax, not from trade taxes." (Fairbank and Reischauer. 4.) So the merchants had no influence. The Chinese peck order put the scholars at the top, then the farmers, then the artisans. At the bottom were the derided merchants. "Confucian doctrine held merchants to be social parasites." (McNeill. 5.) The Chinese rulers did not depend on loans from the merchants as they did in Europe. External trade was all but forbidden. So the merchants had no influence by increasing government income with indirect taxation on trade or providing loans. So they could exert no pressure to build up a navy to protect their trade or a transport infrastructure within the country which was not of direct military use.

The government, deriving its income from the vast peasantry, expended considerably more effort than the Europeans in ensuring that the peasants had enough land to produce the rulers' surplus. There was thus a very small urban population to man the factories. The peasantry was self-sufficient and so provided no internal demand for manufactured goods.

To change, China would have needed to replace direct taxation on the peasants to an indirect taxation on trade. This would have produced the pressure for land enclosure to increase cash-cropping, driving the peasants off the land and into the city factories, where, no longer self-sufficient, they would provide the internal demand for manufactured goods. To increase income the government would no longer forbid foreign trade and would need to build up its navy to protect that trade. The low status of the merchant precluded such policies.

Japan

Japan is a small country with a high population, few raw materials, a lot of mountains and not much agricultural land. At the beginning of the sixteenth century the Tokugawa regime, to protect its position, forbade all foreign trade: "a samurai clan leader, dispossessed in the wars at home, might recoup his fortunes by a successful piratical cruise and might even return home rich enough to try his hand at regaining what had been lost in earlier struggles . . . Accordingly the Tokugawa shoguns first regulated and then forbade sea roving entirely." (McNeill. 6.)

For three centuries Japan remained cut off from the rest of the world, feeding itself, just, by highly labour-intensive agriculture, supporting a small elite with few towns or specialists.

Then in 1853 American ships entered a Japanese harbour and demanded to be allowed to trade. Their guns persuaded Japan to agree. Japan quickly became aware of the western military threat. In 1868 the Tokugawa regime was replaced by a government dedicated to rapid modernisation. Teams of experts were sent off to Europe and America to learn their expertise. Every effort was made in education, research, military build-up to compete with the West. Within a hundred years Japan had become the commercial leader of the world.

Because Japan had so few natural resources and agricultural land, it wasn't a target as a potential colony. It had no value as a periphery to any core. Therefore her elite never had the option of making money by selling crops and discouraging local industry by allowing in better manufactured goods from a core without tariffs. There was no elite to benefit by resisting industrialisation. The elite was therefore unanimous in creating a local industry with tariff protection.

Japan didn't know too much about Adam Smith, so the government felt no constraints about taking a leading position in the modernisation. Perhaps the most important change was the increased income government took from indirect taxation. Though it continued to tax the peasants heavily, it also increased taxation on trade so that the percentage of indirect taxes on trade rose from 20% to 75% in twenty years. This increased the cost of living, making investment in labour-saving machinery necessary.

161

What drove them was the Western military threat, so their first priority was to build up their army and navy and then to ensure their supply of raw materials by getting themselves an empire. Trade was just the means of acquiring money to buy guns; mercantilism again.

The government used every possible means to build up its military and commercial power: "these included the exploitation of women and children factory operatives, the onerous taxation of peasants, the brutal drilling of military recruits, the development of an intellectually stifling, narrowly étatiste education system, the waging of war and the enslavement by colonisation of neighbours." (Lehman. 3.)

To solve its supply of raw materials it started building an empire in Korea, Manchuria and the islands of the south-west Pacific. It even tried to take over China. It entered the war against America to protect and increase that empire.

It was doing nearly everything right, everything necessary to be technological, commercial and military leader. But it tried to do it too fast. It was a mistake to confront America at Pearl Harbour before it had built up an empire with a sufficiently large tax base and supply of raw materials. If it had entered the war on the Allies' side, it might have been able to extend its empire into China as the Russians did in Eastern Europe; and without the ideological Marxist trappings Japan could have installed compliant puppets as America does on South America.

America ended the war in the Pacific by dropping two atomic bombs on Japan. The devastating results have left Japan with a strong peace movement which will make it almost impossible to build up a strong enough military machine necessary to protect potential puppets.

Japan is commercially successful because it is hungrier: "only Japan of the developed countries has a figure of less than 3000 calories per caput per day." (Grigg.) It is working harder because its cost of living and taxation is higher: "about 80% of the people are bearing the burden of heavy taxation and exorbitant prices for housing, land, food, clothing and other products and services, where markets are shielded from foreign competition. The average Japanese earns about the same income as his or her American counterpart. But the Japanese must work almost five times as long to buy half a kilogram of fish, five times as long for half a kilogram of rice, nine times as long to buy half a kilogram of beef and three times as long for four litres of gasolene." (Tsurumi.)

Its labour costs are far higher than its local competitors': "Its workers, on the whole earned about six times as much as Taiwanese workers and ten times as much as Koreans. For countries further afield in South East Asia or especially the Indian sub-continent, the disparity could be as much as fifteen or twenty to one." (Woronoff. 1.) And its labour costs are still increasing rapidly: "Whereas Japanese workers were only earning about a tenth as much as Americans in 1950, it was closer to a fifth in 1960 and a quarter in 1970. By the end of the decade they were only earning about a quarter less than the Americans. But this was already about a quarter more than British or Italian workers received." (Woronoff. 2.)

Japan, driven harder than anyone else by its high taxation, high cost of living and high labour costs, is now the technological leader setting the pace. And we are all forced to follow or go bankrupt.

The Trading Blocks

This century the world has been split up into three major cores with their peripheries, America, Europe and Russia. With the end of the Cold War and Russia's bankruptcy the two remaining cores will consolidate their territories. It has been suggested that Japan might replace Russia as a third core, so that there would be three major trading areas, the yen area of the West Pacific, the dollar area of North and South America and the euro area of Europe and its periphery in Africa.

But since Japan will probably not be able to spend enough on arms, its potential periphery puppets will not have the confidence that they can depend on Japan's support against threatening neighbours, or Japan's support to suppress internal dissent. So they will stick with America; and so will Japan itself.

We are likely to see a great deal of competition for the trading rights of the crops of the various periphery puppets between American and Europe.

If Europe is able to increase its military spending sufficiently, the Middle East and its oil, because of its antipathy to America over Israel, might join Europe. Perhaps China would join Japan and America. India, with its links with Russia, might join Europe. And so on.

While Europe is already trying to establish a single currency as a single trading block, America is starting the process with Canada and Mexico.

Canadians are faced with the dilemma of a periphery country close to the core. They've been told that they can all be rich if they have more economic growth. But they can't get more economic growth without more consumers to buy their products. Their population is not large enough to buy enough goods to make investment into mass production profitable. Without mass production they can't get 'rich'; without a large population they can't get mass production. So they need the large, rich American population.

But if America is to allow Canada to sell its products to America, free of tariffs, Canada has to do the same. Canada risks its industry being destroyed by cheaper American products. Already Canadians are flocking across the border to buy cheaper American manufactured goods, putting the Canadian manufacturers out of business.

Some Canadians will benefit. Some will lose. The closer a periphery country is to a core, the more it will benefit, though it is still a minority. Big Canadian businesses will have a large enough production to compete successfully with smaller American businesses. But the smaller Canadian businesses will close. So workers in the large businesses will benefit. Workers in the small businesses will be made unemployed. But because America subsidises its farmers so highly, Canadian farmers are likely to suffer too. In general the richer benefit from the union. The poorer are worse off. The further from the core the more the poor are made poorer.

If the union of Canada and America was the end of the matter, Canada would lose out badly. It would become just the agricultural periphery, its population made superfluous by machinery. But what America has in mind is a trading block comprising the whole continent of North and South America. This would mean not only an expanded periphery but also an expanded core and Canada would be included in that expanded core. It would be part of the exploiting industrial core rather than the exploited agricultural periphery.

So it is strongly in Canada's interest to persuade other countries like Mexico to join the group, so that it is Mexico rather than Canada that becomes the exploited periphery. (It is the same pattern as the peasant who leaves his village to go to the city and whose interests then change to exploiting the villages for his food.) Mexico would then want others like Central America to join and allow Mexico to shift periphery status out on to them.

The only alternative that Canada has is to close its frontiers and become self-sufficient, to stop all external trade. This would mean a regression of technology because its manufacturers no longer would need to compete with cheaper American goods. There would be no incentive or profit to invest in labour-saving technology. But this would put Canada in considerable danger of military aggression by a technologically superior neighbour. America could invent an excuse and devour Canada in one easy gulp, unless all the population is armed, which is a whole new ball game. Individual self-sufficiency close to the core and under the present political system is not a practical option.

So they're forced to join with America. They will be better off, not because they're joining America but because Mexico will be joining too.

Size is important but it is also important that the large population is rich. Artisans have always worked for the rich, not the poor. When

Mexico joins there will be an internal market of over 300 million, many of them rich. Although China has over a billion people, most of them are partly self-sufficient with little buying power for manufactured goods. So they don't offer so many opportunities for mass production. America, Canada and Mexico will have a higher number of non-self-sufficient consumers and no trade taxes, allowing manufacturers to sell far more goods and therefore to profit from investment in mass production.

The European Union

The European countries are also well aware that individually none has sufficient population to make the necessary high tech investment profitable. Faced with the cheaper American and Japanese products, the European countries, singly, would be bankrupted. So we're all swallowing our national pride and trying to find a commercial union, with Africa as our major periphery. Presumably Russia and the Balkans will also perform this function. The strength of the two blocks will be determined by the size of their peripheries. As in ancient Greece, "the larger the plain, the larger the city".

It is the removal of the customs barriers that has always created the empire, as we saw in Germany in 1832. "The disappearence of the customs gates meant the gradual merging of the state into Prussia for such states retained an independence of action which was more judicial than actual." (Milward and Saul. 3.) In 1992 the customs barriers came down in Europe. After which the process is just a matter of tidying up.

Britain is resisting every step of the way. But the economic and military logic of the present system will force her to join and take a full part. She had been the core to her own trading block, the British Empire, but she dropped her previous colonies when she signed the Treaty of Rome. She had tried to join a block separate from the European Economic Community, EFTA, comprising other periphery countries like Norway, Sweden and Austria, but they didn't have sufficient population, consumer demand, to make it economically viable.

The running is being made by the large businesses who, as in Canada, have the most to gain with an enlarged market of consumers. The small businesses will be closed down. As long as Africa and Russia can be incorporated in the community as the periphery, Britain on the whole should gain.

Once the customs barriers are down the real battle will be for the peripheries, a battle probably fought with money rather than guns. Governments of the Third World and Eastern Europe will join the trading block which offers them more "aid" or military aid or other bribes to allow their populations to be starved.

There is a great deal of discussion about how many countries the Community should include. The present Community's problem is that it believes its own rhetoric about the benefits to everyone. So it spends a great deal on regional aid, sending resources from the core to the periphery. It doesn't yet understand the contradiction. A core can't be rich without exploiting the periphery. If you help the periphery the core suffers. To make the system work the periphery has to be exploited, not helped. So the Community, to be economically strong, needs a large periphery to exploit, ie. more poor countries joining the community. But if it has got to give them regional aid, it needs less poor countries. As we shall see with the Third World, aid can be very successful in increasing economic development and therefore poverty. So the contradiction will be resolved with aid which exploits, and rich members will recognise the benefits of increasing membership to the poorer countries.

References

H. Böhme. "An Introduction to the Social and Economic History of Germany". Blackwell. '78. p.22.

F. Braudel. "The Perspective of the World". Collins. '84. 23: p.410.

A. Calder. "Revolutionary Empire". Jonathan Cape. '81. 7: p.393.

M. Dobb. "Studies in the Development of Capitalism". Routledge & Kegan Paul. '46. 9: p.221., 10: p.221., 11: p.313.

Fairbank and Reischauer. "China". Allen & Unwin. '89. 4: p.199.

J.A. Garraty. "The American Nation. The history of the United States." Harper Row. '83. 1: p.28., 2: p.350 and p.334., 4: p.322 and 324.

G.J. Gill. "Peasants and Government in the Russian Revolution". MacMillan. '79. p.106.

J.D. Gould. "Economic Growth in History". Methuen '72. 4: p.219.

D. Grigg. "The World Food Problem." Blackwell. '85. p.19.

A. Harrison. "The Framework of Economic Activity". MacMillan. '67. p.19.

M. Heller and A. Neckrich. "Utopia in Power." Hutchinson. '86. p.468.

R. Hutchings. "Soviet Economic Development". Blackwell. '82. p.88.

H. James. "A German Identity. 1700–1990". Weidenfeld & Nicholson. '89. p.69.

H.W. Koch. "A History of Prussia". Longman. '78. p.224.

J.P. Lehman. "The Roots of Modern Japan." MacMillan. '82. 3: p.198.

C. Lis and H. Soly. "Poverty and Capitalism in Pre-industrial Europe". Harvester Press. '79. 14: p.159.

W.H. McNeill. "A World History". O.U.P. '79. 5: p.225., 6: p.365.

A.S. Milward and S.B. Saul. "The Economic Development of Continental Europe. 1780-1870". George Allen & Unwin. '79. 1: p.173., 2: p.385., 3: p.374., 4: p.373.

D. North. in "The Cambridge Economic History of Europe". Vol IV. C.U.P. '65. p.693.

S. Pollard. "European Economic Integration. 1815-1970". Thames & Hudson. p.33.

J. Roberts. "Revolution and Improvement." Weidenfeld and Nicholson. '76. p.153.

C. Trebilock. "The Industrialisation of the Continental Powers. 1780-1914". Longman. '81. 1: p.38., 2: p.49.

Yoshi Tsurumi. Los Angeles Times. 25.1.88.

S. Viljoen. "Economic Systems in World History". Longman. '74. 6: p.178., 7: p.184.

J. Woronoff. "Japan's Commercial Empire." MacMillan '85. 1: p.209., 2: p.205.

Chapter 11
THE THIRD WORLD

THROUGHOUT HISTORY as the core developed, its periphery starved to feed that core. And so it starves today. The periphery of the developed world has spread to the furthest corners of the Third World. The important difference is that today the starvation takes place in full glare of television. They are dying on camera. So it is no longer possible to deny that the periphery is starving, or to ignore it. It is getting increasingly difficult to blame it on the natives' apathy, or stupidity, or laziness, or lack of knowledge or all the other excuses used by the core to justify the continued expropriation of the crops.

The first thing the core needs from its periphery is timber. One country after another is now being logged out. Thailand has lost 80% of its forests in the last 20 years. The rainforests are being felled in the Amazon Basin. "Perhaps half our rain forests have been destroyed since 1950 and it is quite possible that there will be none left by the early years of the 21st century." (Trainer. 1.) "West African records suggest that Ivory Coast has lost 70% of its forests this century, Ghana 64% and Liberia 69%. As much as two thirds of West Africa's former forests may have disappeared." (Pearce.)

Once the forests are cleared the next demand is for grain and cattle. But because of mechanisation, refrigeration and cheaper transport, the pattern has changed in some ways. In earlier core/periphery relationships the periphery inhabitants were needed to work the soil. Laws were made to force the peasants to stay in the villages. Today machines have replaced human labour so that the inhabitants of the periphery are no longer of use to the core and can be allowed to migrate to the cities, or starve to death. "Increasingly the world witnesses countries in which one third to one half of the population is needed neither for production nor for consumption. Starvation is one end which awaits them." (Borosage.)

Because of cheap transport and refrigeration many of the high-value inner, market garden crops which quickly deteriorated such as fruit and vegetables, and even cut flowers, can now be grown on the cheaper land of the periphery. What has not changed is that by whatever means (this time an economic theory) the periphery is still being forced to provide the crops which the core depends on for its survival.

Neo-Colonialism

After the Second World War fought, they said, in defence of freedom, self-determination and all the other political virtues, it was a bit difficult for the colonial empires to justify their continued occupation of the Third World.

America, not disinterestedly, put the boot in. The empires were able to exclude the manufactured goods of other empires and countries like America. America wanted to get into these markets. During the war Britain needed American money and support. The price was the end of its empire. The Atlantic Charter agreed by Churchill and Roosevelt in 1941 promised that after the allies won the war they would "respect the right of all people to choose the form of government under which they would live."

With various degrees of good grace the empires gave up their colonial territories. Colonialism was ended and neo-colonialism began. Instead of using colonial governors to remove the crops, local puppet rulers were installed and backed up with investment, 'aid', military support for their troops, counter-insurgency and police training to suppress dissent and keep the rulers in power in exchange for the continued supply of raw materials to the core.

Our government had to provide an intellectual justification for the continued removal of the crops. They could no longer go in, like the older civilisations and ravage the countries, nor could they colonise them and claim that they were converting uneducated savages to Christianity. Their intellectuals had rejected Christianity. So Jesus was no longer available as a justification. But they still had Adam Smith.

The first thing a Third World puppet is concerned about is survival. If bigger countries have bigger guns and better technology, if his neighbours are spending large sums on weapons, he can justifiably feel threatened and must spend equally large sums on weapons. It is partly about status, but much more about survival. Like countries in Europe in the nineteenth century he has to keep up technologically.

So the puppet rulers were pleased to be told that if they exported their crops, they would have the money to invest in the 'wealth-creating' machinery and then they could be as rich as the West and buy as many guns.

Development

Enthusiastically, and understandably, they embraced development. But development doesn't help the poor. Development means producing goods for those who have the money to buy them. The poor don't have the money so the goods are not made for them. "Extensive industries have indeed been developed; but these are industries mainly serving the rich few in the cities of the Third World and transferring resources and wealth out to the consumers and shareholders in the developed nations. The development that has taken place has not involved growth of the industries that would provide safe drinking water, iron hoes and mobile health clinics for the peasantry." (Trainer. 2.)

So development is good only for the ruling elites and their middle classes in the Third World. And it is good for the developed world to the extent that the investment produces profits and increases the supply of crops. Some workers in the cities of the Third World benefit, if work for miserable wages in atrocious conditions and long hours can be considered a benefit. But it's better than starvation. Those who really suffer are the local craftsmen and the peasant farmers.

The theory said that if the Third World increased its export of cash crops, it could buy the machinery to create economic growth. Teams of planners and economists fresh out of business school trotted off to the Third World, at the Third World's expense, to advise how to increase the volume of exportable crops, and how to spend the money on 'wealth-creating' factories, transport infrastructure, banking systems, administration etc.

The planners' ideas which benefited the core worked; those which were supposed to benefit the Third World didn't. Much has been made of the spectacular failure of some of the agricultural projects such as the ground nuts schemes in East Africa and Nigeria. But that is to miss the point. Most of the agricultural projects were splendidly 'successful'. The poor were driven off their land and vast acreages were devoted to growing crops for export. Millions of dollars, pounds and francs were spent building roads from these areas down to the ports to decant the crops; money, from the core's point of view, very profitably spent. And starvation inevitably increased because the land was growing crops for export and not food for the people.

Investment

The rulers and their western planners quickly realized that the Third World countries did not have enough money, either to buy the agricultural machinery, or to build the infrastructure. So they borrowed from the West in the false expectation that the 'wealth' created by the machinery would pay back the loans and leave masses of profit in the country as well. But as we have seen, machines don't create wealth.

When core investors invest their money in the periphery, it is because they want to make a profit, that is, they want to take more money out of the country than they put in. The local elites like this investment because, although in general it impoverishes a country, some of the profits stick to their own grubby hands. In South America: "Presidential autocrats discovered that one of the surest supports for their regimes was the favour of foreign investors and commercial enterprises. Foreign money enabled the Caudillo to enrich his friends and to win over some at least of his enemies." (Pendle. 3.)

The foreign investors then took out their profit from the country and not only was there no profit left for the country itself but more was taken out than was created. The country was poorer. Today between $40 and $50 billion are being siphoned out of the Third World every year. So a few are made richer by foreign investment. The many are made poorer.

The poverty was so obvious that the local elites had to work overtime trying to convince their populations that if they went hungry today they would have jam tomorrow. They happily parrotted the western economists. For example Jaime Carral Pinson said, "You need investment because you cannot fund development with internal investment. You have to invite investors to operate in Mexico."

Loans

Their loans have worked well for the West too. The Third World has borrowed so much that no one believes it can ever be repaid. The banks, although concerned at first, now see that the loans could be a source of endless profit.

The smallholder who over the centuries got into a similar impossible situation of incurring unrepayable debt to a local landowner simply spent the rest of his life working for the landowner to pay the interest but never the capital, and the debtor's sons spent their lives, too, working for the landowner as semi slaves. Perhaps the debt was never repaid as such but the landowner profited a thousandfold, until a revolution or political reform freed the debtor's progeny. So the Third World, if the political status quo can be maintained, could stay shackled to the banks forever, paying the endless interest but never the capital. The banks would be quite happy with such a situation.

The Third World puppets can do nothing because they hold their power with the core's guns. If they attempt to repudiate the debt, they lose the guns and their power and, if they're unlucky, their heads. The West would then support with money and guns any rebel who offered to continue paying the interest.

What will worry the banks is if a province declares secession from a debtor country, as in Yugoslavia. It would be very much more difficult for the banks to press a legal case against the seceding province for debts incurred by the central government, and more difficult to impose the same interest on the remaining smaller country. So the banks will always resist any demand for freedom and secession by a province of a debtor country.

The debts give another hold by the West over the Third World. In return for Egypt's support against Iraq the West has cancelled billions of their debt. Some of the cancellation has been postdated to keep Egypt in line.

Aid

The USA has mountains of surplus wheat and maize caused by subsidies to its farmers. This surplus it distributes to the countries it has impoverished by development. The food aid is then used to increase the impoverishment by making the aid dependent on further development. It is just another bribe to the puppet to increase the supply of crops to the core.

Bangladesh is one of the poorest countries in the world. It is also one of the most fertile, some areas producing three crops of rice a year and a crop of fish on top of that. But the people do not own the crops which are taken to feed the elite and their cities. Much of Bangladesh's land is devoted to growing jute which is exported by western companies very profitably. To maintain this status quo Bangladesh receives a great deal of aid. Half the government's income comes from aid of all sorts; a quarter of that is food aid: "nearly half of all government expenditure comes from foreign aid of all kinds. Aid has taken the dominant place once held by land taxation in government revenue. Its level and continuity are a central concern of government. Food aid alone contributes approximately 13 per cent of government resources." (Friedmann. 1.)

"The West needs to keep Bangladesh within its sphere of influence and does this by using aid to maintain a sympathetic regime in power . . . Aid is an easy way for the government to find money for projects which benefit a few people, rather than by raising taxation rates for the 10% of the people who own half the agricultural land. The British government keeps the rich in power and does not use its influence to direct government policy towards helping the poor." (Leamonth and Rolt. 1.) A senior British aid adviser said: "The closer people get to an aid project, the more the difference between rich and poor increases as the rich benefit from all the aid inputs." He resigned. (Leamonth and Rolt. 2.)

Aid is directed to increasing development, ie. the export of crops, never to land reform. The Bangladeshi water projects concentrate on protecting the cities rather than the peasants. The electric grid benefits the middle classes with money to spend on electrical goods. Bread is subsidised – in the cities. "food aid is directly instrumental in providing basic staples to the entire population of six major urban centres in Bangladesh . . . a basic supply of rice, wheat, sugar, edible oils and kerosene is guaranteed to all households through the issue of ration cards. This ration is extended to cover all government employees wherever they are posted in Bangladesh, workers in state enterprises and large industrial units, students residential in college and university hostels, government school teachers and all personnel of the armed forces and other related law and order agencies." (Alavi. 1.)

America, with its food aid, has now taken over from Britain as Bangladesh's major donor and therefore the major recipient of its crop trade. Because of its power through aid it can force its policies on Bangladesh. In 1974 Bangladesh wanted to sell jute sacks to Cuba. America didn't like that, so halted all food aid and for a year watched Bangladesh starve. "No U.S. food aid arrived until late 1974. Famine deaths had reached a peak at which they were to remain for most of 1975." (Friedmann. 2.) Bangladesh stopped exporting the jute sacks to Cuba and the American food aid was resumed.

The American food aid programme (USAID) is directed specifically to force recipient countries to embrace 'development', ie. the export of crops. "Amongst many 'successes,' USAID claims its use of food aid leverage has: determined agricultural policy in Pakistan and food policy in Bangladesh; guaranteed the Camp David accords; and sustained and influenced governments in Sri Lanka, Peru, Jamaica and Haiti." (Friedmann. 3.)

Aid given by Oxfam and the other aid agencies is genuine and, though they will admit it was earlier misdirected into development, is now fulfilling a real need for short term emergency help. But government aid is not genuine at all. Much of it never even leaves the donor countries. It is tied to buying the donor country's manufactured goods. Fine for the Third World elites, but what the poor want is food. Another large chunk of aid goes to military assistance, training counter-insurgency policing, ie. suppressing dissent. The rest is spent on development, building up the infrastructure, electricity, roads, ports to facilitate the export of more crops from the periphery to the core. On one of the few occasions that aid has been used to give land to the poor, Britain in its financial assistance stipulated that the Zimbabweans continue to use the land to grow tobacco for export.

Military Aid

Once religion has been able to obtain obedience from the population, military aid is the most important component for the exploitation of the periphery by the core. It is military aid which keeps the periphery puppet in power, and every other form of exploitation devolves from that.

Britain, France and Russia have been important suppliers of arms to the Third World, but way above them all has been America. This is because of America's democratic pretensions. Britain and France gained their economic dominance by direct rule in their empires. They didn't need to support puppets with guns. America, unwilling to build an empire, had to obtain the rights to trade the Third World crops by installing puppets rather than ruling directly. Thus it had to spend much more money and energy propping up client states.

Sometimes the intervention is quite blatant. "Since 1945 the USA intervened on average once every 18 months somewhere in the world. This included Iran, 1953, Guatemala, 1954, Lebanon, 1958, Thailand, 1959, Laos, 1959, Cuba, 1961, British Guyana, 1963, South Vietnam, 1964, Brazil, 1964, Dominican Republic, 1965, Cambodia, 1968, Laos, 1968, Chile, 1973, and Jamaica 1975. British interventions included Egypt, 1955, Malaya, 1948, Aden, 1963, Brunei, 1966–78. French intervention included French Indo-China, 1946, Algeria, 1956, and continuously with troops since independence in Senegal, Ivory Coast, Mauretania, Central African Republic, Chad and Zaire." (New Internationalist).

Covert intervention is going on all the time. In Chile: "Full public confessions have proved among other things that the U.S. government directly participated in Chilean politics by bribery, espionage and blackmail. The strategy for the crime was planned in Washington. Kissinger and the intelligence services were carefully preparing the fall of Allende ever since 1970. Millions of dollars were distributed among the enemies of the legal Popular Unity government (ie. Allende's government)." (Galleano.)

Military aid is also given in the form of training of their soldiers and policemen both on the spot and back in the core countries where the sons of the tyrants and generals are welcomed at the officer training academies. America runs many training camps for the soldiers of South American countries. "Since 1949, 33,534 Latin American soldiers and police have passed through the U.S. Army's Fort Gulick in the Canal Zone where they have been taught among other things counter-insurgency and free enterprise economic theory." (Trainer. 3.)

The Policies That Failed

The success of forced development, loans, military and economic aid was clear. The profits flowed from the underdeveloped world to the West, from the periphery to the core. But the policies that the economists recommended for the underdeveloped world's benefit failed, again and again.

The failure for a long time was disguised by the oil crisis, and for twenty years before that by the West's orgy of printing money and credit which increased world demand so that the effects weren't temporarily as bad as they became later. From about 1950 the economic theories of J.M. Keynes were globally influential. He said that the lack of economic growth, and hence unemployment, was caused by a lack of demand – people didn't have enough money in their pockets to buy the products of the factories. So he suggested that the governments borrow money, or print it, to employ people to do whatever they think needs doing – digging holes and filling them in would be enough – to put money in people's pockets and get the factories going again. He thought that this would produce an 'engine for growth' and that the factories would then produce their own momentum and the government could take back out of circulation the money they had borrowed to get the thing moving.

For twenty years governments of the developed world borrowed money and spent it, printed money and spent it. There was a boom, and for twenty years the Third World received a few crumbs from this boom. But printing money and creating credit, not backed by money withdrawn elsewhere, creates inflation. Elites can live happily and profitably with 2 or 3% inflation. They borrow money and have to pay back less because of the inflation. Inflation at that level only hurts the poor who cannot borrow, and see their small nest egg dwindle in value. But higher inflation makes the ruling elites look too obviously incompetent and threatens the whole financial system by undermining confidence.

Then Milton Friedman and his colleagues said that printing money causes inflation, but that, instead, a return to pure Adam Smith, no government interference and a totally free market, would create a non-inflationary economic growth. So governments stopped printing so much money. It did not produce economic growth. Factories do not generate their own momentum. They need a constant infusion of tokens for food and the other necessities of life for which the workers work. So the twenty year boom ended.

Then the true horror of the economic set-up began to strike the Third World. But this time the West was able to blame the oil crisis. The increasing demand for oil enabled the oil sheiks to increase their prices dramatically. Most Third World countries had to import oil. The sheiks, awash with oil profits, lent their money through the international banks to the Third World. Then developed world governments, still trying to control inflation, increased interest rates and the Third World, having to pay these extra rates on all their extravagant loans, were finally faced with the full extent of their financial disaster. Their industries had been destroyed by the cheap imports from the core. Their agriculture was growing crops for the core and not food for themselves; they were so deeply in debt that they could see no way to pay it off. And nor can anyone else.

175

The failure of the economists' plans to help the Third World started with the assumption that if the GDP (the Gross Domestic Product, the total of financial transactions) was increased, the country was richer. If a peasant increases the amount of food he grows, and eats it, that food is not traded and does not appear in the statistics. It does not increase the GDP. If on the other hand he grows more food and is forced to sell it for cash to pay taxes to the government, he ends up with neither the food nor the cash. He is no better fed. But the sold food appears as an increase in trade. The GDP goes up and the economists claim that the country is richer and by implication better fed, even though the peasants have not benefited. "A recent study prepared for the International Labour office concludes that, in those very Asian countries where yields have gone up, where per capita GNP has gone up, precisely there 20% to 80% of the population is eating less." (I.F.D.P.)

The United Nations was finally forced to admit that, at the least, a rising GDP was an insufficient criterion. From that it moved to employment creation and income redistribution, and then to Basic Needs, an idea pushed by the left but still requiring to be achieved by government spending, which can only be found from increased economic growth, increased GDP.

Poverty by Agricultural Development

The effects of development in the Third World have varied according to the distance from the core. Out on the periphery the first tentacles of development are the roads pushing through the virgin forest. The trees are cut down and transported back along the roads to the core. The minister and his friends make millions by selling licences to contractors to sell the timber to the West.

The forest people lose everything. Originally an 'affluent society', the whole basis of their affluence, the forest, is gone. Their food and fuel had been free. But now their nut and fruit trees are cut down. The habitat of the animals which they hunted is destroyed. Then they are decimated by imported disease against which they have built up no resistance. They suffer social disruption by the arrival of money which sets one man in competition with another. Their survival no longer depends on mutual co-operation but individual possession of cash. Money has brought the dog-eat-dog society. Social sanctions are weakened, so difficult behaviour like drunkenness increases, the brunt of which the women bear. Not even the developers pretend that western development benefits these hunter-gatherers in any way.

Nearer the core where cultivation has already happened as forest or bush fallow, the tribespeople with no legal title to their land, since they have no concept of land ownership, are evicted. Without the shared ownership of land and shared responsibility for feeding everyone, the pressure to maintain population stability is removed and the population starts to increase.

In the next band closer to the core were the subsistence farmers. It was these lands that had been turned over to grain for the core and the farmers turned into slaves and serfs. The cheaper grain had forced those closer to the core to abandon grain-growing and turn to cattle and sheep farming. The final band closest to the core had grown the perishable, high value crops like fruit and vegetables. Today cheap transport and refrigeration have amalgamated all these bands. "Three quarters of American fruit and vegetable consumption originates in the Third World." (Trainer. 4.) "In effect, Africa is being converted into a farm for exporting luxury crops such as flowers, protein-rich legumes and even meat." (Perelman.) "three times a week from early December until May, a chartered cargo DC10 takes off from Senegal's dusty airport loaded with eggplants, green beans, tomatoes, melons and paprika. It's destination? Amsterdam, Paris or Stockholm. These airlifts of food from the African Sahel began in 1972, the fourth year of the region's publicised drought. They increased dramatically as the famine spread." (Collins and Lappé.) "In Africa production of food for local consumption remained almost stagnant from 1950–70 and per capita consumption has been falling, but export production has risen at up to 4% p.a." (Trainer. 5.) "In Latin America per capita production of subsistence crops decreased 10% between 1964 and 1974 while per capita production of export crops . . . increased by 27%" (Trainer. 5.)

"In Algeria, to offer one example among many, the French took more and more fertile land for producing wine to send across the Mediterranean to France. But the land they took was land on which Algerians, before, had grown an abundance of food for themselves. So the Algerians had less food, just at the time when their numbers were growing bigger. It has been calculated that the amount of food in cereals, available to an average Algerian person in 1945, was little more than half the amount in 1900." (Davidson. 4.)

"Consumers in advanced economies depend on food exports from the Third World. Workers depend on cheap meat products from land once used by peasants, and privileged consumers benefit from the 'strawberry imperialism' that devotes large fertile areas and outrageously low-paid labour to supply exports of fresh and preserved fruits and vegetables." (Friedmann. 4.) "Outrageously low-paid labour" directly contradicts the theory of Comparative Advantage which says that if each country produces what it is best at, then both countries, in producing more between them, will each get higher wages. As with Division of Labour all the wealth goes to the rich; the poor have to undercut each other; otherwise they starve. The theory only works if there is no unemployment which has never been the case since the beginning of history, and no-one thinks will ever happen in the future.

The demand for crops to export has put a premium on the peasants' land and every trick in the book has been used to get them off it. "Landless peasants were virtually non-existent in Thailand 20 years ago, but now make up 30% of households." (Trainer. 6.) And mechanisation has made their labour irrelevant. To grow the grain they had had to be tied to the soil. Movement from the village was forbidden. Today most of the peasants are of no use to the plantation owner. They are evicted and left to starve or migrate to the cities or further out to the forests where they bring the diseases to wipe out the hunter-gatherers.

In slightly more democratic countries like India the peasants are not being evicted en masse (except by the massive dam projects) but economic pressures of development are having the same effect. To pay for the transport infrastructure and increased government, the government needs more taxes, ie. more crops from the peasants. So the peasants' smallholdings have to feed not only his own family, but the government employees too. So the size of a smallholding necessary to support a family, the viable farm size, increases. The peasants with too little land are forced to become labourers for others to supplement their income, or migrate.

Development aid has made the situation worse. "For example, the introduction of mechanical farming methods in Arsi province, in Ethiopia, under a Swedish aid programme resulted in the eviction of more than 5000 tenant households between 1967 and 1975." (Griffin.) Development in the form of the 'Green Revolution' further impoverished them. High-yielding seed was developed in the West but it needed large cash inputs for the fertilizer etc. The small peasant couldn't afford it. Only the richer peasant was able to benefit. Because of the high yield the price of the crop was lower and so undercut the small producer who was forced to sell his land to the larger producer and become an agricultural labourer: "the introduction of 'new technology' (improved varieties of seeds, fertilizers, agrochemicals and machinery) has hastened the process of differentiation of agrarian classes and served to consolidate the rich peasantry as a powerful dominant class." (Alavi. 2.) "The 'Green Revolution' has been a flagrant example of a 'development' solution that has brought nothing but misery to the poor." (George. 5.)

The ones who benefit most are the class immediately above. In India the 'bullock capitalists', peasant families with about 15 acres of land, have obtained the land from those poorer families and are now a strong political force, stronger than the 'tractor capitalists' with more than 15 acres of land, a tractor and wage labour. But as the cost of living, taxation and therefore the viable farm size increases, the tractor capitalists will buy out the bullock capitalists.

Agricultural development imposed by western economists has benefited the West and the ruling and middle classes of the under-developed countries. More food has been produced but it has been exported. The GDP has gone up and the country is called richer. But the poor have been made hungrier. "In Egypt, for instance, the number of rural poor increased by nearly two million between 1958/9 and 1978 . . . This was associated with, and partially caused by, a rise in the incidence of the landlessness from 40 per cent of agricultural households in 1961 to 45 per cent in 1972." (Griffin. 2.)

In general the introduction of western technological solutions has been a disaster for the poor of the Third World. "The transfer and promotion of technological solutions tends to increase inequality of power and wealth, concentrate land and resources in the hands of the few, and displace the many. The result too often is more production by the few of crops which the many cannot afford to buy." (Borosage. 2.)

Poverty Caused by Industrial Development

The effects of industrial development vary with the distance from the core. Out on the periphery the major disruption is by mining which destroys the hunting grounds and water courses by pollution and tipping of the waste. It destroys the social independence of the tribespeople by the introduction of money and different cultural values. The only excuse the developers can offer is that it brings employment. It's unwanted employment, in fact forced labour; the local population is forced by taxation to go down the mines. More usually labour has to be imported, a male work force without women and without the moderating influence of their own villages.

There are no countries today which are totally in this category. But places like New Guinea and Namibia are largely so. Most of the periphery countries had already been colonised and forced into the agricultural stage. Nevertheless many countries have their own peripheries of this category; the Amazon rain forest of Brazil and the peripheries of many sub-Saharan countries of Africa.

In the band closer to the core where money and the shortage of land had already created craft industries such as weaving, shoe-making, iron and copper working, these industries are all destroyed by the cheaper manufactured goods brought from the periphery country's own core by the new roads. These areas are de-developed by development.

At the cores of these countries, now sub-cores to the developed cores of the West, their low labour costs gave them an opportunity to build up an industry which did not require too advanced a technology such as textiles, shoes, toys and plastic goods. But success in exporting to the West meant unemployment at the western core (contrary to their economic theory), so it was stamped on. Quotas and tariffs such as the Multi-Fibre Agreement were imposed on the periphery sub-cores to protect the workers of the core. Any thoughts about Free Trade are quickly abandoned by the core when their industries are threatened, while still demanding Free Trade for their own goods. The puppets have to accede.

Local Industries

It is local industries which are hurt by investment from the industrialised core. Japan, with increasing food and land costs, quickly found its wages rising. The high labour costs drove the smaller producers in industries like textiles and shoes, rather than investing in expensive automation, to transfer their factories to low labour cost countries of South-East Asia, where their higher technology put the local factories out of business. During the years of the boom these imported factories prospered in the Philippines and Indonesia. Japan also brought in assembly plants for advanced technology products, 'screwdriver' operations whose parts were imported and the completed unit exported again. Young Filippino women were employed to do meticulous assembly work under microscopes of complicated microelectronic parts. After a few years they'd lost their good sight and were fired. But Japan is now pulling out of the Philippines and Indonesia because the populations aren't working hard enough, leaving unemployment and a devastated indigenous industry.

Third World governments had been told by their western economists that if they borrowed money from the West and bought western machinery, they could be as rich as the West. But the wealth never came. The economists forgot to mention that to industrialise a country needs a large internal demand, not just a large population but a large, rich population or a large non-self-sufficient population which depends on the output from the factories. A large self-sufficient peasant society provides no internal demand at all. So the governments bought their expensive factories from the West but couldn't find anyone to buy their products.

The western economists made this even worse by saying that the Third World countries should open themselves up to western competition and allow in cheap western manufactured goods which would encourage the Third World countries to improve their performance. It didn't. It just put them out of business.

At each stage some of the local inhabitants benefit. On the periphery very few, perhaps the local chief and his family, temporarily. In the agricultural belt a higher proportion benefit, the larger landowners, the better off peasants with wage labour who can grow enough crops to sell some for cash; and there are a few government jobs.

At the sub-core even more benefit, the small, service businesses, the government workers, the middle classes, and the workers from skilled workers up.

Then there comes a point, with countries very close to the western core, either geographically or economically, where the majority benefit. At that point the periphery has been incorporated into the expanding core. Those who were exploited become the exploiters.

This applies to the Little Tigers of the Pacific Rim, South Korea, Taiwan, Hong Kong and Singapore, where Japan has concentrated its external investment. The incentives for two of them, Taiwan and South Korea were threatening neighbours, China and North Korea. The incentive for the other two was very high population. At first they were undeveloped countries, previously part of the Japanese Empire. Japan invested heavily, taking advantage of their low labour costs. The investments were far more successful than elsewhere. There was political stability achieved by ruthless governments; conditions of investment didn't change too much, such as demanding a larger local control or larger local input of subcontracted parts. But above all the populations were hungrier.

Whereas in most other countries the arrival of more technologically advanced factories spelt the closure of the indigenous businesses, the factories of these Little Dragons, driven by hunger, aided by considerable government protection, gradually built up their own markets, until they are now competing with Japan and even exporting to Japan itself. Since these Little Dragons ring China, perhaps it is the Chinese market that has created them.

Chapter 11. The Third World
References

H. Alavi in "South Asia". Ed. H. Alavi and Harris. MacMillan. '89. 1: p.109., 2: p.42.

R.L. Borosage. in the introdution to "Ill fares the Land" by Susan George. Writers and Readers Publishing Co-operative Society Ltd. '85. 1.p.XIV., 2: p.XIV.

J. Collins and F.M. Lappé. "Still Hungry after all these years". Mother Jones. Aug. '77. p.30–32.

B. Davidson. "Modern Africa". Longman '83. 4: p.77.

H. Friedmann in "The Food Question". ed. H. Bernstein et al. Earthscan Publications. '90. 1: p.35., 2: p.35., 3: p.34., 4: p.24.

E. Galleano. "The Open Veins of Latin America. Seven years later". Monthly Review. 30.7. pp.12–35.

S. George. "How the Other Half Dies". Penguin. '76. 5: p.17.

K. Griffin. "World Hunger and the World Economy". MacMillan. '87. p.14., 2: p.7.

I.F.P.D. Institute of Food and Development Policy. "Food First Resources Guide". '79. p.9.

T. Leamonth and F. Rolt. "Undeveloping Bangladesh." War on Want. 1: p.6., 2: inside front cover.

New Internationalist. October. '78.p.5.

F. Pearce. "Turning up the Heat". The Bodley Head. '89. p.72.

G. Pendle. "A History of Latin America". Penguin. '63. 3: p.161.

M. Perelman. "Farming for Profit in a Hungry World. Capitalism and crisis in agriculture." New York University Press. '77. p.115.

F.E. Trainer. "Abandon Affluence". Z Press. '85. 1: p.104., 2: p.162., 3: p.171., 4: p.143., 5: p.144., 6: p.140.

Chapter 12
THE CRISIS OF INDUSTRIALISM

OVER TWO HUNDRED YEARS AGO the intellectuals of the core decided that there was no god, no after-life as a compensation for the hardships of this world. If you didn't get it here on Earth, that was it. No longer could the rulers claim that the soldiers fought, the priests prayed and everyone else fed and clothed them. For two hundred years the intellectuals have been looking for a new justification for the expropriation of the crops and a new justification to rule.

The rulers have been forced to accept that they rule on the people's behalf rather than to the glory of God. And they have been forced to concede a small degree of people's participation in government, the chance to say a yes or no twelve times in a person's lifetime. That's called democracy.

The Russian Revolution of 1917 was the first to try to put into practice the previous century's socialist theorising to enable people to have a genuine say in their government through the organisation of soviets. Within three years it was clear that the experiment was not going to work; the peasants weren't going to feed the cities voluntarily. The experiment was ended and was replaced with dictatorship. The other socialist revolutions all ended the same way. The question posed by the French Revolution 200 years ago – how should we be ruled – has still to be answered, because capitalism, the market economy, is not delivering. It offers only environmental crisis, starvation for a quarter of the world and social breakdown.

Environmental pollution has always accompanied industry, and agriculture too, but never until today has it been globally life-threatening. Now the greenhouse effect and the vanishing ozone layer are a threat to life over the whole planet. The manufacture of poisonous chemicals and industrial waste are poisoning the water supplies and the waters of the sea as well. Industry and agro-industry are making the planet uninhabitable.

183

Global Warming

Because of the increasing cost of human labour, caused by higher taxation, it has become necessary to replace human energy with machines driven by energy from fossil fuels, coal, gas and oil. These produce carbon dioxide which allows in light from the sun as ultraviolet light; but on the earth the ultraviolet light turns to infra red light which the extra carbon dioxide in the atmosphere does not allow through and reflects back to the earth again, so building up the heat. The carbon dioxide acts as a greenhouse, so gradually the earth is warming up.

The Greenhouse Effect was first predicted by Fournier, a Frenchman, in 1768, and then by the Swedish chemist, Svante Arrhenius, during the 1890s. Ever since, the scientists have been watching to see when it would start. Then in 1988 James Hansen of NASA said, "The Greenhouse Effect is here." The concentration of carbon dioxide in the atmosphere has risen from some 270 parts per million before the industrial revolution to around 350 parts per million. The 1980s were almost a degree warmer than the 1880s. Seven of the eight hottest years in the past century have occurred between 1980 and 1987.

There are other gases which contribute to the greenhouse effect. Methane, nitrous oxide and chlorofluorocarbons which have also risen in quantity since the industrial revolution, each introduced to reduce the high labour costs caused by high indirect taxation.

Global warming will cause some of the ice at the poles to melt, raising sea levels perhaps by a metre, flooding low-lying areas including all the coral islands of the Pacific, the deltas of the largest rivers and some of the large cities built on the coasts.

Some estimates of the rise in sea levels are much higher. "The U.S. Environmental Protection Agency predicted in 1984 that there might be a rise in the average temperature of 2 degrees celsius (3.6 degrees farenheit) by the middle of the 21st century and a rise of 5 degrees celsius (9 degrees farenheit) by 2100." Such a temperature rise would melt the ice caps. "Sea levels would rise about 50 metres (165 feet) inundating low-lying land areas that include many of the world's major cities." (Allaby. 1.)

Rainfall patterns will change and so will the air and soil temperature, moving agricultural areas more quickly than farmers will be able to adapt. Long term this does appear to be threatening to the human race, but the frightening problems are medium term in the adaption to the new conditions, the evacuation of the flooded areas, the temporary but serious food shortages.

It has been made clear by the scientists of the world at their conference,

'The Changing Atmosphere' in Canada that we have to cut emissions of carbon dioxide by 50%.

Cutting carbon dioxide emissions by half means half the number of lorries and cars, half the amount of electricity, half the amount of heating, half the number of factories. That won't stop the flooding. It will just stop the flooding being much worse.

The Ozone Layer

The other major global atmospheric threat is the thinning of the ozone layer, which seems to be far more dangerous, though perhaps more easily cured. Chloro-fluoro-carbons (C.F.Cs.) are used in refrigerators, aerosols and for foaming plastic. When these products are dumped, the CFCs are released into the atmosphere and float up and destroy the layer of ozone between 10 and 50 kilometres above the earth. The ozone layer stops too much ultraviolet light reaching the earth. When the ozone is destroyed, the ultraviolet light gets through. Each spring in the Antarctic a hole in the ozone layer now develops, each spring getting bigger. The process is now beginning at the Arctic pole and already the layer over Europe is thinner than expected.

The extra ultraviolet light increases skin cancers, but far more important, it reduces agricultural output. It will cause a world food shortage. Global warming was predicted. The thinning ozone layer was not. How many other surprises are in store?

Nuclear Power

Its proponents have tried to suggest that nuclear power is a safer alternative to the fossil fuels which create the global warming because nuclear power does not produce carbon dioxide. But it produces its own pollution, radioactive waste. After forty years they still haven't found a safe way to dispose of it. Britain has been dumping it in the Irish sea, making it the most radioactive sea anywhere. Britain has been called 'the dirty man of Europe'. 'The dirty man of the world' would be more appropriate.

Radiation is such a frightening, invisible thing that nuclear power is understandably very unpopular. It only needs one more Chernobyl to blow for it to be no longer a political option. It's only a matter of time. Since the implication of this book is that there will have to be technological regression, further dependence on nuclear power is inconceivable when there will be no way, technologically, to deal with either the nuclear waste or the de-commissioning of the power stations themselves.

There is no such thing as safe levels of low level radiation. All radiation kills. Their 'safe levels' are simply selected levels of acceptable risk. But it is probable that even these are far too high. They were based on the Japanese experience of Hiroshima and Nagasaki. But it seems that much less radiation was released than was thought, so that the destructive effects were the result of much lower levels than assumed. The 'safe level' should apparently be only about a tenth of what it is now.

Deforestation

Deforestation has been going on since the beginning of cultivation. Examples have already been quoted for Mesopotamia and ancient Greece and Rome. It is thought that the culture on Easter Island died out after they'd cut down all the trees. They had no hinterland from which to get more timber.

Deforestation occurs long before industrialisation. "France, once 80% forested, had trees covering only 14% of its territory by 1789." (Postel and Heise. 1.) As the population of the core grows so the area of deforestation round the core also grows. Today that deforestation has reached the furthest corners of the world. The southern slopes of the Himalayas are being logged out by the West, the northern slopes in Tibet by China. In South East Asia: "So much forest cover has been lost that the climate is beginning to change in some areas. The loss of catchments is so severe that many areas are now inundated by floods of unprecedented magnitude." (Chia and MacAndrews. 1.) "Some 40% of Ethiopia was under forest at the turn of the century; 20% was still covered in the early sixties. By 1984 government experts were quoting figures based on satellite photographs of 2–4%." (Timberlake. 1.) In India: "Between 1972–75 and 1980–82 the country lost 9 million hectares of tree cover, roughly 1.3 million hectares per year. At this rate India will lose most of its remaining 31 million hectares of forest by the end of the century." (Brown and Flavin. 1.)

It seems that the planet has survived without trees before, and man will survive too. But cities and industry are impossible without timber. They will not survive.

The other major cause of deforestation is the burgeoning peasant population. Forests are cleared for cultivation often because the peasants have been driven off the level, fertile, arable land by the large farmers and multinationals. And trees are cut down for fuel. There is a global, desperate shortage of wood fuel.

Erosion

Deforestation is a major cause of erosion. Once the forests are gone, without the decaying vegetable matter to soak up the rainwater, and without the trees, the water runs over the surface taking the top soil with it. The extra run-off causes flooding, in some cases disastrously as in Bangladesh.

The other cause of erosion is agriculture, over-grazing, irrigation and monoculture. "The depth of U.S. soil has been significantly reduced over the last century. Several estimates put the loss at approximately one third of the depth that existed 100 years ago." (Trainer. 3.) "Africa and Asia may lose between them almost a billion tons of soil to the wind annually – the soil blows out over the oceans in great plumes which can be clearly seen from the satellites." (R. North. 1.)

To reduce high labour costs caused by high taxation it is cheaper to use factory-made fertilizer; the soil is being starved of the natural detritus of decaying vegetation which holds it together. The soil is just being asked to produce too much, and too little is being put back.

Biocides

Another frightening aspect of modern agriculture is the use of pesticides and herbicides – life killers, again to reduce labour costs. Pesticides kill the crop pests which are therefore no longer available as food for their bird and animal predators which then decline in number. Some of the chemicals such as DDT build up in the predators and they die that way or their offspring are malformed.

Agro-industry in the Third World is a major user of pesticides and the farmers are often unaware of their dangers. "Between 400,000 and 2 million pesticide poisonings occur worldwide every year, most of them amongst farmers in developing countries." (Postel.) Charitably, one could believe that these farmers hadn't been warned of the dangers.

But it is difficult to believe that constant annual application of these often persistent poisons is not doing long term damage. "The introduction into the environment of copious quantities of chemical compounds, some of which are persistent and have already accumulated in dangerous concentrations (is) now recognised as one of the most serious threats to the well-being of the developing world." (Shane.) Another unknown effect is of the residues of the pesticides left on the fruit and vegetables.

Industrial Wastes

Poisons are being produced as by-products of the manufacturing process and then indiscriminately dumped onto industrial tips. In the developed countries local protest is ignored, and then when it becomes too vocal, is answered by the excuse of commercial confidentiality. Local people are not allowed to know what is being put onto the tips. They are not allowed to know whether the poisons are seeping into the water courses or whether the foul smells are indicative of health dangers. Love Canal, a town in America, had to be completely and permanently evacuated because its soil had been so contaminated by dioxin from its industrial tip. In Holland: "an unsuspected dump of 10,000 drums containing, amongst much else, a good deal of dioxin was soon found. In the ensuing investigations 4,000 illegal waste dumps were discovered." (North. 2.)

Because of public pressure at the core these poisons are now being exported to the Third World where corrupt politicians are well paid to accept our poisonous wastes. "China has been considering storing nuclear waste from rich countries in its deserts. A U.S. company has been reported as offering $25 million to Sierra Leone to take some of its hazardous mining wastes. Nigeria, Liberia, Senegal and Chile have all been looking to Haiti as a potential destination for their wastes. Mexico and the Dominican Republic are said to have taken hazardous waste." (North. 3.)

In order to attract foreign factories the Third World allows considerably lower pollution standards, so that factories from the core, where their pollution is unacceptable, can transfer their business to the Third World, and their pollution too. American firms are re-locating in Mexico on a large scale partly for this reason.

Water Pollution

The poisonous industrial wastes are also being tipped into the oceans where the results are seen in the increasing number of diseased fish being caught, which we eat. This applies particularly to the North Sea.

Perhaps the most serious yet least known water pollution is that of the rivers of the Third World which have to provide most of the protein, the fish, in the local peasants' diet, and their drinking water. The rivers are polluted by agro-industry growing crops for us. In Malaysia: "eleven river basins experience pollution problems, six rivers or tributaries are grossly polluted, eight moderately polluted and fifteen encounter potential problems . . . the major sources of water pollution are attributed to agricultural activities and agro-based industries including the processing of oil palm, rubber, pineapple, tapioca, sugar, sago and to some extent paper and pulp manufacturing." (Chia and MacAndrews. 2.)

In South East Asia: "Industrial and agro-industrial pollution is befouling rivers throughout the region. Agricultural areas irrigated by the same waters are producing lower yields and fresh water and coastal fisheries are being destroyed." (Chia and MacAndrews. 3.) In Thailand sugar mills "have created serious pollution to the point where the rivers cannot support fish life in the lower reaches under low flow conditions and cannot be used as a source of potable water supply for villages." (Pescod. 1.) In South America: "Columbia's Bogota River (often claimed to be one of the world's most polluted rivers) collects sewage and industrial effluent for almost the entire length of its long course towards the sea. Analysis of its water – which villagers downstream have no choice but to drink – reveals a very special cocktail containing mercury, copper and arsenic. A recent survey of fifteen Mexican Rivers has found them unfit for most purposes. (Clarke. 1.)

The most extreme case of water pollution was at Minimata in Japan when a factory used the bay to get rid of its mercury-polluted wastes. The fish took up the mercury and the local people, having eaten the fish, developed physical deformities and brain damage from the mercury. For years the factory denied responsibility.

Air Pollution

The combination of air pollution and industrial wastes is causing an ecological nightmare in Eastern Europe. "In Poland, where chemical contamination has rendered one fourth of the soil unfit for food production and left only one per cent of the water safe for drinking, life expectancy for men has fallen back to the level of 1952 . . . In Czechoslovakia's heavily industrialized northern Bohemia, the incidence of skin disease, stomach cancer and mental illness is at least double that in the rest of the country. And life expectancy there is up to ten years shorter than elsewhere in Czechoslovakia." (Brown and Flavin. 2.) It is in this region of Bohemia that the trees are suffering the worst effects of acid rain and industrial air pollution in Europe.

The most notorious example of air pollution is at the Union Carbide factory at Bhopal in India, forced on India in return for American food aid. Poisonous gas was accidentally released, killing thousands. How many thousands no one knows. Another example was at Seveso in Northern Italy when a Hoffman la Roche factory emitted dioxin causing widespread eye and skin problems. The town had to be totally and permanently evacuated.

Though industry is the main culprit, agriculture is not innocent. In Thailand sugar mills "release large quantities of air pollutants in burning baggase as a fuel without emission controls. In addition to being a possible health hazard, this air pollution is locally reputed to have a noticeable adverse effect on agricultural productivity in the area of the mills." (Pescod. 2.)

Cars and more importantly the lorries which transport the necessities of life to the cities contribute 18% of the carbon dioxide which is causing the greenhouse effect. They also emit considerable quantities of carbon monoxide, unburnt hydrocarbons, nitrogen oxide and lead. "In Germany a good deal of acid rain pollution has been blamed on the exhaust of cars and its relationship to high ozone levels." (North. 4.)

The effects of lorry and car exhaust fumes have made some cities unhealthy to live in. Tokyo's air at one point became so polluted that doses of oxygen were provided in the streets, at a price. Athens and Mexico are now badly affected.

Acid Rain

Acid rain "has been reported from China and the U.S.S.R. but it is especially marked in Scandanavia, Central Europe and parts of north-eastern North America." (Allaby. 2.) Rain is acidified by sulphur and nitrogen deriving from industrial processes, mainly power generation, burning coal for electricity, and lorry and car exhausts. Because of wind patterns the acidified rain often falls far from its country of origin. Scandinavia, which produces few of the acids itself, receives those from Britain mainly, Germany and Eastern Europe. In Sweden; "20,000 lakes out of a total of 90,000 have now been damaged by acid rain; 9,000 of them no longer contain any live fish at all. Norway is equally badly affected: 80% of the lakes and streams in the southern half of the country are either 'dead' or 'critically ill'." (Clarke. 2.)

Acid rain is also implicated in the dying forests of central Europe. No one seems certain of the precise mechanism, but no one doubts the cause is industry and cars. "By 1986 half the forests in the Netherlands, Switzerland and West Germany showed signs of damage." (Brown and Flavin. 3.) In China: "In a forested section of Sichuan, 90 per cent of one local area once covered with pines is now bare, apparently as a result of air pollution." (Brown and Flavin. 4.)

Resources

Greens have been predicting for years that resources would run out. But for the moment, except for two cases, it doesn't seem to be true. The prices of resources are going down.

The two cases are timber and water. The price of both is increasing, and neither can be replaced. We are running out of two of the most vital resources of all.

The logging out of forests across the world has already been mentioned. The water situation is already becoming acute in the Middle East. Turkey, which controls the head waters of the Euphrates, is diverting water for its own agricultural irrigation to grow export crops to feed the developed world, leaving only half of what Iraq was previously receiving. Israel, Syria and Jordan are competing for one diminishing water source. Israel is encouraging immigration from Russia with no water for the immigrants. But most of their water is required to grow their exported agricultural crops. If we have to cut carbon dioxide emissions by half to stop global warming, plants for the desalination of sea water are not an option. There will be war in the Middle East, not for oil, but for water, unless they reduce their population, or stop feeding us.

In California the water is being 'mined'. Because of the wells the water table is getting lower.

Obsolescence

Because of high labour costs caused by high indirect taxation, previous patterns of labour intensive activities have had to be abandoned. It is too expensive in labour to have shop assistants serving their customers individually. So self service has to be introduced. This means far more expensive packaging which has to be self-explanatory, easily exhibited and easily stacked etc. And once it is bought it has to be put into yet another bag to show that it has been bought and so reduce the need for staff to check. Excess packaging is caused by high labour costs. It is not because we are greedy or materialistic or lazy that we do not recycle, but because it is too expensive in labour costs to do so.

Those high labour costs mean that it is more expensive to mend a product individually than to buy a new product. There's no great conspiracy of built-in obsolescence. It's just the inevitable result of high labour costs caused by high indirect taxation.

Industry is making the planet uninhabitable. We can't have nuclear power without nuclear waste. Nor can we have industry without poisonous industrial waste. Clean industry is a contradiction in terms. Global warming can only be halted by 50% cut in carbon dioxide emissions which means an immediate halving of all power production and all factory production.

This does not mean, as some Greens seem to think, that we shall just have to do without the luxuries such as electric toothbrushes. As we have seen only about 5% of our income is 'discretionary'. The other 95% is spent on the necessities of life because we have no land and cannot be self-sufficient. The factories are producing those necessities, clothes, food, heating, fuel, shelter. If half those factories must close, we must have the land on which to be self-sufficient.

Chapter 12. The Crisis of Industrialism
References

M. Allaby. "Ecology Facts". Hamlyn. '86. 1: p.85. 2: p.107.

L. Brown and C. Flavin. "The Earth's vital signs" in "State of the World". L. Brown et al. W.W. Norton for Worldwatch Institute. '88. 1: p.5., 2: p.7., 3: p.5., 4:p.15.

Chia Lin-Sien and C. MacAndrews in "Developing Countries and the Environment." Ed. C. MacAndrews. McGraw Hill. '79. 1: p.44., 2: p.53., 3: p.44.

R. Clarke in "Ecology 2000". Ed. E. Hillary. Michael Joseph '84. 1: p.117., 2: p.137.

R. North. "The Real Cost". Chatto and Windus. '86. 1: p.16., 2: p.178., 3: p.177., 4: p.165.

Pescod. in "Developing Countries and the Environment." Ed. C. MacAndrews and Chia Lin-sien. McGraw Hill. '79. 1: p.182., 2: p.182.

S. Postel and L. Heise "Reforesting the Earth." in "State of the World". L. Brown et al. W.W. Norton for the Worldwatch Institute. '88. 1: p.84.

S. Postel. "Controlling the Chemicals". in "State of the World". L. Brown et al. W.W. Norton for the Worldwatch Institute. '88. p.121.

L. Timberlake. "African Crisis." Earthscan. - International Institute for Environment and Development. '85. 1: p.129.

F.E. Trainer. "Abandon Affluence." Z Press. '85. 3: p.99.

Chapter 13
SOLUTIONS WHICH WON'T WORK

WE HAVE SEEN THAT POVERTY is not caused by laziness, lack of knowledge, lack of education or lack of technology. The pre-agricultural societies are not, or were not, poor. They have been called 'the original affluent society'. Food and fuel are free and abundant.

We have seen that agriculture was developed to avoid the hunger and poverty caused by population pressure and also, by a hierarchy which could demand obedience, forcing the peasants to produce a surplus, usually as grain which could be stored and which they would not otherwise grow. This all meant harder work. We have seen that though people work harder to climb the peck order, they are still, like every other organism in nature, obeying the Law of Least Effort since the peck order is necessary to keep the peace with least effort. Therefore, because it is less work, they revert to a lower level of agriculture if the opportunity occurs, such as more land, fewer people or no demanding hierarchy.

Because these peoples never produce a surplus voluntarily, all solutions by 'advanced' countries to increase crop production by education and encouragement always fail. And all solutions involving the peasants' voluntarily feeding the cities have to end up using force. By choice the peasants, obeying the Law of Least Effort, will not feed the cities.

Government

We have also seen that rule or government originated to take away the crops by the sword or by taxation. Government is the cause of poverty. We have seen that religion was evolved to legitimise the inheritance of kingship in order to maintain the wealth of the companions of the king. We have seen that it was religion which produced the concept of obedience to the gods' laws which enabled the kings to say that the gods had told them to take away the crops.

So if governments are the cause of poverty, it is unlikely that they will want, or be able to cure it. The Pacific Tigers seem to show that government can certainly increase economic growth, but more economic growth somewhere means more poverty somewhere else. The specific object of government, right from the beginning, was to take from the many to give to the few. The specific object of government is to create wealth and the corresponding poverty.

So prescriptions to end poverty by government action, which generally means increasing economic growth, are condemned to failure. They will simply increase the starvation of the Third World. Nor is it possible that taxation, introduced to take from the many to give to the few, will ever reverse the process. Instead, by increasing the cost of living, wages and labour costs, it will worsen unemployment and green problems, and it will force the peasants to increase the amount of crops they hand over as taxes. They will be hungrier.

Capitalism

Conventional economic wisdom holds that trade and industry create wealth and therefore they reduce poverty by creating employment. But they create wealth simply by moving it from the periphery to the core. All wealth is accompanied by its corresponding poverty.

The theory of capitalism is derived from Adam Smith's theory of 'Division of Labour' which states that the wages of all the employees of a firm are increased if it successfully divides up the labour functions. The truth is that the managers benefit, but the wages of the lowest paid are determined, not by the success of the firm, but by the hungrier at the factory gate prepared to work for less.

The theory of capitalism also depends on the idea of 'Trickle-down'. The world economy is now being operated on the theory that the rich entrepreneurs create wealth which 'trickles down' to the poorest as each level uses the wealth to employ the next level, so that, although there is a widening gap between the richest and the poorest, the poorest, they say, are nevertheless better off than before.

But they measure this wealth by Gross Domestic Product (GDP), the total of all monetary transactions, so that a car crash, needing towing away, repairs, ambulances and medical treatment, all increase monetary transactions, so the GDP has gone up and, in their book, everyone is richer. A prison is built and therefore everyone is richer More thefts needing more policing means we are supposed to be richer. More pollution to be cleaned up means we are richer. Because water is now polluted everywhere, it has to be treated, costing money, increasing GDP. In the countryside water used to be free. It now has to be paid for by a water rate increasing GDP. But people are only better off if their wages have increased more than the water rate. For the poor, wages never keep up with the increasing monetarisation of life. The people are poorer while the GDP goes up.

So their measure of wealth is wrong. And so is their means of transferring the wealth. We have seen that it is not the entrepreneurs but the supply of food (and other necessities of life) extracted from the periphery that creates the jobs. The food is taken by governments and traders who eat some of it but use most of it to buy the services of intellectuals, artists and managers who eat some of it and use the rest to employ the workers who eat the rest of the food which has 'trickled down' from the rich. This is true. The urban middle classes and working classes depend on a strong ruling class to extract their food from the peasants. But there's none left to 'trickle back down' to the peasants on the periphery. All that's left of the food and natural resources that were taken from them is sewage, scrap, shoddy and soot. It's all been consumed by the consumers. The wealth of the core is created by the poverty of the periphery.

Since the capitalists say that trade and industry create wealth, they can claim that any restriction on trade and industry will reduce wealth and therefore jobs. Thus they say that any government protection of trade or industry against cheaper foreign competition will reduce wealth and therefore jobs. So they are against 'protectionism' and in favour of 'Free Trade'. Since, as we have seen, the cost of living is always higher at the core because of the cost of water, fuel, food, firefighting, policing etc., wages and labour costs will always be higher, and therefore labour-saving machinery will always be more advanced than on the periphery. So manufactured goods from the core will always be cheaper than periphery goods. If periphery governments don't protect their industries with import duties and tariffs they will be undercut and destroyed by the core industries. So the capitalist theories of 'Free Trade' will destroy periphery industries.

The capitalist system has now reached its final mad apotheosis. The Uruguay Round of the General Agreement on Tariffs and Trade (GATT) has persuaded much of the Third World to end protectionism and allow Free Trade. The West will end its duties on agricultural and low technology products like cloth and shoes, while the Third World would end its duties on the advanced technologies of the West. If a Third World country didn't sign, it wouldn't be able to sell its agricultural products to the West because they would be charged duty and be more expensive than those products of the Third World countries who signed and were therefore not taxed.

Like lambs to the slaughter Third World countries queued up to sign. Their choice was between opting out of the world trading system altogether or chancing their industrial luck with the western giants. About 120 countries signed. And 60 did not.

The full effect will take some years to appear. The Multi-fibre Agreement, for example, which excluded Third World cloth from the West, is to be phased out (they say!) over fifteen years and Third World reduction of tariffs will take nearly as long. But before that final destruction of Third World industry anything could happen.

Socialism

Socialism accepted the theory of Division of Labour and Comparative Advantage. It agreed that trade and industry created wealth. Its quarrel was with how that wealth was distributed. Its answer was 'the redistribution of wealth by the nationalisation of the means of production.' Since the collapse of the Russian economy not many socialists will now agree to nationalisation. But without it they're left with little more than a sort of caring capitalism including the disastrous 'Free Trade'.

Religion

It's fashionable at the moment to blame the monotheistic religions, Judaism, Christianity and Islam, but to acquit the other, polytheistic religions like Hinduism and the ancient religions of Greece and Rome, or Buddhism. But it's been said that whenever an oriental ruler wanted to become more autocratic, he embraced Buddhism, and no one could say that the Egyptian Pharaohs were the personification of good government.

Nevertheless it does look as if the monotheistic religions were keen traders. Judaism certainly does not seem to have hampered Jews as traders. In the Dark Ages after the collapse of the western Roman Empire it was the petty kings all over Europe who were gradually converted to Christianity, well ahead of the people they ruled. So there was something in it for them.

The example of Islam in Africa suggests it was the benefits of trade, "far from condemning trade, Islam smiles on it. The two essentials for drawing closer to God are piety and usefulness to the community. Usefulness means not just good behaviour and worthy endeavour but actively promoting the community's welfare by enriching it and endowing it." (Mussallam). Islam offered the rulers the excuse for taking the crops from the villages to create trade. Just as in Europe the rulers converted long before their subjects. "Their kings could prosper and pay their way as long as they could use the Islamic system of belief and government for the promotion of both central rule and long-range trade and credit. But this very reliance on the towns tended to alienate the peoples of the countryside" (who were not moslem). "In times of crisis, the town-centred empires could quickly fall apart." (B. Davidson.)

At the moment all religions seem to accept that trade and industry create wealth. Most seem to think that any ensuing disparities of wealth should be dealt with by Charity. Put simply, religions offer charity as the solution to poverty, a rough look-out for the poor.

Green Solutions

Greens are a single issue group concerned about the pollution of the environment. Since they want political action they also are forced to pay lip-service to a concern about poverty. The solution of the British Green Party is a National Income, a version of the 'money grows on trees' theory. If it were set at a genuine living wage paid to everyone, it would mean doubling present taxation. But it's usually watered down to income support levels set against other income, which is no sort of redistribution of wealth.

Although theoretically they accept that trade and industry create wealth, they cannot use this method to solve poverty, since it is that very trade and industry and its technology which is, they think, causing the pollution.

As we have seen technology is caused by high wages and the need to cut labour costs. But most greens instead blame technology on science and the materialist thinking of determinism, utilitarianism and reductionism. This is scary. It is a rejection of reason.

Determinism says that the cause is followed by effect which becomes the cause of the next effect; the same cause produces the same inevitable effect which becomes the inevitable cause of the next inevitable effect, so that the development of the universe becomes inevitable, determined. A subsidiary idea is that everything is not only determined but determinable, predictable, with a big enough computer. Scientists tell us that the theory of quantum mechanics shows that the smallest particles are not predictable and therefore the universe is not predictable. But if it's not predictable, how they managed to build the Bomb beats me. There now seems to be some question about it. But that does not affect the main proposition that the world is determined, leaving nothing for which a god could be a cause.

Greens don't like this idea because they think it was this theoretical base which produced science, then technology, then pollution.

Descartes is credited with determinism about 1650 which is said to have produced the spurt of science which produced the technology and pollution. But technology, as we have already seen, gathered speed four hundred years before that in the European monasteries where determinism would have been anathema.

Groups such as Social Ecology, based on the ideas of Murray Bookchin and Deep Ecology of Arne Naess both think that the answer lies in a change of attitude or 'mind-set', so that people will live more simply, using less advanced technology, so that there are fewer factories, so less pollution. But they both think that we can be selective about which technologies we get rid of. Electric toothbrushes are out. Computers are retained. They don't understand that technology is a result of high labour costs. If labour costs go down, both electric toothbrushes and computers disappear.

Nor do they understand that the consumer society is the way, in an anonymous society, that we create the peck order, to keep the pace with Least Effort. If we can't decide our place in the peck order by how big or recent is our washing machine, we'll have to go back to hitting each other.

The green way to make us live more simply, if they can't persuade us, is to increase indirect taxes. If there are too many cars, tax petrol. To make organic agriculture profitable, tax chemical fertilizers. To lessen carbon emissions which are causing the Greenhouse Effect, tax all carbon fuels, etc. All these indirect taxes will increase the cost of living. Wages will go up so labour costs will go up, so more labour-saving machinery will be required, exactly the economic growth that the greens deplore. There will be more unemployment. The poor will be poorer.

Chapter 13. Solutions Which Won't Work
References

B. Davidson. "Africa: A History of a Continent." Spring Books '72. p.117.

Basim Mussallam. "The Arabs". Collins/ Harvil. '83. p.76.

Chapter 14
TO END POVERTY

SINCE GOVERNMENT IS THE CAUSE OF POVERTY, we must end government. But it seems likely that for a group to work without government it must be smaller than about 500 people, which is about the maximum number that one person can know. "There is an architects' rule of thumb to the effect that the capacity of an elementary school should not exceed 500 pupils if the principal expects to know all of them by name – and it has been stated that when a group exceeds 500 persons, it requires some form of policing." (Pfeiffer. 1.)

This figure of about 500 seems to be a natural grouping. "Among the least advanced of the food gatherers, the average size of the tribe is between 300 and 400 persons. In the Andamans the figure was 400 to 450 and Kazywicki calculates the average size of 123 Australian tribes as between 300 and 600 souls." (A.S. Diamond.) "studies reveal a central tendency to cluster at the 500 level, and this tendency is widespread. It holds for the Shoshone Indians of the Great Plains, the Andaman Islanders in the Bay of Bengal and other peoples as well as the Australian aborigines." (Pfeiffer. 2.)

How then do we get back from here to autonomous, self-sufficient, armed villages? There are three main methods which could operate concurrently, revolution on the periphery, progressive break-up of the political units, and cutting taxation to reduce the power of government until there is no taxation and therefore no government.

Revolution on the Periphery

Since the beginning of this century the number of independent countries has gradually increased as the European empires have broken up. With the end of the Cold War America is reducing its arms aid to S.E. Asian governments, so those governments can no longer control their own peripheries, which are then able to stop sending their crops to the core, weakening the core still further.

The process continues with the collapse of the Soviet Union, and it is in the hills of its furthest, now independent republics that the same revolution is happening. The republics have fewer guns than the Soviet Red Army and will be able to exert far less control of their own peripheries. They will be able to expropriate fewer crops and therefore the cities will be able to support fewer people.

The problem still remains of guns in the hands of a small group, and a period of 'warlordism' is likely until the guns are spread further around. The danger is that religions such as Islam and Christianity will be used to legitimise the power of the warlords who can then disarm everyone else. With the monopoly of arms and the support of the priests these fiefs will become small inherited kingdoms. Still, they will probably be expropriating fewer crops than the present system. They won't be having to feed the Western world as well as their own elite, so the peasants will be a little better off.

Without the influence of religion and without the monopoly of arms and therefore without the ability to remove the crops, the political unit can continue to break down to the village size.

Political Break-Up

At the moment there is a conflict of trends. While the political trend is to a smaller unit, the economic trend is still towards enlargement. The conventional political economic theories, capitalism and socialism and the religions all subscribe to 'big is beautiful', and fall in with the demands of Big Business for single currencies, free trade and open borders and therefore a single bank to control the currency and therefore a single parliament to control the bank.

The only opposition – the opposing trend – is likely to come from increasing nationalism which, as in the Soviet republics, is prepared to sacrifice supposed economic benefit for national individuality. Slovakia made this decision in departing from the Czechoslovak republic. The confusion in the European Union is the effect of this conflict of trends.

In Britain the first step in the break-up of the political unit would be to leave the European Union. The next step would be for Scotland, Wales and Ulster to become independent countries with their own coinage and their own Final Appeal. Nationalism will obviously play a strong part in this process. But because Britain has such a high population and therefore has to import so many necessities of life, it's very complicated. We can break up the political unit but until we have cut the population we still have to be industrially competitive to earn our food from abroad. For that size is still important.

Once we have reduced the population sufficiently, England can be broken up into independent countries, probably North, Middle, South, each with their own governments and currencies and Final Appeal. In turn they can be broken up into smaller independent units and then again until there are only autonomous, self-sufficient, armed villages.

But Britain can't do this alone. The nation states were forced to coalesce because of threats from larger neighbours. If Britain broke up into villages, a right wing Le Pen in France would soon find a pretext to invade and, with the superior arms of a high labour-cost core, would easily win. So we can't break up the political unit too far until our neighbours do so too. And nothing at all can happen until America with its threatening nuclear power has broken up.

Unself-sufficient Britain

We can break down the political unit but because of our high population we've still got to exploit others for our necessities of life, food, fuel, wool and timber.

In Britain there are about 33 million acres of farmland, excluding rough grazing. There are about 58 million people, about half an acre per person. Enough for food but not nearly enough to grow timber for building and fuel and not nearly enough to raise sheep for wool for warm clothing. It's reckoned that a family needs about 8 acres to be self-sufficient. That means Britain could support a population of about 15 million self-sufficiently, without exploiting anyone else. More than that and it would have to be very intensive agriculture and very hard work. The fewer people there are, the less intensive the agriculture until, with a population of 15,000 people, Britain could be hunter-gathering again.

But it's not enough to reduce the population. As we have seen, the cause of poverty is government, taking the crops by the sword, or by taxation, or by taking the land from the many and giving it to the few by the Acts of Enclosure, forcing the poor into the factories or the workhouses, or today into unemployment.

But one cannot simply give each family 8 acres and tell them to be self-sufficient, even if there was enough land. At the moment, because of taxation and the proper need to keep up with the Jones, a farmer needs about 200 acres to make a living. With less than that hundreds are going bankrupt each year.

It clearly has to be a gradual process. One could imagine many who would be prepared to accept the different cultural norms of self-sufficiency, i.e. the different ways of establishing the peck order. Perhaps they could be allowed land on the furthest peripheries, on the Outer Hebrides, in the hills of Wales or Cumbria where they could be left alone, untaxed. Gradually that self-sufficiency could spread from the periphery towards the core as the power of government weakened and the population diminished.

Cutting Taxes

The third way is to cut taxes to cut the power of government and to cut the cost of living and labour costs. The first taxes to go must be the indirect taxes on the poor, VAT, fuel taxes, etc. Taxation is the life-blood of government. With no taxation government cannot exist. They can't even hire a shed to have their meetings. Without taxation they cannot enforce any decisions.

But by cutting taxation, as well as cutting the power of government and reducing poverty by cutting the cost of living to the poor, the effect is also to make smaller more beautiful. By cutting the cost of living, the corner shop needs less turnover and profit to make a living; the viable farm size goes down and organic methods become profitable. Repairing and recycling become economic. Craftsmen can make an easier living. All this means that business returns to the smaller unit and therefore away from the bigger one, so that the high technology of the supermarkets can no longer be paid for by the high turnover. They close. You get a regression of technology.

If, instead, you increase indirect taxation with such as carbon taxes, as the Green groups like Friends of the Earth and Greenpeace suggest, you increase the cost of living, wages, labour costs and the need for labour-saving technology. So the supermarkets put the corner shops out of business. Big is beautiful again.

But once more, this cannot be done alone. Britain still needs to import most of its necessities of life. If our technology regressed, we would not be able to sell our products abroad to pay for those necessities. As other countries were forced to industrialise after Britain's Industrial Revolution, so one country, which is not self-sufficient, cannot de-industrialise alone.

The effect is not only economic and political, it is also social. As self-sufficiency increases, people move about less. Communities regain their strength. The social sanction by the community against anti-social behaviour gets stronger. There is less crime. Because of the community support there is less poverty and loneliness in old age. The community replaces the state in providing necessary welfare.

It's a grubby sort of utopia, not cultured, or liberal, or advanced, or powerful. Instead it will be warm and well-fed, kind, peaceful, healthy, lazy and parochial. And it will work because it has worked for hundreds of thousands of years.

Chapter 14. To End Poverty
References

A.S. Diamond. "The Evolution of Law and Order." Watts '51. p.8.

J. Pfeiffer. "The Emergence of Man". Harper Row. '72. 1: p.334., 2: p.333.

Postscript

You will find it difficult to say whether this book is leftwing or rightwing. It is neither. It is moderate, but decentrally extremist. There is a new agenda dividing both left and right as illustrated by the splits in both the Labour and Conservative parties on Europe, between the centralists and the decentralists. The division between left wing and right wing will be replaced by the division between the centralists and decentralists, right wing centralists with left wing centralists against right wing decentralists with left wing decentralists.

CENTRALISTS	DECENTRALISTS
Equality	Liberty
Economies of scale	Small is beautiful
Higher taxes to distribute wealth	Lower taxes to cut government power
Free trade	Protectionism
Pro-GATT	Anti-GATT
Pro-technology	Anti-technology
Pro-Europe	Anti-Europe
The Core	The Periphery
Capitalists	Nationalists
Liberalism	Anarchists
Marxists	Greens/SNP
Conservatives, Labour	Religions, Charities
Liberal parties	Regionalists
B.N.P.	Tribalists, Hippies
Fascists	Racists
Socialists	Third Positionalists
Internationalists	Survivalists
Workers	Peasants
Townspeople	Country people
Third World rulers	Third World people

So, dear reader, which side of the barricades will you be on?

Authors quoted

Alavi, H., "South Asia". MacMillan. '86
Allaby, M., "Ecology Facts". Hamlyn. '86
Anell, L., and **B. Nygren,** "The Developing Countries and the World Economic Order". Francis Pinter Ltd. '80
Arnold, A.R., in "Trade and Market in Early Empires". Ed. K. Polanyi. Free Press. '57
Arnold, C.J., "Roman Britain to Saxon England". Croom Helm. '84
Arnold, R., "A Social History of England. 55 BC. - 1215 AD." Constable. '67

Bautier, R-H., "The Economic Development of Medieval Europe." Thames and Hudson. '71
Baumol, W.J., and A.S. Blinder. "Economics". Harcourt Brace Jovanovich. '82
Beresford, M., "New Towns in the Middle Ages". Lutterworth. '67
Bernstein, H., "The Food Question". Earthscan Publications. '90
Block, M., "Feudal Society". Routledge Kegan Paul. '61
Boardman, J., "The Roman World". O.U.P. '88
Borosage, R.L., in "Ill Fares the Land". by S. George. Writers and Readers Publishing Co-operative Society Ltd. '85
Böhme, H., "An Introduction to the Social and Economic History of Germany". Blackwell. '78
Braudel, F., "Capitalism and Material Life". Weidenfeld and Nicholson. '73
"The Perspective of the World". Collins. '84
"The Wheels of Commerce". Collins. '82
Bray, F., "The Rice Economies". Blackwell. '86
Bridenbaugh, C., "The Colonial Craftsman". New York. '50
Brooke, C., "The Structure of Medieval Society". Thames and Hudson. '71
Brown, L., "State of the World". W.W. Norton. '88
Durman, E., "The Templars Knights of God". The Aquarian Press. '86
Burn, A.R., "The Lyric Age of Greece". Arnold. '60

Cairncross, F. and **H. McCrae,** "Capital City". Eyre-Methuen. '73
Calder, A., "Revolutionary Empire". Jonathan Cape. '81
Carus-Wilson, E.M., "Essays in Economic History". Edward Arnold Ltd. '54
Christopher, A.J., "Colonial Africa". Croom Helm. '84
Cipolla, C.M., "Before the Industrial Revolution". Methuen. '72
"The Industrial Revolution. 1700-1914". Harvester Press/Barnes Noble. '73
Cipriani, L., "The Andaman Islanders". Weidenfeld and Nicholson. '66
Clapham, J., "A Concise Economic History of Britain". C.U.P. '66
Clark, C., "Population Growth and Land Use". MacMillan. '67
Clay, C.J.A., "Economic Expansion and Social Change". C.U.P. '84
Clayborne, R., "Climate, Man and History". Angus and Robertson. '73
Coates, B.E. and **M.E. Rawstrom,** "Regional Variations in Britain". '71
Collins, D., "The Origins of Europe". George Allen and Unwin. '75
Collins, J. and **F.M. Lappé,** "Still Hungry after all these Years". Mother Jones. Aug. '77
Cortazzi, H. "The Japanese Achievment". Sidgewick and Jackson. '90

Cotterell, A. and **D. Morgan**, "China". Harrap. '75

Davidson, B., "Africa in Modern History". Longman. '83
        "The Story of Africa". Michael Beasley. '84
Davidson, S., "Human Nutrition and Diatetics". Edinburgh. '69
Derry, T.K. "A History of Modern Norway". Clarendon. '73
Diamond, A.S., "The Evolution of Law and Order". Watts. '51
Diehl, C., "The Economic Decay of Byzantium"
Dobb, M., "Studies in the Development of Capitalism". Routledge Kegan Paul. '46
Douglas, M., "The Lele of Kasai" in "African Worlds", Ed. C. Darryl Forde. O.U.P. '54
Dovring, F., in "The Cambridge Economic History of Europe". Ed. Postan. Vol. VI. '65
Doyle, W., "The Old European Order. 1600-1800". O.U.P. '78
Duby, G., "The Early Growth of the European Economy". Weidenfeld and
  Nicholson. '74
Dumas, M., "A History of Technology". John Murray. '69
Dumont, R. and **N. Cohen**, "The Growth of Hunger". Marian Boyars. '80
Duncan, A.A.M., "The Kingdom of the Scots" in "The Dark Ages". Ed. L.M. Smith.
  MacMillan. '84

Eberhart, W., "A History of China". Routledge Kegan Paul. '59
Edward, M., "A History of India". Thames and Hudson. '61
Evans, J., "Life in Medieval France". Phaidon. '25
Evans-Pritchard, E., "The Nuer". O.U.P. '74

Fairbank and Reischauer, "China". Routledge Kegan Paul. '59
Finberg, H.P.R., "The Formation of England". Hart Davis McGibbon. '74
Finley, M.I., "Early Greece. The Bronze and Archaic Ages". Chatto and Windus. '81
Forde, C. Darryl, "African Worlds". O.U.P. '54
Frank, A.G., "Capitalism and Underdevelopment in Latin America". Monthly Review
  Press. '67
Frazer-Darling, F., "A Herd of Red Deer". O.U.P. '37
French, A., "The Growth of the Athenian Economy". Routledge Kegan Paul. '64
Frere, S., "Britannia. A History of Roman Britain". Routledge Kegan Paul. '78
Friedmann, H., in "The Food Question". Ed. H. Bernstein et al. Earthscan
  Publications. '90

Galbraith, J.K., "The Age of Uncertainty". B.B.C./Deutcsh. '77
Galleano, E., "The Open Veins of Latin America. Seven Years Later". Monthly
  Review. 30.7
Garraty, J.A., "The American Nation. The History of the United States". Harper
  Row. '83
Gellner, D. and **C. Humphrey**, "Gurkha Swords into Ploughshares". New Society.
  17.8.87
George, S., "How the other half dies". Penguin. '76
        "Ill fares the Land". Writers and Readers Publishing Co-operative
           Society Ltd. '85
Gill, G.J., "Peasants and Government in the Russian Revolution". MacMillan. '79
Gille, B., in "A History of Techonology". Ed. M. Dumas. John Murray. '69
Gimpel, J., "The Medieval Machine". Gollanz. '74
Glyn-Jones, W., "Denmark". Benn. '70
Gorz, B., "Paths to Paradise". Pluto Press. '85
Gould, J.D., "Economic Growth in History". Methuen. '72

Gourou, R., "Man and Land in the Far East". Longman. '75
Griffin, K., "World Hunger and the World Economy". MacMillan. '87
Grigg, D., "The World Food Problem". Blackwell. '85

Hamilton-Jenkin, A.S., "The Cornish Miner". David and Charles. '72
Harrison, A., "The Framework of Economic Activity". MacMillan. '67
Haviland, W.A., "Anthropology". Holt Rhinehart and Winston. '82
Hawkes, J., "The First Great Civilizations". Hutchinson. '73
Heller, M. and **A. Neckrich,** "Utopia in Power". Hutchinson. '86
Hillary, E., "Ecology 2000". Michael Joseph. '84
Hindley, G., "England in the Age of Caxton". Granada. '79
Hobsbawm, E.J., "Industry and Empire". Weidenfeld and Nicholson. '68
Hodgett, C., "A Social and Economic History of Medieval Europe". Methuen. '72
Holderness, B.A., "Pre-Industrial England. Economy and Society from 1500-1750".
    J.M. Dent. '76
Hopkins, A.G., "An Economic History of West Africa". Longman. '73
Hufton, O.H., "Bayeux in the late 18th century. A social study". Quoted by N.J.G. Pounds.
    Oxford. '67
Huntington, E., "The Climate Factor as illustrated in Arid America". Carnegie Institute
    of Washington. 1914. Publication No. 192.
Hutchings, R., "Soviet Economic Development". Blackwell. '82

Inglis, B., "The Opium War". Hodder and Stoughton. '76
Institute of Food and Development Policy. "Food First Resources Guide". '79

James, H., "A German Identity. 1700-1900". Weidenfeld and Nicholson. '89

Kelley, K., "The Longest War". Z Books. '82
Kennedy, P., "The Rise and Fall of the Great Powers". Unwin. '88
Kenyon, N., "Labour Conditions in Essex" in "Essays in Economic History". Ed. E.M.
    Carus-Wilson. '62
Koener, R., "Settlement and Colonisation of Europe" in "The Cambridge Economic
    History of Europe". Ed. Postan. Vol I. C.U.P. '71
Knowles, D., "The Monastic Order in England". C.U.P. '40
Koch, H.W., "A History of Prussia". Longman. '78

Laing, L. and **J.,** "The Origins of Britain". Routledge Kegan Paul. '80
Lawrence, C.H., "Medieval Monasticism". Longman. '84
Leamonth, T. and **E. Rolt,** "Underdeveloping Bangladesh". War on Want
Lee, R.B. and **Devore,** "Man the Hunter". Chicago. '68
Lehman, J.P., "The Roots of Modern Japan". MacMillan. '82
Lilley, L., "Technological Progress and Industrial Revolution". Vol III of "Fontana Economic
    History of Europe". London. '73
Lis, C. and **H. Soly,** "Poverty and Capitalism in Pre-Industrial Europe". Harvester
    Press. '79
Lopez, R., "The Commercial Revolution of the Middle Ages". Prentice Hall. '71
        "Hard Times and Investment in Culture". Metropolitan Museum of Art.
Lorentz, K., "On Agression". Methuen. '66
Loyn, H.R., "The Governance of Anglo-Saxon England. 500-1087". Edward Arnold. '84
Luckhurst, D., in "Monastic Water Mills". Society for the Protection of Ancient Buildings.
    N.8 (London) n.d.6
Luzzatto, G., "An Economic History of Italy". Routledge Kegan Paul. '61

MacAndrews, C., "Developing Countries and the Environment". McGraw Hill. '79
MacDermot, B.H., "Cult of the Sacred Spear". Hale. '73
Mair, L., "An Introduction to Social Anthropology". O.U.P. '65
Maland, D., "Europe in the Sixteenth Century". MacMillan. '73
Matheson, S.A., "The Tigers of Baluchistan". O.U.P. '75
Matthews, J., in "The Roman World". Ed. J. Boardman. O.U.P. '88
McNeill, W.H., "A World History". O.U.P. '79
Miller, E. and **J. Hatcher,** "Medieval England". Longman. '78
Milward, A.S. and **S.B. Saul,** "The Economic Development of Continental Europe. 1780-1870". George Allen and Unwin. '79
Miskimin, H.A., "The Economy of Early Renaissance Europe". Prentice Hall. '69
            "The Economies of Late Renaissance Europe". C.U.P. '77
Moore, Barrington, Jnr., "The Social Origins of Dictatorship and Democracy". Penguin. '66
Morris, J., "The Age of Arthur". Weidenfeld and Nicholson. '73
Mumford, L., "The Myth of the Machine". Vol. I. "Technics and Human Development". Secker and Warburg. '66
Basim Mussallam. "The Arabs". Collins/Harvil. '83
Munck, E., "Biology of the Future". Collins. '74
Myers, J.N.L., "The English Settlements". Clarendon. '86

North, D., in "The Cambridge Economic History of Europe". Vol. IV. C.U.P. '65
North, R., "The Real Cost". Chatto and Windus. '86

Oates, J., "Babylon". Thames and Hudson. '86
Oppenheim, A.L., in "Trade and Market in Early Empires". Ed. K. Polanyi. Free Press. '57
Osborne, H., "Bolivia, a Land Divided". O.U.P. '64

Parry, J.H., "Transport and Trade Routes" in The Cambridge Economic History of Europe. Vol. IV. Ed. Postan.
Patlagean, E., in "The Middle Ages". Ed. R. Fossier. C.U.P. '89
Pearce, F., "Turning up the Heat". The Bodley Head. '89
Pearson, H.W., in   "Trade and Market in Early Empires". Ed. K. Polanyi. Free Press. '57
Pearson, R., "Introduction to Anthropology". Holt, Rhinehart and Winston. '74
Pendle, G., "A History of Latin America". Penguin. '63
Perelman, M., "Farming for Profit in a Hungry World. Capitalism and crisis in agriculture". New York University Press.
Pfeiffer, J., "The Emergence of Man". Harper Row. '72
Phelps, E.H., "The Economics of Labour". Newhaven. '62
Pirenne, H., "Economic and Social History of Medieval Europe". Routledge Kegan Paul. '36
Platt, C., "The Abbeys and Priories of Medieval England". Secker and
                Warburg. '84
            "Medieval England". Routledge Kegan Paul. '78
Polanyi, K., "Trade and Market in Early Empires". Free Press. '57
            "The Livelihood of Man". Academic Press Inc. '77
Pollard, S., "The History of Labour in Sheffield". University of Liverpool. '59
            "European Economic Integration. 1815-1970". Thomas and Hudson.
Pope-Hennessy, J., "Italian Gothic Sculpture". Phaidon. '55
Polybius. "The Histories". Loeb Library. London. '60
Pounds, N.J.G., "A Historical Geography of Europe". C.U.P. '79

Power, E., "The Wool Trade in Medieval History". O.U.P. '41

Raistrick, A., "The Role of Yorkshire Cistercian Monasteries in the History of the Wool Trade". International Wool Secretariat. '53
Riasanovski, N., "A History of Russia". O.U.P. '63
Roberts, J., "Revolution and Improvement". Weidenfeld and Nicholson. '76
Rodney, W., "How Europe Underdeveloped Africa". Bogie-l'Ouverture. '72
Rogers, T., "Six Centuries of Work and Wages". 1884.
Ross, A., "The Pagan Celts". Batsford. '86
Rouche, M., in "The Middle Ages". Ed. R. Fossier. C.U.P. '89
Roux, G., "Ancient Iraq". George Allen and Unwin. '64

Saggs, H.W.F., "The Might that was Assyria". Sidgewick and Jackson. '84
Sahlins, M.D. "Tribalism". Prentice Hall. '68
Sampson, A., "The Seven Sisters". Hodder and Stoughton. '75
Saylles, G.O., "Medieval Foundations of England". Methuen. '48
Shorter, A., "Chieftainship in Western Tanzania". Clarendon. '72
Stenton, F., "Anglo-Saxon England". Clarendon. '71
Stern, W.M., "Britain, Yesterday and Today". Longman

Thomas, H., "An Unfinished History of the World". Hamish Hamilton. '79
Timberlake, L., "African Crisis". Earthscan. International Institute for Environment and Development. '85
Trainer, F.E., "Abandon Affluence". Z Press. '85
Treasure, G., "The Making of Modern Europe. 1648-1780". Methuen. '85
Trebilock, C., "The Industrialisation of the Continental Powers. 1780-1914". Longman. '81
Trigger, B.G., "Ancient Egypt. A social history". C.U.P. '83
Trump, D.H., "The Prehistory of the Mediterranean". Allen Lane. '80
Turnball, C., "The Forest People". Jonathan Cape. '61

Unwin, G., "Studies in Economic History". Ed. Tawney. Cass. '66

Viljoen, S., "Economic System in World History". Longman. '74

de Waal, F., "Peace-making among Primates". Penguin. '91
Wacher, T., "The Roman Empire". Dent. '87
Wallerstein, I., "The Modern World System". Academic Press Inc. '74
Ward, C., in an editorial appendix to 'Fields, Factories and Workshops Tomorrow", by P. Kropotkin. Freedom Press. '85
Washburne and Devore. "The Social Life of Baboons". Scientific American. Vol. 204. No. 6
Wells, H.G., "The Outline of History". Penguin. '36
Wightman, E.M., "Gallia Belgica". Batsford. '85
Wilkinson, R., "Poverty and Progress". Methuen. '73
Woronoff, J., "Japan's Commercial Empire". MacMillan. '85

Yong Yap and A. Cotterell, "Chinese Civilization from the Ming Revival to Chairman Mao". Weidenfeld and Nicholson. '77

Zipf, J., "Human Behaviour and the Principle of Least Effort". Hafner, '65

Index

Aboriginese, 2
acid rain, 190
Act of Enclosure, 29, 45
Africa
    cash taxes, 43
    Dahomey, 45
    Entente Cordiale, 134
    erosion, 187
    export of cash crops, 177
    forced cash crops, 73
    gifts as taxation, 15
    ground nuts schemes, 170
    hours worked, 5
    hours worked in Roman North
      Africa, 64
    hours worked in West Africa, 64
    Islam in, 196
    Land Act in South Africa, 64
    luxury crops from, 177
    Masai in East Africa, 3
    regression, 72
    roads in Roman Africa, 30
    slaves from, 138
    stagnant food production, 177
    unwillingness to trade in
      East Africa, 37
agriculture, 4-6
    in America, 157
    benefits to the rich, 89
    beginning of, 4
    biocides in, 187
    causing water pollution, 188
    Cistercian, 90
    effects of grain from Poland, 125
    effects of industry, 73-74
    effects of settlement, 17
    effect of Black Death, 126
    effect of expanding periphery, 129
    German reforms, 150
    'improvement', 137
    in 6th cent. Italy, 89
    harder work, 5, 57
    poverty from agricultural
      development, 176-179
    regression of, 7-8

    in Russia, 153-154
aid, 172
air pollution, 189-190
Akbar, 26
Alavi, H., 146, 173, 178
Alfred the Great, 113, 114
Allaby, M., 184
Algeria,
    hamletisation, 28
    crops for export, 73
    wine for export, 177
altered state of consciousness, 33
Amalfi, 35
Amazon basin, 168
Ambrose, 84
America, United States of, 155-160
    aid to Third World, 172
    Civil War, 157
    erosion, 187
    health of workers, 144
    makes sterling convertible, 44
    Mid-West, 157
    military aid to the Third World, 173
    water shortage, 181
    working hours, 65
Amsterdam, 98
    dependence on Baltic grain, 101
Andaman Islands, 1
    religion, 18
Anell, L., 16
Anglo-Saxons, 108, 109-114
Archaic Age, 107, 110-114
Arkwright, Richard, 141
Argentina, 30
arms, monopoly of, 15, 31
    in Crete, 15
    in Ireland, 15
    in Japan, 15
    William the Conqueror, 31
Arnold, A.R., 34, 46
Arnold, C.J., 109
Arnold, R., 113, 114
artisans,
    producing for the rich, 67
    status in England, 119

Asia, erosion, 187
Assize of Cloth, 118
Assize of Bread, 118
Assyria, 24-34
    hamletisation, 27
    exhaustion of forests, 35
Athens, 53-55
    cultural peak, 70
atonement, 21
Atlantic Charter, 169
Australia, 63

Baboons and peck order, 9
Babylonia, 25
Baltic grain, 98, 100, 124
Baluchistan, 56
Bangladesh, 172-173
banking,
    the church in, 92-94
    during the Great Depression, 144
    loans to the Third World, 171, 175
    medieval collapse, 123
basic industry in Paris, 61
Baumol, W.J., 71
Bautier, R-H., 30, 96, 101, 123, 124, 126
Bayeux, 61
Belgium, 149
Benedictine technology, 86-90
Bengal, 26
    trading privileges, 41
Beresford, M., 47
Bhopal, 189
Bible, 20-23, 28
biocides, 187
Black Death, 123, 125-127
blast furnace, 126
Blinder, A.S., 71
Block, M., 80
Böhme, H., 150
Bookchin, Murray, 197
Borosage, R.L., 168, 179
Boserup, E., 4, 5, 8
Braudel, F., 27, 28, 35, 36, 38, 46, 66, 67,
        68, 98, 100, 101, 102, 129, 131, 132,
        140, 143
Bray, F., 30
Brazil
    attack on industry, 136
    cash crop acreage, 73
    own periphery, 179
Bridenbaugh, C., 67

Bridgetown, 117
Britain
    archaic age, 110-114
    early history, 107-108
    growth 16th-18th cent., 132-134
    heroic age, 109
    as periphery, 116-117
    political break-up, 200
    self-sufficiency, 201
    standard of living, 66
British Petroleum, 42
Brooke, C., 114, 116
Brown, John, 142
Brown, L., 189
Buddhism, 196
bullock capitalists, 178
Bülow, 134
Burman, E., 92, 93
Burn, A.R., 15, 53
bush fallow, 4
Byzantine Empire, 99-100

Cairncross, F., 142
Calder, A., 98, 103, 133, 135, 142, 155
Canada, 163-164
    trade in, 40
canals, 140
Canal Zone, 174
Cape Colony Act, 43
capital accumulation, 142
capitalism, 194-196
carbon dioxide, 184, 185
Caribbean Islands, 135-136
Carus-Wilson, E.M., 118, 120, 121
cash crops
    African exports, 177
    Britain, 18th cent., 137
    Cistercians, 117
    farmer, 89
    forced by coinage, 42, 43
    justified by theory, 59, 170
    Italy, 6th cent., 89
    in the Third World, 73, 177
Caudillo, 171
'Changing Atmosphere', 184
Charles I, 133
Charles II, 40
charter to hold markets, 46
Cheng Ho, 80
Chernobyl, 185
Chia Lin-Sien, 186, 188

chieftain, 3-4
Chile, 174
China, 80-83
    acid rain in, 190
    economic stagnation, 97
    failure to grow, 160
    nuclear waste, 188
    opium for, 146
    without indirect taxation, 49
chloro-fluoro-carbons, 185
Christianity,
    apostolic, 88
    in Britain, 111
    justification to exploit, 169
    less worry about poverty, 79, 88
    and population, 83
Christopher, A.J., 28
Church
    as banker, 92-94
    and welfare, 88
C.I.A., 41
Cipolla, C.M., 66, 67, 86, 101, 133, 141
Cipriani, L., 1, 18, 19
Cistercian technology, 90-92
    settlements in Britain, 116
cities, 26-27
    achievements of, 69
    after Black Death, 126
    disappearance of, 109
Clairvaux, 87-91
Clapham, J., 56, 118, 135
Clark, C., 5, 6, 65, 107
Clay, C.G.A., 7, 63, 67, 132, 133
Clayborne, R., 78
cloth industry
    Assize of Cloth, 118
    in Britain, 102, 118, 132, 140
    in Brazil, 136
    destruction of foreign industries, 143
    Indian, 146
    Irish, 135
    French, 61
    Spanish, 102
    suppression of rural industry, 69
    weaving towns, 95-96
    working hours, 64-65
coal, 139-140
Coates, B.E., 48
coinage, 34, 42, 44, 104
    Anglo-Saxon, 112
coke-smelting, 139, 151

Collins, D., 109
Collins, J., 177
colonialism, 134
Columbia, 189
Columbus, Christopher, 130
command economy, 154
Commonwealth Development
    Corporation, 40
companions, 15-16, 103
    in Britain, 109, 110-111
    and kingship, 18, 19, 103
    of Moses, 20-21
Comparative Advantage, theory of, 71-73, 177
conflict of trends, 200
Congressman Porter, 6
Constantinople, 84
    church and charity, 88
    fall of, 100
consumer goods, 62-63
consumers, 66
consumer society, 10
Continental system, 150
cooker, 145
Corbie, 86
core, 35-36
    in Britain, 137
    core meets core, 99-100
    in Germany, 152
    protection by, 143
    workers' dependence on periphery, 55
Corn Laws, 62
Cortazzi, H., 17, 82
Cortez, 102
cost of living
    in 18th cent. Britain, 141
    after the Black Death, 126
    in cities, 54
    in Holland, 131
    in Japan, 162
Cotterell, A., 81, 82
craftsmen in France, 60
credit, 38, 93, 158
Crete, 15
Cromwell, Oliver, 133, 141
Crusades, 92
cut and burn agriculture, 5
cutting taxes, 202
customs union, 151
Czechoslovakia, 189
    depature from Slovakia, 200

Dahomey, 45
Davidson, B., 4, 27, 43, 64, 73, 177, 196
Davidson, S., 2
DDT, 187
Deep Ecology, 197
deforestation, 186
    affecting forest people, 176
    in Assyria, 35
    in Attica, 53
    in the Roman Empire, 78
    in the Third World, 168
Delamere, 63
Denmark
    literature, 70
    concentration on livestock, 129
Depression, The, 124, 158
Derry, T.K., 47
Descartes, 197
determinism, 197
Deuteronomy, 21
development, 169
DeVore, 9
Diamond, A.S., 4, 56, 199
Diaz, Bartholomew, 130
Diehl, C., 100
Dinka, 4
direct taxation
    in China, 49, 160
    in Japan, 49
    in Nigeria, 27
disarming the peasants, 15
discretionary income, 62, 145
Division of Labour, 57-60, 177, 194
Dobb, M., 8, 46, 69, 118, 136, 143, 155, 157
Domesday Book, 114, 121
Dorians, 52
Douglas, M., 4
Dowring, F., 67
Doyle, W., 137
Druids, 108
Duby, G., 8, 29, 85, 88
Dumont, R., 38
Duncan, A.A.M., 15
Dynamic Minimum, 9

Eastern Europe, 97-98
    grain price fall, 123
    enserfment, 129
Eberhart, W., 80
economic growth
    in Flanders, 97

in 15th cent. Britain, 129
in 18th cent. Britain, 141-142
economic theory, 57-62, 71
'Economist, The', 8
education
    in Germany, 152
    in Japan, 161
Edward I, 117
Edward II, 127
Edward III, 44, 127
Edward, M., 143
Egypt, 24
    corn production for Rome, 84
    cancellation of debt, 172
    religious land holdings, 24
    rural poor, 179
    settlement, 17
élite, superiority of, 29
Elm Decline, 107
enclosure in Britain, 132
Encyclopedia Britannica, 70
England
    importing grain, 124
    peasants' working hours, 119
    periphery to Flanders, 102
    wool exports, 45
Entente Cordiale, 134
erosion, 186-187
    in America, 187
    in Ancient Greece, 53
    in Italy, 78
Eskimos, 2
    and religion, 19
Ethiopia
    deforestation, 186
    farm evictions, 178
Etruscans, 78
Euphrates, 190
Europe, acid rain, 190
European Union, 165-166
Evans, J., 86, 87
Evans-Pritchard, E., 4
exhaust fumes, 190
export of grain
    by Britain, 133
    by Scythia, 54
    from eastern Europe, 98
    by Poland, 101
Factories
    in Britain, 141-142
    manned by prisoners, 64

producing for the rich, 67
in the Roman Empire, 79
failed policies, 174-176
Fairbank, 81, 160
Farmers General Wall, 46
Fatehpur Sikri, 26
Fertile Crescent, 5
feudalism, regression to, 115
Final Appeal, 29, 103, 200
Finberg, H.P.R., 111
Finley, M.I., 8, 52
First Industrial Revolution, 91
Flanders, 44
imports from Britain, 118
importing Baltic wheat, 124
population growth, 96
superseded by Britain, 132
suppression of countryside, 69
Flavin, C., 186, 189
Florence
artistic debasement, 70
Black Death, 125
labour-saving machinery, 69
the Templars, 92
Foigny, 91
food aid, 172
forced trade, 41
forced crop production, 73
forests
in Assyria, 35
in early Britain, 107
forest fallow, 4
France
18th cent. battle with Britain, 132
deforestation, 186
Division of Labour at the
French court, 59-60
increasing poverty in the
16th cent., 129
justice, 29
lost war against Britain, 134
population growth, 96
standard of living, 65
the Templars, 93
working hours, 65
Frank, A.G., 40, 136, 143
Frederick the Great, 150
Free Trade, 195
for America, 158
French, A., 64
French Revolution, 68, 183

Frere, S., 108
Friedman, Milton, 175
Friedmann, H., 172, 173, 177
Friends of the Earth, 202
Fusfield, D.B., 37

Galbraith, J.K., 26
Galleano, E., 174
Garraty, J.A., 155, 157
GATT, 195
GDP
as wealth, 66, 194
in medieval Britain, 120
in the Third World, 176
Gdansk, 102
Gellner, D., 4, 56
genealogy, 110, 111
General Charter to all Burgesses of
Scotland, 46
Genghis Khan, 81
George, S., 30, 72, 73, 144, 178
Germany, 149-152
bannmeile, 46
companions, 15
guild privileges, 46
hamletisation, 27
meat consumption, 66
overtakes Britain, 147
standard of living, 66
gift exchange, 37
GKN Sankey, 40
Gildas, 109
Gill, G.J., 153
Gille, B., 91
global warming, 184
Glozer, 48
Glyn-Jones, W., 70
Gobelin, 60
gold, 43, 44
Chinese disinterest, 81
Gorbachev, M., 154
Gorz, A., 73
Goths, 6
Gould, J.D., 8, 43, 125, 139, 159
Gourou, R., 4
Governor Rogers, 6
government, 193-194
grain
from the Baltic, 98, 100
crises after price fall, 124
export by 18th cent. Britain, 133

fall in price in the 14th cent., 123
    from Scythia, 54
Great Depression, the, 124, 143-144, 158
grid-iron pattern of towns, 28
Griffin, K., 178, 179
Grigg, D., 162
Grimal, P., 68
green revolution, 178
green solutions, 197-198
greenhouse effect, 184, 198
Greenpeace, 202
Greece, working hours, 64
ground nuts schemes, 170
'The Guardian', 41

Hamilton-Jenkin, A.S., 142
hamletisation, 27
Harrison, A., 44, 158
Hatcher, J., 118
Haviland, W.A., 2, 3, 17
Hawkes, J., 24, 25
health of hunter gatherers, 2
Heise, L., 186
Heller, M., 154
Henry I, 117
Hephaestus, 56
Heptarchy, 112
Hero of Alexandria, 79
Herodotus, 34
Heroic Age in Britain, 109-110
Hibbert, A.B., 47
hierarchy, 3
    jackdaws, 9
    baboons, 9
High Renaissance, 70
Himalayas, 186
Hindley, G., 127
Hinduism, 196
hinterland, 35-36
    Athens, 53
    expanding in Europe, 125
    towns' dependence on, 53
Hiroshima, 186
Hittite sculpture, 26
Hobbes, T., 57
Hobsbawm, E.J., 41
Hodgett. C., 83, 92, 99, 123, 124, 127
Holderness, B.A., 133, 137, 141
Holland, 131
    forced deliveries of spice, 130
    industrial wastes, 188
    unable to raise enough taxes, 134
    weight of taxation, 131
    well-fed, 144
hollandgänger, 98
Hong Kong, 181
Hopkins, A.G., 5, 64
Hospitallers, 88
Huberman, 63
Hudson Bay Trading Company, 40
Hufton, O.H., 62
Humphrey, C., 4, 56
Huntington, E., 6
hunter-gatherers, 1-4
    abundant food supply, 1
    chiefs, 3
    diet, 1
    disruption by money, 176
    harmful effects of logging, 176
    health, 2
    murder, 2
    social control, 2-3
    size of group, 3
Hutchings, R., 154

Improvement, agricultural, 137-138
India, 146
    air pollution, 189
    deforestation, 186
    de-industrialisation, 143
    Fatehpur Sikri, 26
    viable farm size, 178
indirect taxation, 45-46
    in America, 159
    in Anglo-Saxon Britain, 113
    in Britain in the 17th cent., 133
    in China, 160
    in Holland, 131
    in Japan, 161
    in Nigeria, 27
    in Russia, 154
Indonesia
    forced delivery of crops, 39, 130
    no industry, 71
    screwdriver plants, 180
Industrial Revolution
    working hours, 65
industrial wastes, 187-188
industrial wealth, 60-62
industry
    effects on the periphery, 73-74
    in Italy, 100

production for the rich, 67
squalor, 138
industrialisation
    in America, 156
    in Belgium, 149
    in Germany, 152
    in Russia, 153
inflation, 175
Inglis, B., 41
inherited kingship, 18, 110
*Institute of Food and Development
    Policy,* 176
internal colonialism, 157
International Labour Office, 176
international trade, 44-45
invention of religion, 18
investment, 170, 180
IOU, 43
Ireland, 134-135
    armed nobles, 15
    Famine, 135
iron age, 8
iron
    industry in France, 91
    beads, 8
irrigation, 6
Islam, 196-197
Israel, 191
Istanbul, 100
Italy
    banking crisis in 14th cent., 123
    building programme in the
        6th cent., 89
    industrial development, 99-100
    population growth, 96
    profitability of crops, 36
    working hours, 64-65
Ivory Coast, 168

Jackdaws, and peck order, 9
Japan
    armed elite, 15
    economic growth, 161-163
    exports to China, 82
    feudalism, 115
    foreign trade forbidden, 49
    hit by cheap textiles, 72
    increased indirect taxes, 49
    settlement, 17
    water pollution, 189
James, H., 152

Jason, 55
Java, 71
jazz, 29
Jerusalem, 22
Judaism, 196
    the Bible, 20-23
Julius Caesar, 108
justice, 28-29

Kalahari Desert, 1
Keeping up with the Jones, 10-11
Kelley, K., 134, 135
Kennedy, P., 133
Kenya, 1
Kenyon, N., 119
Keynes, J.M., 42, 58, 175
Kimbu, 14
King, Gregory, 133
kingship, 18, 103, 110
Koch, H.W., 150
Koener, R., 6, 28
Knights Templar, 92
Knowles, D., 91
Kula ring, 39
Kung bushmen, 1, 9
kwashiorkor, 144

Labour costs, 140-141
    in America, 155-156
    in cities, 54, 69
    at the core, 36
    effects, 94
    cause of Industrial Revolution, 140-141
    in Japan
labour-saving devices
    in America, 155-156
    in Rome, 79
La Graufesenque, 79
Laing, L. and J., 107
land
    allocation in America, 155
    changes in Prussia, 150
    of Chinese peasants, 82
    in Mesopotamia, 24-25
    private ownership, 115-116
landlessness
    in America,
    in Egypt, 179
    in Thailand, 178
Languedoc, 65
Lappé, F.M., 177

216

Latin America, 177
Law of Least Effort, 8, 25, 193
Lawrence, C.H., 116
Le Pen, 201
Leamonth, T., 172
least effort, 8-9
Lee, R.B., 2
legal tender, 44
Lehman, J.P., 49, 162
leisure, 5
Leisure Preference, 6-7, 8
leopardskin chief, 3
Lepanto, 79
Les Halles, 60
Levant, 70, 84
Leviticus, 21, 22
Lex Hadriana, 64
Lezoux, 79
Liberia, 44
    loss of forests, 168
Lilley, L., 79
'*Links*', 146
Lis, C., 72, 98, 118, 119, 125, 129, 131-132,
    132, 140, 141, 143, 150
Little Tigers, 181, 194
living standards, 65
loans, 171
local industries, 180
London, 27
    abandonment, 109
Lönnroth, E., 45
Lopez, R., 69, 70, 83, 99
Lorentz, K., 9
Louis XIV, 59
Low, D.A., 37
Love Canal, 188
Loyn, H.R., 110, 113, 114
Luckhurst, D., 87
Lüll, 57
Luzzatto, G., 99, 125
Lydia, 42

MacAndrews, C., 186, 188
MacDermot, B.H., 3
MacFarlane, 4
Mcneill, W.H., 26, 34, 54, 143, 160, 161
markets, 45-46
    charters to hold, 46
    Les Halles, 60
    in medieval Britain, 117
    lack of in Mesopotamia, 34

lack of in Persia, 34
    in planted towns, 47
    profits from dues, 47
market dues
    in Dahomey, 45
    to local lords, 47
    in Poland, 45
market gardens, 35
Masai, 3
Matheson, S.A., 56
Matthews, J., 67
Mauss, M., 19
Mbuti, 2
municipal clock, 126
Medici Bank, 70
medieval Europe
    exploitation of hinterland, 68
mercantilism, 81, 130, 162
merchants, in China, 160
Merivale, 63
Mesolithic period, 107
Mesopotamia, 20-25
    climate change, 5
    hamletisation, 27
    little trading, 34
Mesta, 102
Mexico, 165
    water pollution, 189
Middle East, water shortage, 190
military aid, 173
military power
    America, 159
    Britain, 134
    mercantilism, 130
    Prussia, 150
    to support Third World
        governments, 169
    Russia, 153
    in the Third World, 171
    threat to Japan, 162
mills, 120-122
    Cistercian, 87
    increase after Black Death, 126
    saving labour costs, 88
    water mills, 86, 88
Miller, E., 118
Milward, A.S., 151, 165
mining, destruction of the periphery, 179
Miskimin, H.A., 67, 95, 100, 101
monopoly of arms, 31
    in Crete, 15

in Ireland, 15
in Japan, 15
monasteries, 87
 Benedictine, 86-87
 Cistercian, 87, 90-92
 in debt, 125
 pioneers of technology, 86, 89
 growth of weaving, 96
money, 42-44, 104
 Anglo-Saxon, 112
Moore, Barrington, Jnr., 16, 68, 72, 132
moot, 111
Morgan, D., 81, 82
Morris, J., 109, 110
Moses, 19-20
Multi-fibre Agreement, 180, 196
multi-nationals, dependence of, 42
Mumford, L., 8
Munck, E., 48
murder
 amongst the Eskimos, 2
 amongst the Masai, 3
Mureybit, 17
Bassim Mussallam, 196
Mycenaean Age, 52
 writing, 8
Myers, J.N.L., 110

Naess, Arne, 197
Nagasaki, 186
Namibia, 179
Napoleon, 150
National Income, 197
Neckrich, A., 154
neo-colonialism, 169
Nepal, 56
Newcomen, 139
New England, 156
'New internationalist', 174
New Guinea, 179
Nigeria
 direct taxation, 27
 ground nuts scheme, 170
 no private land, 116
Norman Conquest, 114
Norway, rights to trade, 47
North, D., 156
North, R., 187, 188, 190
North Africa, 79
Northern Wei, 82
Nubia, 24

nuclear power, 185
Nuer, 4
Numbers, 20, 21
Nygren, B., 16
Nyungu, 14, 18

Oates, J., 26
obedience, effects of, 20
obsolescence, 191
Odoacer, 84
Offa, 112
oil, 159
 crisis, 174, 175
 in Iran, 42
 at Pithole, 27
 the Third World, 175
Onges, 18
opium, 146
Oppenheim, A.L., 26, 28, 34
Orcagna, 70
Osborne, H., 37
Oxfam, 173
ozone layer, 185

Pacific Tigers, 181, 194
Panic of '57, 157
Pantheon, 79
paper, 94
Paris, industry in, 60-61
Parry, J.H., 134
Patlagean, E., 86, 88
Pearce, F., 168
Pearson, H.W., 23
Pearson, R., 1
peasants
 conditions in England, 118-119
 and Division of Labour, 57
 enserfed in Poland, 124
 impoverished by towns, 117
 reasons for toil, 57
 in Roman Britain, 108
 v. workers, 48-49
Peasants' Revolt, 121, 125
peck order, 9-11
 in Africa, 3
 jackdaws, 9
 baboons, 9
Pendle, G., 71
Penny, D.H., 71
Perelman, M, 177
perestroika, 154

218

periphery rulers
  bribed by core, 55
periphery, 35-36
  Britain as, 116-117
  effects of industrialisation, 145-146
  effects of agricultural
    development, 176
  empty, 36
  expansion in Europe, 97-99, 124-125,
    152
  grain-growing, 124
  harm by trade, 36-39
  low cost of living, 36
  lowest food prices, 36
  poverty in the 18th cent., 138
  primitive societies, 37
  in Russia, 154
  Southern states of America, 157
  Third World as, 168
  towns' dependence on, 53
Persians, 34
pesticides, 187
Pfeiffer, J., 1, 3, 199
Philippines, 40
  cash crops, 73
  screwdriver plants, 180
Phoenicians and trade, 34
Pinson, 171
Pirenne, H., 96, 102, 123, 124, 127
Pithole, 27
Pitt, 135
planted towns, 114, 117-118
Plato, 53
Platt, C., 90, 116, 119
plough, 86
Poland
  air pollution, 189
  defence budget, 45
  exporting wheat, 124
Polanyi, K., 25, 37, 63
political break-up, 200
Pollard S., 142, 152
pollution, 183
Polybius, 55
Polynesia, 56
Pombal, Marquis of, 4
Pope-Hennessy, J., 70
Population
  Athens, 53
  Black Death, 125
  decline in Rome, 83

effects on Economic growth, 94
  growth, 16
  growth in Europe, 95
  high population without industry, 71
  in prehistoric Britain, 107
  reduction in Britain, 201
Portugal
  control of Indian Ocean, 131
  exploited by Comparative
    Advantage, 71
  in Kongo, 72
  protectionism against Brazil, 136
  Triangle of Corruption, 40
Postel, S., 186, 187
pottery industry
  in Anglo-Saxon Britain, 109
  in Athens, 54
  in Roman decline, 84
potters' wheel, 8
Pounds, N.J.G., 46, 61, 64, 67, 79, 83
poverty
  by agricultural development, 176-179
  in America, 156
  in 16th cent. Britain, 132
  in 17th cent. Britain, 140
  in 16th cent. France, 129
  in Germany, 150
  by governments, 193
  by industrial development, 179-180
  of slavery, 138
primitive societies
  G.D.P. 66
  fair shares, 37
  property in use, 37
  social control, 2
  unwillingness to trade, 37
Principle of Least Effort, 8
private ownership of land, 115-116
  in Britain, 132
progress, 6
protectionism, 143, 195
  in Britain 18th cent., 136
  in Canada, 164
  by core, 143
  in Germany, 150
  in Japan, 161
  in Russia, 154
Prussia, 150, 151
pygmies
  abundance of food, 1
  fighting, 2

rejection of trade, 38
secret trade, 36
social control, 2

Radiation, 185, 186
Raistrick, A., 126
Ramasses III, 24
Raven, S., 30
Rawstrom, M.E., 48
redistribution of wealth in agricultural
    societies, 4
resources, 190-191
regalian rights, 42
regression
    in America, 155
    in Anglo-Saxon Britain, 109-110
    to feudalism, 115
    in Flanders, 69
    in Italy, 69
    in monasteries, 88
    in Norman England, 114
    in the Roman Empire, 83-85
Reischauer, 81, 160
religion, 196-197
    in Anglo-Saxon Britain, 110
    cause of kingship, 18
    cause of settlement, 17
    invention of, 18-20
    lack of in Russia, 154
    as social sanction, 19
    for taxation, 20
revolution on the periphery, 199
Riasonovski, N., 54
Rich, E.E., 39, 130
roads, 30
    in Anglo-Saxon Britain, 113
    disappearence in Britain, 110
Roberts, J., 156
Rolt, F., 172
Roman Empire
    bread and circuses, 62
    in Britain, 108
    and the Goths, 6
    monopoly of arms, 31
    population decline, 83
    regression in France, 8
    roads, 30
    supremacy, 79, 80
    technology, 78-79
    town v. countryside, 67
Ross, A., 15

rotary steam power, 140
Rouche, M., 84, 89
Roux, G., 25
rulers, dependence on traders, 40
    protecting periphery industry, 55
Russia, 152-155
    exploitation by cities, 68
    forced deliveries of food, 26
    more crop exports, 152
    raw materials, 98
Russian Revolution, 183

Saggs, H.W.F., 35
Sahlins, M.D., 3, 5, 65
St. Germain des Prés, 83
Samian ware, 79
sanctuary, 21
Santa Sophia, 79
Sargent, William, 23
Sargon, 26
Saul, S.B., 151, 165
Saxony, 129
Say's Law, 58
schizophrenia, 14, 16
Scotland, 14
Scythians, 53-54
sea level, 184
self-sufficiency
    in Britain, 201
    in China, 160
    in Europe, 66-67, 95
    farmer, 95
serfdom, 98, 124
settlement, 17
    defended, 107
    religion as a cause, 17
Seveso, 189
sexual taboos, 16
shaman, 16, 17, 19, 22
sharing the wealth, 4
sheep, 116, 120
Shorter, A., 15
Silesia, 72, 143, 150
silver from America, 102
Singapore, 181
slavery
    beyond Europe, 98, 138
    in Britain, 108
Smith, Adam, 57, 169
Smith, Lynn, 7
social control, 2

Social Ecology, 197
social relationship economy, 38
socialism, 196
Soly, H., 72, 98, 118, 119, 125, 129, 140, 141, 143, 150
South America, 6
South-East Asia
    water pollution, 188
South Korea, 181
Spain
    change from arable, 124
    undevelopment, 102-103
    the *vito*, 3
specialisation, 56
stagnation, 123
standard of living, 144
    decline in 15th to 18th cent., 129
    in England in the 19th cent., 66
Stalin, 26, 153-154
starvation
    in Ukraine, 154
    in Third World, 170
status
    of English specialists, 119
    amongst jackdaws, 9
    in Nepal, 56
    in Polynesia, 56
steam engine, 139
Stenton, F., 109, 111
sterling, 44
Stern, W.M., 142
Stonehenge, 107
Suetonius, 79
Sumer, 24
swidden gardening, 5
Syria, 68, 70

Tacitus, 6, 15
Taiwan, 181
Tang, 80
Tanganyika, 14
Tanzania, 14
    adverse terms of trade, 72
taxation
    in Africa, 27
    cash-taxes, 43, 104
cutting taxes
    in Britain, 202
    in England 1500-1700, 133
    in France, 131-132
    gifts as, 15

in Holland, 131
in Japan, 49
Norman failure, 114
religion as cause, 20-23
under the Saxons, 109, 113-114
on trade, 45, 60
on wool, 119
technology, 105
    caused by labour costs, 94, 141
    in China, 80-82
    effects in 19th cent., 143
    growth in Europe, 86
    increase after Black Death, 126-127
Temple of Solomon, 22
television, 145
Thailand
    air pollution, 189
    landlessness, 178
    loss of timber, 168
    water pollution, 188
Thak, 4
Thermal Maximum, 5
Third World
    aid, 172
    air pollution, 189
    biocides, 187
    cities, 27
    development, 169
    failed policies, 174
    industrial wastes, 188
    investment, 170
    loans, 171
    local industries, 188
    military aid, 173
    neo-colonialism, 169
    as periphery, 169
    poverty, 176-180
    roads, 30
    water pollution, 188
Thomas, H., 8, 27, 84, 85
three field system, 86
timber
    cutting causes poverty, 176
    English exports, 118
    in Germany, 151
    in Ireland, 134
    from the periphery, 35, 168
    from the Third World, 176
    in Russia, 153
    shortage, 139-140
    shortage in Athens, 53

shortage in Rome, 79
Timberlake, L., 186
Tokugawa, 49, 161
towns, 46-48, 104
   in Anglo-Saxon Britain, 113
   planted, 117
   v. countryside, 67-69
tractor capitalists, 178
trade, 25
   in Amalfi, 35
   in China, 82
   dislike by primitive societies, 37
   harm to the periphery, 36-39
   Kula ring, 39
   in Mesopotamia, 34
   in Japan, 161
   among the Pygmies, 36
   reappearance in Britain, 112
   royal trade, 26, 34
   stagnation after Black Death, 127
   trade wars, 130-132
   traders' dependence on rulers, 39-40
   tricks, 38
trading blocks, 163-165
Trainer, F.E., 168, 170, 174, 177, 178, 187
Treasure, G., 65, 129, 144
Treaty of Methuen, 40
Triangle of Corruption, 39-42
tribes, size of, 199
trickle-down, 57, 58, 194
Trigger, B.G., 24
Trobriand Islands, 37
Tsurumi, 162
Turkey, 143
   Hittites, 26
   water shortage, 190
Trump, D.H., 5
Turnball, C., 2
tyrants, growth of, 14-16
Ukraine, 153
undevelopment,
   in Eastern Europe, 98
   in Germany, 152
   in India, 146
   in Ireland, 135
   in Italy, 135
   on the periphery, 101, 145
   in Poland, 101
   in Spain, 102
unemployment, 158
   Keynes, 175

United Fruit Company, 41
United Nations, 176
Unwin, G., 119, 120
ultra-violet light, 185
Upper Volta, 146

Vandals, 84
Vasco da Gama, 130
Venice
   agreements with Byzantium, 100
   end of spice monopoly, 131
   sources of raw materials, 99
Versailles, 59
Vespasian, 79
Vicens-Vives, 102
Viljoen, S., 64, 100, 132, 136, 156
villages after Black Death, 126
'*vito*', 3
Vulcan, 56

Waal, de F., 3
Wacher, T., 68
wages
   after Black Death, 126
   in New England, 156
   in Japan, 163
Wakefield, Gibbon, 64
Wallerstein, I., 102, 103
walls
   in Peking, 46
   in Madrid, 46
   in Paris, 46
Warbel, 7
Ward, C., 65
Washburne, 9
water pollution, 188-189
water shortage, 190
wealth-sharing, 4
weaving industry
   in Africa, 72
   decline in Italy, 141
   growth in Britain, 140-141
   growth in Flanders, France and Italy, 96
   in Spain, 102
   towns, 95-97
Wells, H.G., 78
Wessex culture, 107
wheel in ancient America, 8
Whitelock, D., 109, 113
Wightman, E.M., 30
Wilkinson, R., 7, 63, 139, 140

Wilson, C., 97, 137, 141
Wilson, C.H., 46
wool trade, 119-120
    Anglo-Saxon exports, 112
    in 18th cent. Britain, 137
    English exports to Flanders, 45
    restrictions on English trade, 102, 127
woollen industry
    in Ireland, 135
    in Spain, 102
workers
    in Athens, 55
    and Division of Labour, 58
    in factories, 63
    goods for the, 62-63
    v. peasants, 48-49
    v. rural workers, 68

workers' consumer demand, 144
working hours, 64-65
    in Ancient Greece, 64
    of English peasants, 119
    in Germany, 150
    in medieval France, 65
    in medieval Italy, 64-65
Woronoff, J., 162, 163
writing
    in Mycenae, 8, 52
    in Sumeria, 25

Yaghan, 1
Yap, 82

Zipf, J., 9
Zollverein, 151